ENGLISH COMEDY

English Comedy

ITS ROLE AND NATURE FROM CHAUCER TO THE PRESENT DAY

by

ALLAN RODWAY

*Reader in English
in the University of Nottingham*

UNIVERSITY OF CALIFORNIA PRESS

Berkeley and Los Angeles 1975

UNIVERSITY OF CALIFORNIA PRESS
Berkeley and Los Angeles, California

820.9
R697e
1975

Library of Congress Catalog Card Number: 74-25377

ISBN: 0-520-02935-6

Printed in Great Britain

TO
MY WIFE

Contents

Acknowledgements

A debt of gratitude is owed to the friends and colleagues, specialists in their periods, who were kind enough to read and criticise the chapters in Part II. In 'chronological' order: Professor Raymond Page, Professor Elizabeth Salter, Dr George Parfitt, Professor James Boulton, and Mr Brian Lee. They are, of course, not responsible for defects of opinion or expression still remaining; they are, however, responsible for reducing their number.

Thanks are also owed to the following publishers and authors for permission to reproduce copyright material:
Hutchinson Publishing Group Ltd., for material from L. J. Potts, *Comedy*; Jonathan Cape Ltd., and Simon & Schuster, Inc., for material from Joseph Heller, *Catch-22*; The Bodley Head, and Random House, Inc., for material from James Joyce, *Ulysses*; Faber & Faber Ltd., for material from Tom Stoppard, *Jumpers*; T. Bailey Forman Ltd., for material from the *Nottingham Evening Post*.

Foreword

The present work is not primarily a history of English comedy, though it does proceed chronologically from the medieval period to the modern. Nor is it an arid structuralist attempt to see comedy as merely a manifestation of its age—to see through it to various social, economic or psychological structures—though it does relate comedy in each period to the general concerns and characteristics of the day. It is rather a literary-critical work, endeavouring to advance the appreciation of those comic poems, plays or novels which, though *of* an age, may nevertheless be *for* all time. The social and historical material, therefore, provides a setting, the necessary minimum required to vivify a mode wherein even the greatest examples 'date' to a degree that tragedy does not. Of the mass of comedies in English, most are limited to, and thus wholly dependent on specifically contemporary issues (such as the South Sea Bubble). Nearly all died with their time, and diligent reading reveals few deserving of resurrection. For all but scholars of the period they seem beyond recovery no matter how much artificial respiration might be applied in the way of 'background'. Like all literary rules, this one has its exceptions—Dryden's 'Absalom and Achitophel' being the most obvious—and these have not been excluded or begrudged the space for an adequately vivifying context.

The tendency to 'date' more than tragedy, however, is not the only hindrance to modern appreciation of the incomparable wealth of comedy still available, or potentially available, in English. For it is also a mode more commonly than tragedy confused with near but significantly different relatives: farce, and what is here styled 'divertisement'.

As far as stringent limitations of space and the more flexible ones of its thesis permit, then, this book attempts three things: *firstly*, to clarify the theory of comedy, and disentangle it from that of laughter; *secondly*, in so far as is necessary for 'background', contextual purposes, to relate comic literature of all kinds to the life of its time; *thirdly*, and chiefly, to proceed far enough from supporting generalisation to critical particularity to give the reader an appropriate base for that personal 'adventure among masterpieces' which is the proper completion of criticism.

PART I, therefore, is largely theoretical. It outlines a hypothesis, derived from the reading of numerous individual works and designed to lead back to the best of them with an accumulation of interest. In addition it defines the terms used in the critiques to follow—a most necessary task, as no consistent usage for any term connected with comedy seems to have been available in any age (a contributory cause, no doubt, of the relative paucity of criticism in this field). PART II briefly applies the theory to different periods and compares contrasted representative examples of the best work within each period. (That the periods are literary rather than historical will be sufficiently evident: Jane Austen began writing before the Prince of Wales became Regent, Byron continued after he had become King; yet, though on opposite sides, they were both clearly of a period—and no apology seems necessary for the shorthand of 'Regency'.)

This method of dealing with an immense amount of literature over a very long period of time must inevitably leave specialists dissatisfied. But since the field as a whole has been neglected, it is hoped that the enterprise will seem worthwhile as a complement to their more intensive cultivation of particular patches.

Note: On the assumption that readers will have access to many different editions, references for novels are normally to chapter or section only, save in the case of *Ulysses*, whose sections are long and not numbered as chapters. In that case, the page-references are to the Penguin edition (which contains an appendix giving page-correspondences with the 1936 and 1937 Bodley Head editions).

PART I

I

Introduction

Literary critics have tended to concentrate much more on tragedy than comedy. In consequence the body of criticism for comedy is slighter than that for tragedy—and than it ought to be. Causes and effects are commonly confused, means are not distinguished from ends, and comedy itself is often treated as if it needed no distinction from farce and divertisement. Speculative philosophers and psychologists have given it more attention, but the habit of identifying it with laughter has largely nullified any value their work might have had for the student of literature.

Of all critics, Ben Jonson probably best avoided such pitfalls. Being however a creator first and a critic second, he subordinated his theory to his practice and in effect limited comedy to the didactic sort. Meredith on the other hand permitted himself to be led right away from the empirical evidence of actual comedies in fatal pursuit of that *ignis fatuus* the disembodied Comic Idea. Yet his graphic phrase 'the sunny malice of a faun' illuminates the nature of much comedy more than many a pedestrian paragraph based on sounder theory.

Of the speculators, probably Bergson is the most useful: particularly insofar as *Le Rire* (Paris 1900) shows that comedy may be corrective without being moral. This is an aside so valuable that it might profitably have been developed at length. For, contrary to the traditional view, comedy need not spring from disinterested impulse, and it is obvious that virtues as well as vices may conflict with the conventions or legal requirements of society and therefore be open to 'correction' by laughter. Moreover, there is no reason to suppose that the effects of something we enjoy must turn out to be such as we should approve. So unless we define our subject in such a way that anything we don't like doesn't count, comedy can be a means of selfseeking propaganda without forfeiting any part of its essential nature. Its effects may be dehumanising (by mockery of natural deformity or of kindliness, for instance) as well as humanising (by, for example, the deflation of pomposity or hypocrisy). It may be fulfilling, or it may be narrowing.

Style is important, since style reflects sensibility and sensibility qualifies sense. Comic—and other—writers therefore may cause us to swallow revolting views, or unintentionally revolt us with worthy ones, by style alone.

Of course, style never is alone, but it was unfortunate that Bergson should ignore it, as well as making the usual conflation of comedy and laughter.

Mr Potts' *Comedy* (London 1948), is not subject to such strictures. Yet even that admirable study pays a penalty for hypostatising the subject, as it does. This useful technical device enables a mass of material to be organised under such headings as 'Idea', 'Subject Matter', 'Style', and so forth, but it suffers from the drawback of revealing works under this or that aspect only, and not as wholes. Further, such a method tends to divorce literature from the life of its times.

Every method, of course, must have its shortcomings. That of the present study (outlined in the Foreword) inevitably entails, for instance, some sketchiness; every chapter could well be expanded to a volume of this size. However, the attempt to unite particular criticisms with general theory, and both with social tensions, seems justified by one certainty: most art, and comedy in particular, *is functional in society*, whether it purports to be or not. This fact was more obvious in the past when power and literacy were closely connected and esthetic quality was of little conscious regard beside considerations of practicality.

All art in primitive communities appears to have been Art for Religion's sake, and primitive religion was the focal point of tribal life: the point where all available knowledge of man and his world, inner and outer, was unified in one system. Art, which gave body and voice to the system, was thus inseparable from social living. Nevertheless, all literary art is apparitional, to borrow a term from Suzanne Langer's *Problems of Art* (London 1957). Any reality literature may have is phantasmal, existing like the image in a mirror in a space that isn't really there. It may be, as we say, concrete—bodying forth and giving to airy nothing a local habitation and a name—but it is insubstantial, a *verbal* reality as different from that of society as the portrait from the living model. Moreover, to deserve praise, a literary work must go beyond mere imitation of life; it may hold the mirror up to nature, but the image shown must have passed through the lens of a gifted sensibility. Even in primitive societies this subjective element must be present to some extent, if the work is to grip. In advanced societies it is usually more evident, since their increased freedom and flexibility tends to favour the development of minorities—a condition of evolution. The art of an advanced civilisation, therefore, may reflect several ways of life, or ideas of ways of life, and not only one. Thus it is less *obviously* functional but may be more functional in effect, since it can contain elements making for progress as well as those, alone permitted formerly, making for stability.

That seems to have been the case with English comedy; in most periods it was used to advance competing viewpoints. This fact, however, has been somewhat obscured for three reasons: linguistic, social, and critical. The word 'society' is a singular noun with a regular plural, so it carries a pressure of suggestion—that society is unitary—which has made it all too easy to see competing viewpoints only as instances of individualistic self-expression, and not as products and agents of social change. Socially speaking, the fact has been further obscured by the enormous development of 'Grub Street' literature, the swamping of works of value by works of entertainment. The two are easily confused, since both entertain (or ought to). But the main difference between them is important: works of literary value are usually produced by men who have something to say (though not all men who have something to say produce works of literary value); works of pure entertainment are produced by men who want money. The former have an element of dedicated purpose which is lacking in the latter, an umbilical cord connecting them slenderly to the ritualistic past. This element underlies, and distracts attention from the matter of competing viewpoints. Thirdly, the works which survive into our own day, the 'great works', do so because they usually also possess those complex harmonies of form and content, that sense of variety-in-unity, which together produce the disinterested pleasure, independent of period, opinion, or utility, which we call *esthetic*, and this too may cause us to overlook other qualities.

In popular usage, muddled though it is, 'comedy' carries more approval than 'farce'; rightly so, since comedy is more likely to produce literature of value, farce, of entertainment. Unlike comedy, farce requires no effort of appreciation, issues no challenge.

Other distinguishing characteristics set off 'comedy' from different modes of amusing literature, and confirm the need for critical separation. For the moment, it is sufficient to insist that though certain plus-qualities of sense, feeling and form give great comedies continuing life, it is the social situation of their age that gives birth to them, as modes of psychological warfare. Asking after beauty and meaning is critically no more important—perhaps less important—than asking after function.

Comedy, then, is more social and less absurd than farce, though retaining slender links with primitive permanencies. It exposes absurdity rather than being itself absurd. Yet it need not be realistic; and although it works at this more rational and social level, there is no valid reason why it should not be as lasting as tragedy. But choosing to appear in period fancy-dress, where tragedy deals with stark humanity, comedy gives an initial impression of dating more.

For assistance in passing beyond that first impression, Bergson's distinction is useful, between things 'comic' (i.e. funny) by conventional agreement (*de jure*) and things comic by nature (*de facto*). This may clear away such impediments as the now wearisome cuckoldry quips of Elizabethan literature or Restoration astrology jests; and it certainly indicates the need for a minimal acquaintance with the background in order to make allowances—but not excuses—for 'period'.

An acquaintance with background—which may come as much from fiction as histories—is necessary also in a more important way, since a representative comedy may reveal something as *de facto* and not *de jure* in its particular setting though it never appears as a fact of human nature in any other period. Creative literature, that is to say, can display potentialities in man that only particular period conditions have allowed to be actualised.

Those comedies which deal not in the representative but the exceptional are in the same position. True, they may deal from the outset in what never has been actualised, even in their own period, warning rather of a standing possibility; but they gain credit only if there are current signs of danger—and one period may provide these more than another. In short, periods other than our own place humanity in different experimental environments where unexpected possibilities may reveal themselves to the modern reader. (As they may, of course, in fantasy-worlds, if they retain a lifeline with reality to make them acceptable.)

All this may give valuable stereoscopic insights. We can see the human situation in better perspective by being out of the game—provided we have some acquaintance with the rules. With comedy such awareness is particularly necessary, since so much of it 'places' men and manners against certain standards, and these inevitably tend to vary according to period needs.

These considerations suggest that the comic writer is at once committed and detached. He is committed because his task has generally been to cherish values derided either by an incipient or an established group in his society, or by 'society as a whole' (that is, the controlling majority-group). Sometimes he may seem, like the early Shaw, to be in a minority of one, but in such cases he is almost invariably the voice of a larger minority unheard or inarticulate.

He is detached because his method requires that he should seem amused but not passionate. Passion may scare people, for fear of attack but is not likely to convert them. So even for dominant groups, underground activity may seem preferable to open hostility, and comedy a suitable technique; it can infiltrate ideas into heads that would reject them in any other form. It enables the writer to minimise conflict over his own position. Since he appears not to be personally involved, it is society's relationship to itself that his work seems to display. Such a writer needs to *appear* disinterested.

Tragedy really *is* disinterested. To that extent it has a less social function than comedy, and is never the voice only of a group. Concerned not to demonstrate absurdity but to reveal human capacity, it deals with what man can be. Comedy deals with what he too often is but—it mockingly implies—ought not to be. Tragedy thus keeps closer than comedy to deep emotive levels. This does not necessarily make it more important, as the essence of both modes lies in profound human needs. Man has been a social being as long as he has been an individual, and needs as much to work out satisfactory relationships with his society as with his deeper self. That his deeper self changes less rapidly—or less obviously—than his society is immaterial.

Finally, a word about words. Here and elsewhere a convenient linguistic abbreviation has been operating. 'Tragedy' and 'comedy' really stand for 'the words *tragedy* and *comedy* taken as stipulative definitions based on the characteristics of those existing literary works that are now universally styled so and are evidently of a common kind'. Thus where such a phrase as 'Comedy *is* so and so' occurs, a more precise and cumbersome substitution could be made: 'The word *comedy* is usefully employed only for works whose characteristics correspond to those of works universally styled so, and not for works with different characteristics'. The word 'is' therefore relates to a pragmatic definition based on a combination of use and usefulness, not to a theory of being. It does not suggest a Platonic form of comedy.

It is merely a matter of critical convenience to use phrases that are not too cumbersome to handle, and definitions that have enough in common with received usage to be readily understandable without sharing its confusions.

2

Origin and Nature of Comedy

The question of the nature of comedy raises several linked questions. What are the distinguishing characteristics of surviving evident 'comedies' that are never called anything else? How do they differ from more disputable examples that might equally well be called farces or divertisements? How do they differ from their contraries, indisputable tragedies? Will these differences indicate the distinctive qualities of the works we are to deal with? And how are they related to human nature and the nature of society?

Though it may provide some relevant ideas, discussion of the origin of comedy cannot itself give an answer to these questions. No historical evidence is likely to show that a study of its origin would account for its nature today; and no logical argument can be constructed to lead from what was to what is, for the course of evolution may alter an original form out of recognition. Why should English comedy any more closely resemble that of Greece than English democracy resembles that of ancient Athens? Even a demonstration of continuous evolution, if it could be made, would not demonstrate a continuing similarity of nature. All the same, if we take it as axiomatic—and surely we must?—that works which outlast their own age have qualities relevant to something comparatively changeless, then a brief scrutiny of origins should be worth while. For while there persist through all changes the changeless needs 'to work out satisfactory relationships' with the deeper self and also with society, equally the nature of those needs and satisfactions is likely to be seen more clearly in earlier and simpler periods.

The earliest surviving form, that of Athenian drama, was still near enough to its raw material to reveal fairly clearly the basic needs and impulses it satisfied and embodied; yet as it happens it was sufficiently developed to have acquired the independence of art.

Between the ritual origins of tragedy and comedy and the earliest extant examples, however, lies a gulf seemingly impassable. On the one side, primitive religion; on the other, civilised literature; what bridges exist being shakily inferential. And unfortunately the nature of the rituals lying behind the drama of Aeschylus and Aristophanes is itself the subject of scholarly disagreement. Cornford, in a coherent and attractive thesis, argues that

> Athenian Comedy arose out of a ritual drama essentially the same in type as that from which Professor Murray derives Athenian Tragedy.
>
> (F. M. Cornford, *The Origins of Attic Comedy*. Oxford 1914, p. 190.)

or at least 'from one closely allied to it' (p. 68). His postulated root-ritual is that basic widespread fertility-rite described by Frazer, in which the expulsion of Death (or one of its analogues, Winter, Barrenness, Old Age) and the induction of Life (Spring, Harvest or New Year) was magically brought about by the sacrifice of the god-king, or by the ritual marriage of the young supplanter of a sacrificed elder. Pickard-Cambridge, however, remarks that

> it is extremely doubtful whether, in any ritual known in Greece, the representation of the death, and the representation of the resurrection of the god or other object of the cult were ever combined in the same ceremony. They were, in fact, almost inevitably supposed to take place at different times of the year, if they represent the phenomena of winter and spring.
>
> (A. W. Pickard-Cambridge, *Dithyramb Tragedy and Comedy*. Oxford 1927, p. 188. [Further material of interest is contained in W. C. K. Guthrie's *The Greeks and their Gods*. London 1950.])

And far from deriving both literary modes from one source, he derives each from several sources. To Cornford's suggestion that tragedy arose when emphasis came to be laid on the element of 'purification' through sacrifice, while comedy arose as the result of an emphasis on the aspect of 'fertility', Pickard-Cambridge retorts:

> whether the scattering of nuts or cakes to the spectators has any connection with phallic rites and the scattering of emblems of fertility may be left an open question. But we may be sure that it was never the scattering of portions of the slain god; for there is no evidence at all that the god was ever slain in any ritual with which comedy can be connected.
>
> (Ibid. p. 188)

However, it is generally agreed: that tragedy and comedy did spring from *some* primitive religious ritual or, more probably, rituals; that tragedy was at first more closely connected with rites of sacrifice, solemnity and death, while comedy was connected with rites of mockery, ribaldry and fertility; and that in a later stage when both rites became assimilated to the worship of Dionysus, tragedy was associated with the festival of Dionysus as the Slain God, and comedy with the vintage festivals of Dionysus under the aspect of Bacchus, or Phales his companion, the gods of wine and fertility. And certainly the characteristics of the Old Comedy—now represented only by Aristophanes—seem appropriate to such origins. As *The Oxford Companion to the Theatre* (ed. P. Hartnoll, London 1951) points out, the very word is significant:

> The name means 'revel-song' (*comos* and *ode*). One form of revel was associated with fertility-rites; it was a mixture of singing, dancing, scurrilous jesting against bystanders, and ribaldry. Aristotle derives comedy from this, and certainly comedy contained all these elements, including the use of the phallus, the symbol of fertility. (p. 335) . . . Today much of it would be obnoxious to the laws of libel, blasphemy or indecency, and of the rest, a great deal would be rejected as too 'high-brow'.

> (H. D. F. Kitto, 'Greece', p. 366)

At this stage it is obviously profitless to distinguish farce from comedy. Only one word is needed because there is only one mode— the reflection of an undifferentiated veneration for the zest of life. In the Middle Ages, too, what little evidence we have suggests that at first there was no differentiation. Such differentiation begins when, with the growing dominance of Christianity, unredeemed nature and fertility cease to be venerated. The development of a commercial theatre in the Renaissance then furthers the process of splitting off from the revel its 'high-brow' element, so as to bring about—probably with more gain than loss—the modern modes of farce and comedy. Not that these are always *clearly* distinguished, of course. What we shall call comedy of psychological release shades into farce, just as corrective comedy at the other end of the spectrum shades into tragi-comedy.

Once ritual sanctity and exclusiveness has given way sufficiently to admit non-Dionysiac themes, of course, an irreversible process has begun, which eventually leaves the ritual origin far behind. The drama passes from the religious to the secular, from the hands of the priest to those of the artist: witness the comparable development of English drama from the miracle plays to those of the Globe Theatre. Nor need this be regretted; a work of art is not necessarily better in all ways for being ritualistic. In England indeed, if not in Greece, it was usually considerably worse in many. Nevertheless, the spirit embodied in the earliest fertility-ritual drama may well be what gives continued life to those great tragedies and comedies which appeal still when the social moulds they were cast in have long been broken; for that spirit is sufficiently basic, psychologically speaking, to have a protean existence from age to age as a possible keynote for men's compositions in living. This is particularly true of tragedy, which deals more directly with what is emotively deep and permanent in man. For comedy, greater attention to period is required in order to illuminate the particular forms in which that outlook reincarnates itself.

What is essential to, though less apparent in, later works does in fact emerge clearly in Attic drama. There, tragedy is an expression of man as an individual, emphasising the solitary virtues of pride, courage and defiance. The protagonist need not be good provided he is great; as a 'hero' he is superhuman, like the Ajax of Sophocles or Shakespeare's Macbeth. But he is extraordinary rather than monstrous. With the introduction of the monstrous, tragedy ends and the horror play or melodrama begins.

Since men are social beings as well as individuals such heroes are not only admired but also subconsciously feared and envied and there-fore must fall. Tragedy, then, solves a psychological dilemma in the audience, the key lying in *sacrifice*, the heart of the tragedy. The element of envy is the smallest part of the total satisfaction, however; the hero's sacrifice and suffering is mainly an atonement for what we might have done. His death, like the old ritual death of the god, is doubly satisfying: it exalts and purifies; we are at once ennobled and purged.

The heroes of tragedy are morally ambiguous. In them is clearly revealed the power of those basic passions of human nature which are not in themselves either good or evil but without which nothing much can be achieved at all. The tragic effect is both cathartic and mithridatic, insofar as the tragedy gives relief for the present and strength for the future. In sophisticated tragedies (as often in Ibsen) the sacrifice may consist of a spiritual death rather than a physical one, and the slayer may be merely a pettier villain, or society, or ill fortune—provided that there is a sense of inexorable law linking the death with the qualities of the protagonist. For there is no room in tragedy for the accidental; it is rooted in a sense of inevitable process and the need for death. That is why *Romeo and Juliet* is not one of Shakespeare's great tragedies; it so narrowly escapes being a comedy of errors.

Comedy seems to be almost completely complementary to tragedy. It has more room for character and accident, as might be expected from its original connection with fertility and life (which, unlike death, is not absolute). Where tragedy is primarily an expression of man's individuality and greatness, and only secondarily (in the underlying pleasure in seeing the mighty brought low) of his social nature, comedy is the reverse. Mainly the expression of man as a social being, it is commonly concerned with his littleness and is critical of it. The relation of plot to character is one of contingency, not necessity, and the protagonists are often monstrous but not great (witness the number who are governed by one characteristic 'humour' like an animal in the cage of its natural limitations). Such characters are more suitable for laughter than death. Finally, tragic death puts an end to suffering, whereas the conclusion of a comedy—marriage, punishment, or reform—usually implies a fresh beginning.

The social-corrective aspect of comedy, however, is not to be overemphasised, since laughter that appears to be on behalf of society may be a form of self-defence; we feel safe about our own shortcomings when attacking someone else's. Comedy, particularly in a late period may be more often mithridatic than we imagine, covertly *inuring* us to the faults of society and self. In these cases, tone and purport may not match*; the writer's attitude is more complex, perhaps, than he himself is aware of. Moreover, since men are individuals as well as social beings we are sometimes impelled to sympathise with a supposedly anti-social protagonist, and our laughter is kindly, a wooden sword of pseudo-criticism. Falstaff is a case in point (though there is, of course, much more to him than this). Again, comedy may be the product of minority groups, or large but powerless ones, concerned to degrade. In such comedy, accepted social values or institutions are mocked in parody or satire, mostly in forms other than the dramatic. Much bawdry may be of this type†—amusing because it cloaks a subconscious and temporary dethroning of what is consciously and conventionally sacrosanct. It expresses man's need for freedom—however temporary —from restraint.

---

* Some Restoration plays, for instance, seem to be of this sort: pretended satires implicitly conveying attitudes contrary to those expressed. And Pope's *Rape of the Lock* seems to be an example of that paradox, the *affectionate satire*.

† This point is expanded in the Introduction to *The Common Muse*, ed. Pinto and Rodway (London 1957, 1965). The street-ballads collected there contain many clear examples. The psychological mechanism behind some of this sort of comedy is elucidated in Freud's *Jokes and their Relation to the Unconscious*, Trans. James Strachey, London 1960. Historically speaking, a disparity between the official ideal and the accepted practice (as, for instance, in the case of arranged marriages) is a sufficient exterior cause of such comedy.

The apparently perennial characteristics of tragedy and comedy in their protean period forms correspond loosely with what their origin would lead us to expect. In one word, good comedy tends to be civilising; good tragedy, exalting. The one, so to say, expresses man as cultivator; the other, man as warrior.

The Dionysiac festival of incarnation involved the sacrifice and eating of the god, so that his divinity should be *assimilated* by the worshippers, and this finds its image in tragedy, the derivative art-form, in the divinising of man. Comedy, on the other hand, sprang from festivals involving drink, and erotic ritual by way of sympathetic magic to *aid* the gods in their task of renewing the fertility of the earth: a task essential to society. Hence, its gods are humanised. (Indeed Cornford goes so far as to say that the gods in Aristophanes are always inferior to the human protagonist). In other words, Fate is taken to be *manageable* by human beings. Tragedy emphasises inflexible courage needed to face a *remorseless* Fate; comedy emphasises flexibility to get by it, round it, or on with it. Comedy tends to integrate man's nature within itself or with the nature of his world, so that he can swim in his sea of troubles; tragedy encourages him to take arms against it.

Certain qualities, then, were characteristic of comedy-and-farce though not all of them are to be found in every work. There is: the exuberant zest for life, usually connected with sex; the tendency to degrade elevated personages; the merriment (in comedy, not as an end in itself but as part of a purposive activity; and this implies some degree of detachment); the connection with ritual, which may be considered analogous to the secular rituals we call 'convention' or 'custom' (both, of course, liable to be regarded as replaceable in a sophisticated period); and finally, there is the element of licence: anti-repressive, but usually only to the extent of restoring a balance (rather as the sensuality of fertility ceremonies was often preceded by a time of voluntary abstinence).

Similar qualities are to be found in that strange pagan survival, the medieval Church's Feast of Fools, and in the secular ceremony of the election of a Lord of Misrule which followed it, both of which have affinities with early English comedy. Clearly, too, the Bacchic recurs in Rabelais, the most Aristophanic of later writers.

None of these qualities, of course, is a *necessary* characteristic of any object, person or situation; so comedy cannot be defined ostensively: by pointing and saying 'That is comic'. Nothing is inherently comic. 'Comedy', like other critical terms, implies treatment—a characteristic *relationship* between symbol and subject. This stems from the artist's attitude to his material—a sort of summer of the mind which can mellow any subject. Its purposive, but not bitter, attitude is inseparably linked with laughter* (though not synonymous with it). In short, comedy can be thought of as *a particular mode—at least slightly genial—of mocking propaganda for (or against) some desiderated norm.*

This is not the only possible idea of comedy, nor does it constitute a formal definition, but it does tally with observed facts, social as well as literary; it is a refinement, not a contradiction of common-sense usage; and it is sufficiently flexible to be of more help than hindrance in getting to grips with so protean an art. Moreover, such a defining idea gives distance, and so enables the critic to meet the artist on his own ground.

All art requires some detachment from life. To be an artist is to be a spectator; the actor, immersed in the flux of living, tends to see only what is relevant to his next action. Comedy requires more detachment than most modes of art, especially if it is 'high comedy': that which is systematic rather than emotional, preferring theory to character-study. Not necessarily better than any other type—any more than Jonson is 'better' than Shakespeare—such comedy more obviously *is* comedy, and not farce or divertisement. In this late form, 'body' is strained off, characters tend to be types, and plot is intricate and artificial, so that the demonstration of absurdity may be contemplated rather than experienced.

The quality of detachment combines with the social mode of comedy, its unheroic adaptability, and its wariness about rigid philosophy, to render it peculiarly fluid. It changes from generation to generation and easily adapts itself to specialised means and ends; it encompasses a number of moods—ranging from the satirical to the humorous, the didactic to the celebratory—and may be in any major kind: poem, play, or novel.

That comedy should adapt itself to the changes of society is hardly surprising, but the variety to be found *within* each period is apt to

---

* 'Laughter', of course, is not to be taken too narrowly. A worldly-wise book may arouse no more than an inner, intellectual smile and yet be 'comic'. In the *Divina Commedia*, however, not even so tenuous a link with outright laughter exists, and one has to say that it is not in any acceptable modern sense a 'comedy'. Dante's conception of comedy as the movement from sorrow to joy is no more adequate for dealing with the literature now available than is Chaucer's view of 'tragedy' as the fall from 'heigh degree Into myserie' (*Prologue to the Monk's Tale*).

be so. Of course, certain sets of ideas or ways of life, and the styles used for expressing them, tend to persist (though with lessened vitality) when the social situation that called them forth no longer prevails. These styles run alongside more pertinent comedy, and may even provoke a new 'literary' comedy designed to hasten the ruthless course of evolution—parody being the commonest means to this end. A more important cause of variety within a period, however, is the lack of homogeneity in civilised societies. What appears 'typical' of a period when seen from a considerable distance in time, is the resultant of the various competing forces that produce what we call historical evolution.

The 'culture' of any highly developed society is somewhat akin to the policy of an American Government: an unstable compromise derived from an amalgamation of competitive groups. Every culture is engaged in a perpetual defence of its established values. But established values may not always be the best ones. They are often compromised in more senses than one. As D. W. Harding writes in his excellent study *Social Psychology and Individual Values* (London 1953):

> where a culture has stabilised behaviour based on morbid unconscious processes, some of its deviant individuals may be much nearer mental coherence than the conforming members of the group.
>
> (p. 123)

He gives the following instances:

> The institutions and sentiments of medieval chivalry, as it affected the relations between the sexes, did violence to human nature. The Victorian conceptions of decency meant too serious a distortion of natural facts to be maintained without repression. It seems likely that a well-integrated mind will tend to strain away from those features of its culture which too much distort human nature and which would involve severe conflict but for rationalisation and repression.
>
> (p. 122)

This reads almost like a statement of the need for innovatory comedy. Two further brief quotations, in amplification of Harding, may serve to sharpen the point. The first bears on the development of the (extra-marital) ideal of Courtly Love, often a target of medieval comedy. The second goes far to account for the tone of some of the comedy of the 1880s and 1890s.

> Not only the pleasure of the sexual act was held sinful (by the medieval church), but also the sensation of desire for a person of the opposite

sex, even when unconsummated. Since the love of a man for a woman was held to be simply desire, this led to the incontrovertible proposition that no man should love his wife. In fact, Peter Lombard maintained, in his apologetic *De excusatione coitus*, that for a man to love his wife is a sin worse than adultery—'Omnes ardentior amator propriae uxoris adulter est'.

(G. R. Taylor, Sex in History, London 1953, p. 52.)

The perfect hostess will see to it that the works of female and male authors are segregated on her shelves. Their proximity, unless the authors are married, should not be tolerated.*

In complex societies the availability of diverse viewpoints eases the pressure of Establishment values, allowing gifted individuals a hope of gaining allies, of swinging certain Centre groups (to revert to political imagery) from Left to Right, or more usually from Right to Left, in their allegiance, in order to turn a minority viewpoint into a majority one, or at least to gain tolerance for it.

Since we value the opinion of others we like to have the widest possible range of our desired activities sanctioned, if only by a section of society. Hence, the natural tendency to try to bring about a congenial social context, to change public opinion. An established majority may use force against innovators—but ridicule is often more successful, besides being free from the aftertaste of guilt. For minorities, comedy provides the obvious answer—though it may need to smuggle an attitude through in disguise. That unlikable and undesirable attitudes may also be smuggled through to produce decadent comedy, is always possible (witness the sentimental comedy of the eighteenth century). Narcissism may disguise itself as an honest attempt at self-knowledge, exhibitionism as philanthropy, arrogance as fearlessness, or bigoted reaction as the guardian of tradition. Only a probing literary criticism, trained on the particular work can reveal whether it is a sham or a genuine comic impulsion towards what Harding gives as the crux of the individual's relationship to society:

> the central effort of a living being to remain an integrated whole and avoid the tension that results from actions conflicting with the stable features of his personality, such as his sentiments and the established hierarchy of his values.

(Op. cit. p. 54)

* The *Manchester Guardian*, March 19, 1954 (Miscellany), reporting the quotation, by Mr E. H. Mason, the Cheshire County Librarian, of 'an almost incredible passage from a book of etiquette published in 1863'.

The rituals from which comedy sprang seem to have aimed at just such an integration with self and society; and since the type of effort remains the same, though its form changes, this concept provides *one* permanently valid touchstone for the evaluation of any comedy: Did it—and, more important, does it—aid such integration?

Criticism is concerned not so much with the specific events or ideas given (which are likely to be often 'dated') as with more general analogies, and with such qualities of the work as style and structure, comprehension of human nature and its impulses, and the intelligence, grasp and subtlety, clarity or force of its insights or of its marshalling of evidence. These can be judged with comparative objectivity, the first two by comparison with other literature, the remainder by comparison with one's experience of living intimately with other people, which is paradoxically general, in contrast to dogmas or conventions, which are usually restricted to particular periods, places, or sects.*

To what use (if any) his audience puts a writer's work is more a matter for the historian than the critic. For the one is concerned with temporary social effects, the other—no matter how practical the author's intention—with more permanent literary effects. Literature fulfils its proper function more in offering opportunity for enriched awareness of problems and potentialities than in offering ready-made solutions. History conditions comedy, but judgement of it must be critical more than historical.

Complex open societies give man little easy guidance, though they do not diminish his human stature as is often supposed. On the contrary they increase it by giving more freedom of action and belief, and therefore more responsibility. But with responsibility comes anxiety, in the same package, for the difficulty of making choices of action and attitude naturally grows with the increase of possibilities.

For the present-day critic, faced with the competing standards embodied in English comedies the difficulty is aggravated, since it hardly seems appropriate to limit to pure description criticism of works concerned with altering standards. Evaluation, as well as description, of their qualities and total effect seems called for—and indeed is

---

* The dogmas and conventions themselves must, of course, be distinguished from the human impulses that give rise to them. The effects of the first pre-frontal leucotomies (impairment of ethical judgement, loss of conscience and sensitivity, decline in sincerity) indicate that human potentiality for 'moral' qualities is permanent, innate and *structural*. The form they take, however, is changeable; and comedy is one of the agents of change.

difficult to avoid, as so many of the terms he must use are inseparably both descriptive and evaluative. However, he is helped by being out of the game (until he comes to his own day). Moreover, the qualities he is concerned with are always potential aids to integration; so that a modern critic can safely adopt as one touchstone some such criterion as Harding implies; for all but the sternest moralists now approve of integration even at the price of not mortifying the flesh. Furthermore these qualities remain the same in essence, and so are not likely to be impenetrably disguised by a work's period dress.

Finally, so far as social context is concerned, it is helpful that most social groups tend to be *Innovatory* or *Conserving*. Each attitude, at certain times has been conducive to a society which permitted an integrated fullness of living and has then narrowed and hardened. During phases of satisfactory social integration we should expect the best comedy, on our standards, to be mainly *conserving* (though a brilliant sourpuss might produce a work of which we should have to praise the esthetic, while deploring the social tendency). Similarly, during the hardening phases, we are likely to find the best comedy *innovating* (and to be obliged to qualify our praise of technically-good conserving comedy).

Such generalisations, however, are useful only as a first step towards the criticism of particular comedies, but clearly closer scrutiny of the special concepts relevant to the criticism of comedy is needed.

3

Critical Terminology

Besides the obvious social polarity of conserving and innovatory, there is an equally general psychological polarity. Though some correspondence between the social and psychological may be admitted, they are not identical. What there is to be conserved in any period, for example, will materially affect the type of man who will become a conserver.

W. Trotter (*Instincts of the Herd in War and Peace.* London 1916) speaks of a psychological tendency to approximate in greater or lesser degree either to a *Resistive* or to a *Sensitive* type. Resistives refuse to acknowledge uncongenial aspects of their experience, rationalising, repressing or reinterpreting them instead. Sensitives, more flexible, admit to themselves the real nature of their experience and are consequently the readier to be unconventional when conventions no longer match needs. This division tallies roughly with Freud's father-identifiers and mother-identifiers respectively. Using the terms *Patrist* and *Matrist*, Taylor (op. cit.) has been able to characterise the mood of certain periods or societies, from the dominance of one type or the other, according as they tended to be restrictive, inhibited, distrustful of pleasure, and authoritarian; or on the contrary, permissive, hedonistic, and liberal. H. F. Eysenck (*Uses and Abuses of Psychology.* London 1953), an astringent university psychologist, highly sceptical about psycho-analysts, still finds that controlled experiments confirm the same sort of relationship, between social attitudes and inner personality. More plausibly, however, he locates his initial determinant not in early identification with one parent or the other but in the general type of upbringing—something obviously much more conditioned by large-scale social factors. Contrasting the *Authoritarian* with the *Tolerant*, he finds in the one a strong tendency to be prejudiced, in the other, to be open-minded; repression and awareness being the chief mechanisms of the respective attitudes;

> The outstanding feature of the research [*centred on the factor of anti-semitism*] was that the extremely unprejudiced individual tended to manifest a greater readiness to become aware of unacceptable

tendencies and impulses in himself; the prejudiced individual, on the other hand, showed the opposite tendency of not facing these impulses openly, and thus failing to integrate them satisfactorily into his total personality. .... Among these tendencies which are repressed .... are mainly fear, weakness, passivity, sex impulses, and aggressive feelings against authoritarian figures, expecially the parents.

(p. 273)

He goes on to contrast the authoritarian's tendency to externalisation with that of the tolerant to internalisation, adding that the former seems to have 'relatively little enjoyment of sensuality, or of passive pleasures such as affection, companionship, or art and music' (p. 274). That is to say, the authoritarian projects his repressions on to others:

anti-semites, in addition to being ethnocentric and conservative, also tended to be patriotic, religious, anti-feminist, and sadistic-aggressive, as shown by their endorsement of flogging, the death penalty, and so forth.

(p. 270)

Other outstanding characteristics proved to be 'conventionalism' as opposed to 'love-orientation', and 'rigidity' as opposed to 'flexibility'.

We do not need to commit ourselves fully to Bergson's view that comedy is the attack of living flexibility on deadening rigidity to perceive that far more comedy is likely to be produced by one type than the other. Not only are authoritarians equipped with far fewer of the attributes needed by the comic artist, but also they are naturally attracted to those professions that exercise power—the Army, the Police, the Bench, the Church—where their drive (the beneficial result of repression) will often enable them to reach the top. And those who hold power have less need of comedy than those who do not. When comedy is in fact produced by resistives, patrists or authoritarians it is usually when the balance of social power, or the climate of opinion, is such that force seems inapplicable or a confession of moral weakness. Generally, too, it is written by men who are merely somewhat to the right of Centre, as it were—a timely reminder that the classifications refer to polar extremes, where type-differences are more immediately perceptible than amongst the more moderate majority.

Such comedy need not be conserving, as we have seen, and in its own day it might conceivably be *politically* innovatory—if there were arguably a need for dictatorship, say. But it is difficult to see how such comedy could be permanently valuable: i.e. integrative in the psychological sense given by Harding, for this type cannot be itself balanced and integrated—save perhaps when set in an exceptionally stable environment.

For reference to a work's period aspect, then, such sociological terms as 'conserving' or 'innovating' are to be preferred. For its more permanent psychological aspect, the psychological terms 'restraining' and 'releasing' will be better. On the whole, we are likely to give more weight to what encourages psychological integration than what encourages social integration, since the latter is more likely to be of interest only in relation to the setting of its own period.

Both types may—and most likely will—be combined. For example, a comedy could be socially innovating and individually restraining, if written by an authoritarian in a predominantly tolerant period (witness T. S. Eliot's drab comedies, which seem to be preparations for a backward progress by reactionary innovation). Though there is a tendency for conserving and restraining comedy to embody authoritarian, resistive attitudes, and for innovating and releasing comedy to embody sensitive, tolerant ones, it is not very marked, and any combination is possible.

Anyway, major comic writers are unlikely to be extreme examples of either psychological type, since to be—or even seem—detached requires some degree of balance.

What happens to anti-puritanism in comedy illustrates these points. Jonson's comedy deals almost purely in types, not individuals, and is ostensibly concerned to *conserve* Renaissance harmony* and *restrain* individualistic excess. In Restoration comedy, which otherwise takes a great deal from Jonson, anti-puritanism is both *innovating* and *releasing*, a double-barrelled attempt to substitute a Hedonist ideal of the Wit for the Puritan ideal of the Saint. For Jonson puritanism just might gain the day; for Etherege it had gained it.

Any insinuation of values or attitudes must tend to modify public opinion. As it is obvious that neither the world nor its literature has always changed for the better, it seems proper to allow that though comedy must be *purposive*, by definition, it need not be 'corrective'. We are, however, now able to add to our previous idea of comedy the concept of sociability. To the statement that comedy is the product of a purposive genial attitude we can add that it is further distinguished from tragedy by its gregarious quality.

---

* See also *Twelfth Night*, II. iii. 'Dost thou think because thou art virtuous, there shall be no more cakes and ale?' Another recognition of the danger of an innovatory attitude—represented here by the puritan Malvolio—which happened to be the opposite of liberalising.

The tragic hero is invested with his isolation; though it may cause his downfall, it does not reduce his stature. In comedy, such extreme individualism is seen as eccentric or abnormal. Again, the comic writer, unlike the lyric poet, has an audience in mind when he composes; and more than the writer of tragedies he seems concerned to have the audience accept his view—but is wary of overt didacticism.

Though laughter is compatible with attitudes other than the comic —and may be a mere physical reflex, as in the case of tickling—it is not compatible with what we normally think of as preaching. In short, comedy is purposive in a uniquely accommodating way, and thus produces more complex, if less perceptible effects than the exhortations of solemn or sentimental works.

Now 'farce', for all its backslapping, lacks this sort of sociability. Insofar as it reaches to the depths of the psyche it is more akin to tragedy than comedy. L. J. Potts (*Comedy*, London 1948, p. 152) neatly defines farce as 'Comedy with the meaning left out'. In comedy, that is to say, laughter is a means to an end; in farce the means *is* the end: it is purposeless—but not therefore motiveless. Knockabout farce is often unconsciously motivated: the expression of subconscious impulses of envy, aggression or herd feeling. So patches of such farce may serve comedy well *as one of its means*, both in giving psychological depth and in relieving the diplomatic manner by the acrobatic. But farce on its own draws one into a primitive private world, where conscious awareness, particularly of a social kind, is relatively absent, and no responsive effort is required of the audience. It is thus different from the sort of writing to deserve the title of 'comedy'.

The definitive qualities of comedy, then, must include a considerable degree of conscious control, in the whole if not in every part. Though value-judgements must be insinuated *un*didactically, the spectator should not be allowed to lose himself in the laughter. A certain 'distance' is requisite. Neither writer nor audience should be so involved in a comedy as in a farce. Its 'balance' holds judgement in one scale, geniality in the other.

Yet it is often possible to feel for the characters of comedy, though never for those of farce. The point is that we feel for them as characters separate from ourselves, whereas in farce we are involved with fragments from an inner world. In existentialist terms, we are *pour soi* (dominating and contemplating the subject) or *en soi* (submerged and thinglike). Being primitive, farce may have greater staying-power than comedy, but it will have less effect; for it only exercises our nature, it does not try to alter our behaviour.

There remains one further class of amusing works. 'Divertisement' may serve to describe works which, like farce, leave the meaning out (sometimes, as in the miscalled 'sentimental comedy', most of the laughter too), and like comedy abjure the acrobatic. In a word they are frivolous rather than farcical or comic. At their best they manipulate current verbal counters with sufficient skill to disguise their superficiality for many decades. Lyly, Steele, Wilde and Fry have thus coruscated in this sort of *intellectual farce**.

Any further clarification of words referring to modes and their psychological *causes* or moral or social *ends* would probably prove unnecessarily restrictive. But some elucidation of the vocabulary of *means* is urgently needed.

In common usage the distinctions between such indispensable terms as parody, burlesque, satire, invective, irony, cynicism, wit and humour are so blurred as to make them almost useless without some reworking. Since yesterday's usage was no more consistent than ours no 'right' meaning can be borrowed from history. (Coherent evolutions, particularly of 'Wit', have been made, of course, but only by leaving out the inconvenient usages proliferating in most periods.) Today's usage is known, if not clear, and it should be possible to work out concepts that are neither so tight that they hurt nor so loose that they come down, to evoke a distinctive meaning from the chaos of common usage without distorting it out of recognition. True, a word defines itself in use, but if you haven't some general meaning at the back of your mind how do you recognise and place any particular usage?

The need for clarification is apparent from the questions that spring to mind in connection with any one term. For instance, ought we to consider satire as a mode, distinct from comedy, like farce and divertisement? If it is a mode, is it so always or only sometimes? Or should it be looked at from a different angle altogether, if common usage can possibly be shown to permit such a viewpoint?

If comedy is accommodating, does it therefore follow, as almost all critics suppose, that it must be a different *genre* from satire? Certainly, satire can be savage and laughterless, but need it be so? Or it may have laughter but no human feeling—only perhaps such feelings as the

---

* Many modern farces, influenced by Feydeau, lie on the border of divertisement. There is a tension between the esthetic distance created by their ingenious plot and the involvement—compounded of malicious joy and secret relief—created by their content, the embarrassing, nightmare predicaments of the characters.

female mantis has for her mate. Pope's lines on Lord Harvey (Sporus) exude such a cannibalistic affection as the victim is mangled; the poet gains strength in a vampirish way. Could this possible be comedy? On the other hand, in the satire on Addison (Atticus) surely, for all its bite, there is a less dreadful feeling involved? And if there were not, could we possibly exclude the whole of the *Epistle to Arbuthnot* from the realm of comedy because it is satirical?

At this point as we are obviously approaching the field of wit, humour and irony: words that tend to gravitate towards any discussion on satire. It is an old-established critical custom to offer contrasting definitions of humour and comedy, wit and humour, comedy and satire, satire and ridicule, ridicule and humour. . . . Something is clearly amiss when one's definitions go round in circles. That is what comes of pairing items from different logical categories. In brief, a necessary distinction between methods and attitudes has been overlooked. This has not only led to a critical merry-go-round but also has had the effect of hiding much that deserves notice. The fact, for instance, that it is questionable whether humorous wit or comic satire *are* contradictions in terms. Certainly if we are to be forbidden by definition to use those terms we shall have to invent others that mean the same, for they fit some literary facts.

Some such scheme as this, however, seems workable:

> *Comedy, farce* and *divertisement* are to be taken as MODES;
> *Satire, humour, cynicism* and *celebration* as MOODS;
> *Irony, invective, parody, incongruity, slapstick, nonsense** and *wit* as

METHODS

The Modes, as the previous chapter indicated, represent the work's most general aspect. The mode of a work, in short, is the widest category—of a psychological, not a technical sort—into which it can be placed. The moods are a refinement or subdivision of a mode: the prevailing climate of that region. They represent the spirit, or tone, in which the methods are used. The methods are the writer's technical means of incarnation.

Perhaps sufficient has been said already of the distinguishing characteristics of the modes of comedy, farce and divertisement. Before passing on, however, to the distinguishing characteristics of the moods

---

* Nonsense might seem better placed among the MODES, but any complete nonsense work could be considered either farce or divertisement according to the type of nonsense.

and methods given, it might be as well to investigate a little further the notions of mode, mood and method themselves—if only as a reminder of their ultimate inseparability

First, it has to be admitted that the scheme can claim only critical usefulness, not absolute truth. Had PART II of this study been concerned not with English comedies but English satires, it might have proved more convenient to take 'satire' as the mode and 'the comical' (slightly redefined) as one mood that might give it a predominant flavour, to make a 'comic satire'. For such an investigation* would involve a different general interest and therefore different subdivisions; it would require a preliminary separation of *all* satire from all that is not satire and thereafter varieties of satire would need to be distinguished. Orwell's *Animal Farm*, then, might be called a comic satire to distinguish it from *Nineteen Eighty-Four*, a horrific satire. As we are dealing only with 'comedy', *Nineteen Eighty-Four* will not come within our purview at all, and *Animal Farm* will be more conveniently described as a 'satirical comedy' to distinguish it from humorous and cynical comedies that we might be dealing with.

Mode, then, is not normally a given form, but a more inclusive category. Structure usually contributes to it, but is not a definitive characteristic. Clearly it would be absurd to distinguish comedies from tragedies by intricacy of plot, though in fact there is a tendency to such a difference of structure. Like a human being, and unlike a machine, the work of art is a continuum. So the mode may be altered by alterations of mood and methods—just as, for instance, an aggressive mood in a man will affect his method of behaviour and his total being: colour, shape (posture of attack, perhaps) and internal relationships (heartbeat, blood pressure, glandular activity, muscular tension) —but these are inseparable from his mood. The continuum is unbreakable. A work is technically good or bad according to its success in embodying its purport. But the purport itself is deduced from what the work does as it goes on.

Normally we may suppose, the mood or attitude to the subject comes first (but, of course, some subjects prompt certain moods more than others) and then mood and subject together call for that handling of the subject which *in total* distinguishes one mode from another.

Mood is obviously more fundamental than method: a witty tragedy is not impossible, but a humorous tragedy would be a contradiction

* Something of the kind has in fact been done by A. M. Clark in a long essay, 'The Art of Satire and the Satiric Spectrum' in *Studies in Literary Modes*, London 1946, which anticipates and expands some of the points made here.

in terms. Yet sometimes structure—large-scale method—does come first. This is one of the harmful effects of tradition: the provision of set moulds into which authors obediently pour their feelings (tradition is helpful, on the other hand, when it provides formal models of the failure and success of various methods of embodying different moods).

It is in farce that such an order of precedence is probably most common and least harmful. Since farce is largely mechanical anyway, the writer can decide, let us say, to have one act of a play complicating relationships of A, B, C, and D; a second act of slapstick, containing one jelly-slapping scene, two in undies (female nylon, male Jaeger); and to wind up with a third act leading to an in-and-out-the-windows denouement—and then think of suitable characters, style and tone.

All the methods listed are no more than tools, which could be used in tragedy as well as comedy. It is the end to which they are used, the way they are deployed for a given purpose, which makes them 'comic'.

That the moods or attitudes are sensibly so described gains support from adjectival usage. We do speak of a man's having a humorous, satirical, or cynical attitude, but not of his having a witty or parodic one. Admittedly, we do sometimes speak of an 'ironic attitude to life', but this is one of the places where common usage has to be rather arbitrarily tidied up for critical purposes, for though the grammatical form is parallel to that for the moods the sense is not. We use this phrase more vaguely, to denote the detached, cynical or satirical attitude of which the irony is an *expression*. If greater precision is needed, irony must be thought of as a technique.

THE MOODS

Satire, the manifestation of a satirical mood may be subdivided *ad infinitum*. For instance, John Lawlor ('Radical Satire and the Realistic Novel', *Essays and Studies*. Vol. 8, London 1955) distinguishes the Augustan or urbane variety from the traditional rough one, and minor from major modes. Such refinements, however, are more useful in actual critical practice than for general definition. For the moment, satire can be sufficiently characterised as a corrective but entertaining attack on vices, using intellectual weapons and a tone of superiority (though occasionally the element of correction may be so slight that the satirical mood almost evaporates, leaving a work of intellectualised humour or clinical naturalism). Comedy that laughs not at a vice, but at some other departure from a desiderated norm—such as ugliness, uncouthness or simplemindedness—cannot be successfully satiric, for these things, though useful to point the norm, do not deserve *attack*.

Satirised characters are dealt with extrinsically: revealed not as they would see themselves, but as they would be seen by prefects in an upper form.

The commonest methods of a satirical mood are wit and irony: and while it uses them satire may remain within the bounds of comedy. When invective becomes predominant, however (as in the last book of *Gulliver's Travels*), the satire parts company with laughter and detachment and therefore passes from comedy into the less sunny realm of lampoon or flyting—a realm of attack more destructive than corrective, using less intellectual weapons, chiefly ridicule.

The humorous mood seems to be fundamentally one of self-defence. (To have a 'sense of humour' usually means to be able to shrug off one's mishaps.) Often, however, it assumes the guise of a good-natured attack on another character with whom we have some underlying cause for partial identification. Then our tolerant laughter at him protects us, in much the same way as our laughter at ourselves protects us, by forestalling the probably less indulgent laughter of others and burking further criticism. Thus humour is a tone indicating amusement without judgement or attack without malice.

Cynicism is easier to recognise than define, but its nature becomes more apparent if we take it to be the opposite of humour: essentially a form of self-attack. There are certain feelings or beliefs—those sponsored by 'conscience'—which we cannot ignore unless we are hypocritical. But we can snub them; we can devalue our sterling qualities. The cynic thus pretends to be bad, much as the hypocrite pretends to be good. Irony is the chief means of maintaining a cynical attitude, for it enables us to accept what we emotionally dislike by taking both sides of the ironic statement as of equal value so that it cancels itself out. By cynicism we bring about an uneasy truce between the forces of theory and practice. It is not peace but an armistice; we have inwardly agreed to differ. That writers of cynical comedy, like the early Huxley or Isherwood, sometimes become mystics is not accidental. Such comedy is based on despair and its purpose is not so much to defend values as to defend defeat.

All this means that cynicism is psychologically expensive, and may become ruinously so. Therefore it gets itself condemned as immature, immoral and destructive, and so artistically valueless. Yet in certain circumstances it may be a mature and responsible mood, the only way of preserving integrity, and therefore suitable for bitter comedy. Such circumstances, for instance, might arise when the general populace was being taken in by inflated values actually manipulated by pressure groups for their own end, and opposition was rendered impracticable. For a one-eyed man in the kingdom of the blind, cynicism is mature, moral, and (if only for him) integrative—a way of still seeing and surviving.

In comedy that is not cynical as a whole, too, cynicism may play a valuable part by deflating sentimentality: to the angel face it opposes a baboon's bottom (cf. Touchstone in *As You Like It*).

A mood of *'celebration'* may sound inappropriate for a purposive mode like comedy, and perhaps a better word might be found.* But it may serve as a reminder that 'comedy' is not being implicitly equated with 'humorous satire'. Its purposiveness may stop at revealing absurdity without trying to correct it—either because the writer likes the absurd or because he doesn't think it can be corrected, or because he thinks it's a necessary element in the individual or society, regrettable but amusing, which once corrected would leave life duller and colder than it was. Hence the prevailing climate of his comedy may be that of the 'celebration' of inescapably unideal common humanity, despite squalls of satire and bright periods of humour. Or, people may be shown overcoming their weaknesses.

This term will cover great comedy like Chaucer's 'Marriage Group' in the *Canterbury Tales*, Shakespeare's *Twelfth Night* and *As You Like It*, and Joyce's *Ulysses*. All these are shotsilk comedies, the product of myriad-minded men, who seem conscious of the complexity of experience and the limitations of every view, so that one mood tends to be given depth by a shading of some other.

Such writers relish the absurd at the same time as they expose it, have a good deal of charity for the failings of human nature and appreciate the need for variety in the world. Thus, though they place what is laughable by some implicit norm of sanity and balance, they also seem to accept it as a concomitant of human nature—and none of them thinks human nature itself can be much changed, though it may be amended somewhat. So they are not too severe, not too whole-hearted in their comedy, for behind the effort to change particular manifestations of human folly lies the feeling *Plus ça change, plus c'est la même chose*.

Such writers tend to be empirical humanists rather than systematic moralists. Their comedy mingles farce and sadness, and the shotsilk quality of their vision tends to make the comic point less apparent.

---

* 'Festive' would serve admirably, save that it seems a little too gay in its implications to be right for a comedy tinged with sadness, like *Twelfth Night* (though the title and the name Feste do indeed tend to justify the word).

Indeed there may be no one point—apart from the general trend in favour of benevolent discrimination. Thus against a gain in human richess must be set a loss in force. So the established preference for Shakespeare's comedies rather than those of Jonson has no objective validity. Shakespeare has more depth, but then Jonson has more direction. For comic purposes, neither strength seems universally or necessarily more valuable than the other.

THE METHODS

Irony needs fairly extensive consideration, even for such a general characterisation as this. Fortunately, it is one of the few words whose etymology proves helpful.

So many critics, especially in America, find irony under every stone that a reminder of its original meaning may not come amiss— *eironeia* 'assumed ignorance', from *eiron*, 'a dissembler'. The sense of the dissembling that is meant to be seen through must remain fundamental if the word is to have any consistent function. And R. H. Brower, for instance, is misguided in extending the term to cover Keats' *Ode to Autumn* (*The Fields of Light*, New York 1951, p. 27). 'Irony' is not synonymous with 'ambiguity': though it is ambiguous, as the ironic vision is bifocal.

On that last point, Brower is right; irony is not merely a matter of seeing a 'true' meaning beneath a 'false', but of seeing a double exposure (in both senses of the word) on one plate. The fact of opposition must be as apparent as the fact that it is overcome. Only then will there be an effect of laughter, usually inward laughter, through the release of tension.

The risk, of course, is that the dissembling will not be seen through. One recalls the story of the old dear who re-read Mr Gibbon for the sake of all the pious reflections in his footnotes. Irony needs a discerning audience. But given such an audience it may prove the most profitable of means.

Where primary states like hostility subdue, irony, more complex, may reform. Hence its prevalence in satirical comedy. Such comedy combines strong feeling with didactic purport by means of barbed laughter.

A few of the more important operations of irony may be indicated. Probably deflation is the commonest: the apparently indifferent introduction of the physical, perhaps, when we are concerned with the moral, or the apparent equating of ideals with mundane facts, or the humbling of a proud style by a bastard content. Pope's *Rape of the*

Lock is full of such deflations, and a run of them is to be found in Swift's verses on his death.

The technique of inversion—of roles, ideas, or value—is so often found in the works of Shaw with his dustman-philosophers and the like, that it hardly needs illustration. Again, there is fusion—usually of appearance and reality. Witness Robert Ferrars, who is adorned in the first style of fashion and has 'a person and face of strong, natural, sterling insignificance' (*Sense and Sensibility*. Chap. XXXIII).

Finally, where irony is used not for satirical but for cynical comedy it is often masochistic. The author identifies himself with the bad, the impotent or the defeated. Possibly some of Henry James comes into this category. This sort of irony was presumably at the back of Kierkegaard's mind when he wrote that irony ends by killing the individual—a dubious judgement, though provocatively near the mark for some cases.

An author's reasons for using irony may be extremely varied. In addition to those implicit in the foregoing account, there is its use to blame without seeming to, by divorcing tone and statement, as in Fielding's *Jonathan Wild* (passim). This use suggests that the writer is more polished and urbane, more 'polite' than his opponent, and is common in Augustan irony. Irony may also be used to imply that the case is so foolproof that only a reminder of it, a hint, is needed— anyone thinking otherwise convicting himself of proven foolishness. Argument can be answered; irony cannot, for it undermines a position in the very act of defending it. Again, irony is a form of flattery for the intelligent reader, and a veiled threat to the hypothetical opponent; he had better be careful how he deals with so levelheaded a fellow as the writer. There is the suggestion, too, of dispassionate objectivity; the ironist has obviously not been misled by passion or prejudice. Since in all he writes there is an implication as well as a statement, it seems to follow, however illogically, that he sees both sides of a question. And finally irony substitutes a tone of reasoned contempt for an expected indignation: witness Swift's *Modest Proposal* or the *Letters* of Junius. The ironist seems to give light instead of heat, since he has maturity enough to see round a question and not to be blinded by wrath.

Obviously, irony can be used in any sort of comedy, and in some tragedy; when it passes into *sarcasm*, in its crudest form, it is usually found to be keeping bad company with invective in a noncomic satire.

The place of *invective* in comedy appears to be small, and is in fact smaller than it appears to be, for much of what might be taken for invective turns out to be humorous hyperbole. Falstaff's bravura passage on Bardolph's nose, for instance, is less biting, and more comic, than a shorter and intenser attack on the drunkard's debasement would have been. The swelling takes away the sting:

> FALSTAFF Thou art our admiral, thou bearest the lantern in the poop,—but 'tis in the nose of thee; thou art the knight of the burning lamp.
>
> BARDOLPH Why, sir John, my face does you no harm.
>
> FALSTAFF No, I'll be sworn; I make as good use of it as many a man doth of a death's head, or a *memento mori*: I never see thy face, but I think upon hell-fire, and Dives that lived in purple; for there he is in his robes, burning, burning. If thou wert in any way given to virtue, I would swear upon thy face; my oath should be, by this fire that's God's Angel. But thou art altogether given over; and wert indeed, but for the light in thy face, the son of utter darkness. When thou ran'st up Gadshill in the night to catch my horse, if I did not think thou hadst been an *ignis fatuus* or a ball of wildfire, there's no purchase in money. O, thou art a perpetual triumph, an everlasting bonefire light! Thou has saved me a thousand marks in links and torches, walking with thee in the night betwixt tavern and tavern: but the sack thou has drunk me, would have bought me lights as good cheap, at the dearest chandler's in Europe. I have maintained that salamander of yours with fire, any time this two-and-thirty years; God reward me for it!
>
> (*Henry IV*, Pt. I, iii. iii)

The general tone is sufficiently indicated by the movement from the genial 'I think upon hell-fire' (which could have been bitterly indicting) to the not-completely-ironical 'God reward me for it!'

On the satiric scale, true invective generally lies at the opposite end from detached irony. And invective-satire is of a lower order than ironic-satire, if only because it does not work so well. The follies of big-enders and little-enders in Lilliput seem follies indeed, for they are presented with a detached irony. But at the end of *Gulliver's Travels* few readers can help siding with the loving wife who is called 'that odious Animal' and the children who have the misfortune to smell more like human beings than horses. That satire is unsweetened by laughter, and its bitterness leaves a nasty taste behind. Furthermore, its tonal effect is neurotic rather than integrative. Ultimately—no matter what Swift may have intended—one gets a sense that man's inescapable humanity is being found disgusting.

Parody need present no difficulties, provided that it is distinguished from its near relations, *burlesque* and *mock-heroic*. According to Dryden and Boileau there is burlesque when a high theme is treated in a low style; when a low theme is treated in a high style, there is mock-heroic. A distinction adequate for most critical purposes. Parody is a form of mimicry that is just off the note, and it may therefore approximate to burlesque or mock-heroic, according as it is sharp or flat. Almost invariably it is connected with that 'degrading' whose ritual origin was remarked in Chapter 2. Aristophanes used the device frequently. With the tragedies fresh in his audience's mind, he was able to degrade the gods humorously, and Euripides satirically, by parodying the latter's work.

In parody we enjoy seeing the mighty fall, to our own level or a little below it; so that it is generally a means of what we have called 'releasing' comedy—in Aristophanes, of an anti-innovating kind as a rule. It acts as a preservative, keeping sentiment from going sugary, solemnity from becoming pompous. All good qualities are in danger of losing vitality or relevance and hardening into mannerism. Parody indicates the end-product of such a process. It is unique among methods of comedy in that it usually mocks not the bad but the good, holding up a glass in which its worst potentialities are seen realised. Among modern parodies, Henry Reed's 'Chard Whitlow' (*A Map of Verona*, London 1946) stands out as both clever and salutary comedy, finely evoking the prim precisian latent in T. S. Eliot. So many spoof lines, too, carry a momentary air of admonitory authenticity: 'As we get older we do not get any younger', 'And I cannot say I should care (to speak for myself) to see my time over again—if you can call it time', or 'The wind within a wind, unable to speak for wind'. A clear warning of the disguised emptiness to come in *The Cocktail Party* and *The Confidential Clerk*.

Parody could, perhaps, have been subsumed under 'Incongruity'—in this case, of content and manner—but *incongruity*, like *knockabout*, hardly warrants much discussion. Both are immediately recognisable and primarily arouse *un*thoughtful laughter by surprise. Knockabout, in particular, is far more often a means of farce than comedy.

Nonsense is more interesting. In her sensible book on the subject (*The Field of Nonsense*, London 1952) E. Sewell maintains that nonsense is a game in which the forces of logic play—and beat—the forces of dream and disorder.

However, if one is not going to concentrate on Lewis Carroll, and unlike Miss Sewell, has no theological axe to grind, the worlds of dream and disorder can surely be considered as Nonsense. Why, after all, is the mind able to receive nonsense in only '*one* of three ways' (loc. cit. p. 4)? The common use of the word covers all three ways, and all three have this in common: they are not of the world of the senses and commonsense. Logic, like algebra, is independent of it; dream transforms it; and disorder denies its laws. The last species seems of no value in itself and of no use for comedy. As Miss Sewell says (p. 5) 'nothing is more boring' than 'an endless succession of random events'. Dream-nonsense, however, may well be of use for comedy, since it can symbolise realities of the world of sense and commonsense in a striking way or obliquely comment on them.

Much condensation but comparatively little distortion of everyday reality, produces not nonsense but *wit*, the most important and inclusive of all our terms.

Wit was once thought of as a mental quality, as opposed to humour, a bodily fluid. And doubtless there still lingers an echo of that fundamental distinction. However, there is certainly no contradiction today in speaking of a humorous man as an intelligent one also. Moreover, Freud, who has given by far the most satisfactory modern account of wit (op. cit.) shows that there is such a thing as humorous wit. Thus the idea of a contradiction between wit and humour is shown to be itself contradictory. The puzzle is solved by taking the one to be a method, the other a mood.

Both fact and theory make it apparent that wit may be used to convey *any* comic mood (and also, as in *Hamlet* and *Lear*, attitudes that are not comic). Its intellectual quality and its indirectness render it peculiarly fitted for comedy, which is a civilising agent, an alternative to violence as a group-weapon. Of this sort of use Clough's *The Latest Decalogue* is a deservedly well-known example, and its most famous couplet is not only a biting comment on the economic orthodoxy of a sanctimonious age but also an accidental description of the satirical wit's own attitude;

> Thou shalt not kill; but needst not strive
> Officiously to keep alive.

Wit taps the deeper levels of the psyche; it is the only civilised equivalent of those 'releasing' elements of primitive ritual which in most developed societies—particularly Christian ones—are considered too aggressive, too irreverent or too indecent for open expression. This, indeed, seems to be intrinsic to wit: that though it is made *by* the intellect it is made *from* the unconscious. Irony on the other hand is intrinsically conscious. The ironist applies his technique quite consciously; wit comes 'in a flash'. Brevity is the soul of wit, which must, as it were, shortcircuit the civilised mind's censorship system; whereas irony can be leisurely. There are, then, two layers in wit: an intellectual veneer which varies as the culture changes, and a primitive substratum always effective regardless of changes in outward fashion.

Even if we ignore Freud's separation of word-wit and thought-wit, as a distinction without much difference, we are left with two broad categories. Though the two are not entirely separable, the distinction between *Play-Wit*, as we may call it, and *Tendency-Wit* seems both valid and necessary.

Play-Wit is probably a form of regression to the freedom of child-hood, an escape from the repressions required to maintain adult dignity, reason and responsibility. In consequence, it is primarily associated with ingenuity rather than intellect, and is more useful for farce or divertisement than for comedy. Almost by definition, what is playful is not particularly purposive, though it may release pent feelings and be brilliant—witness Whistler's remark that photography was a *foe-to-graphic* art, or Keith Preston's neat couplet:

> A modernist married a fundamentalist wife.
> And she led him a catechism and dogma life.

Next to the pun, dream-nonsense is perhaps the chief expression of play-wit. Often it occurs briefly in a complex pseudo-pun in the clinching phrase, as in the incongruous sexual-moral-economic-vocational complex in the word 'frontage' below:*

> There was a young lady from Wantage
> Of whom the town clerk took advantage.
> Said the borough surveyor:
> 'Indeed you must pay her;
> You've totally altered her frontage'.
>
> (*Anon*)

Significantly, England's great age of nonsense is the first three-quarters of the nineteenth century; an age too authoritarian to be ideal for comedy but for that reason needing the more a harmless way of retreat into farce and fantasy. In Lewis Carroll's case, of course

---

* That this is play-wit is confirmed by the fact that the joke will not stand up to analysis. The wit is merely verbal legerdemain. For, of course, the value of property to which a bay-window has been added is increased, not diminished, and therefore rates not compensation but extra tax.

to the strain of living up to standards of Victorian respectability were added those of being a mathematician, a male spinster, and a clergyman who dared not allow his logic to impinge on his religion.

In the twentieth century, America has been the land of nonsense, for it has resembled nineteenth-century England not only in its wealth and accompanying sense of virtuousness but also in the degree of pressure exerted by its conformism:

> . . . You crush all the particles down
> into close confirmity, and then walk back and forth on them.
>
> Sparkling chips of rock
> are crushed down to the level of the parent block
>
> (Marianne Moore, 'To A Steamroller')

Where pressures are too great, comedy is apt to be replaced by indignant revolt or regressive retreat.

Much play-wit shares with tendency-wit its kinship to the dream, but is obviously nearer the surface. Such wit more often chooses *de jure* subjects, and is limited to comedy of mild release. Moreover, it relies much more on the associations of words than ideas. Wodehouse's description of a character as 'meadowfied'—'cowed and sheepish'—is typical play-wit. Typical of tendency-wit, on the other hand, is that ancient joke (instanced by Freud) of the prince who noticed a slave resembling himself and asked patronisingly, 'Was your mother ever employed in the king's household?' 'No, Sire', came the reply, 'but my father was'. Here, quickness of wit deceives the emotions. The brevity and complexity of the largely implicit statement gives expression to thoughts and feelings that would otherwise have had to be repressed. A retaliatory impulse, a forbidden insult degrading the mighty, and a lightning piece of logical reasoning are compressed into that six-word answer. In that disguise they pass muster, expecially since the tension gathered for understanding is released in the hearer not through wrath but through laughter; at any rate when all the points are taken *at once*— not quite consciously —*together with* a recognition of the cleverness of the wit-work and of the incongruity of rude implication and polite tone.

As Freud points out a dream, too, uses disguises—such as Inversion, Substitution, Symbolism, Representation through Opposites, Indirect Expression (as in this joke) and so forth—in order to smuggle into consciousness tendencies to aggression or other forbidden behaviour. All these mechanisms are found in tendency-wit, too.

The correspondence between dream-work and wit-work, however, is not exact. Visual symbolism, the chief mechanism of the dream, is of much more service to the cartoonist than the writer. Again, a dream is usually personal and unintelligible. Wit is social and so must be intelligible; the disguise must not be impenetrable. Further, if wit is in words there is a natural tendency to coherence (unless a Dodgsonian logic-game is being played), as words are normally the agents of consciousness and sense: a late product of evolution; whereas the language of dreams is mainly pictorial: scarcely less primitive than the repressed impulses it works on. However, wit and dream share the kindred characteristics of latent significance, unexpectedness, disguise and compression. So although wit is made, not found, a good deal of its making, though not all of it, must be unconscious. The speaker often surprises himself, and yet is not quite so surprised or amused as his hearer. Surely the schoolboy author of the following tendency-witticism was neither completely conscious nor completely unconscious of his full meaning:

> During my first period of religious instruction this term [a teacher wrote to the *Manchester Guardian*] I was asked, 'What are the Seven Deadly Sins?' whereupon I enumerated them with brief explanations. Later in the morning I caught the questioner loafing and brought him out before my desk
>
> 'Smith,' I began in ominous tones, 'earlier this morning I enumerated for your benefit the Seven Deadly Sins. Can you remember any of them?'
>
> 'Yes, sir,' he replied. 'Wrath.'
>
> (M.G. Miscellany, 10.9.53)

It seems needless to multiply examples, enumerate tendencies, or subdivide mechanisms. Indecency and aggression are the forbidden tendencies most obviously served by wit, and all the mechanism can be subsumed under the one term, *Condensation*. Whether there is play on sound, as in Whistler's pun, or on sense, as with the word 'rest' in Dryden's epitaph on his wife:

> Here lies my wife, here let her lie.
> Now she's at rest—and so am I;

whether there is telescoping of form, as in De Quincey's remark that in old age one drops into anecdotage, or of ideas, as in Johnson's comment that second marriages represent the triumph of hope over experience, or of tone and implication, as in the husband's comment on his wife's epitaph:

> As I am now, so you must be,
> Therefore prepare to follow me. . . .

To follow you I'm not content;
How do I know which way you went?

(*Anon*)

—in each case there is condensation, and in each case some craving, playful or purposive, is gratified despite the potential hindrance of reason, respect, or politeness. Johnson's remark, however, is obviously not play-wit, and the element of tendentiousness—undermining the sacred and sentimental views of marriage—is so slight that we seem to be nearing the *epigrammatic*. If wit is defined as the marriage of intellect and abandon, begetting surprise and delight, then epigram is a chess-playing widower.

To confuse 'What oft was thought, but ne'er so well express'd' with the sort of wit that serves psychological needs was pardonable in Pope's day but is not so now. When La Rochefoucauld writes:

> Qui vit sans folie n'est pas si sage qu'il le croit. (The man who lives without folly is not so wise as he thinks.)

(*Maximes:* 209)

our satisfaction lies only in the recognition of a truth expressed with the utmost point and economy. This is even more apparent in number 228. We all know, perhaps rather vaguely, that pride is not precisely the same as self-love, but could we define the difference so as to reveal their distinct essences? How swiftly and how brilliantly La Rochefoucauld pierces the mist!

> L'orgueil ne veut pas devoir, et l'amour propre ne veut pas payer. (Pride dislikes owing, and self-love dislikes repaying.)

No desire, save that to understand, is here gratified. The case is different with some comments whose tone seems equally detached— so different as to require another name. Thus Gibbon's footnote on the Empress Theodora's banquet for ten nobles and forty slaves is witty, not epigrammatic. 'Her charity,' says Gibbon, 'was universal'. By doing so he intimates, demurely enough to pass the wards of decorum, that she took fifty men in one night; the word 'charity' opposes pagan and Christian attitudes to 'love' and implicitly praises the Empress (for charity is a ruler's Christian duty); he smiles at Christian chastity (for the Church's charity too, is 'universal', though not so literally loving) and excuses Theodora (who, after all, was putting precept into practice). Moreover, one is made aware of the smug Emperor Justinian, a *persecuting* Christian, deceived and given an object lesson in the love of one's fellow men by his pagan wife.

Tendency-wit could hardly go further or be more briefly complex. It is as civilised and delicate, too, as it well could be in the circumstances. After all, it just *might* refer only to the feast.

With this polished weapon Gibbon fought against the forces of barbarism and fanaticism that, in his view, had destroyed Augustan Rome, and were then menacing Augustan England. The polish of high civilisation, however, is not to be attained without exiling some part of human nature. There is some loss of depth and wholeness: a loss rarely made good by the following reaction, which usually tips the scale the other way. In England, a divorce of mind and body, of 'higher' and 'lower' faculties, is evident in most of the literature between Urquhart's translation of Rabelais and Joyce's *Ulysses*—a divorce responsible, at least in part, for the movement from Shakespearian richness of texture, through Congrevian urbanity, to a comedy of urban sentimentality. However, there is some gain too. 'Deformity' headed Bacon's list of objects of merriment (*Nat. Hist.* viii, 721); 'infirmities' were emphasised by Hobbes (*Human Nature* Ch. 9) but in his case the word was not restricted to a physical sense; and Congreve at the beginning of our Augustan age objects even to the mockery of fools if they were not self-made but born so (Dedication to *The Way of the World*).

He is, of course, in advance of his age. But then so is all comedy in one way, for whether innovating or conserving, releasing or restraining, it works humanely and without fanaticism, tending always rather to promote persuasion than persecution; and it must rank high among the many social factors which contributed to that one indisputable gain between the sixteenth and eighteenth centuries: the gradual humanisation of laughter and social life. By its nature comedy is a humane way of influencing public opinion. In the very act, even, of bringing a disciplinary vigour to a culture it contributes to a civilised growth.

4

Comedy and English Society

That comedy is potentially an agent of growth in a culture is not a simple truth, since no culture is uniform, and growth often results from conflict. If Gibbon represents one facet of his age, Sterne represents another; and there was also a 'preromantic' facet that expressed itself rather through the grotesque than the comic.

All the same, to judge by nothing more than the numerous protests of those in high places, comedy from Chaucer to Joyce certainly played its part in the evolution of English society and English sensibility. Moreover, if we stand back, a more simple general pattern is discernible than is visible close to. To put it crudely, the main tendency of comedy before the Reformation, when the Lords temporal and spiritual had all the power, is to be anti-feudal and anti-clerical; and its main tendency after the Reformation, when the balance of power was changing, is to be anti-bourgeois. In each period, however, there is a subsidiary tendency in the other direction—though if we substitute, for the post-Reformation period, 'to attempt to civilise the bourgeoisie' for 'anti-bourgeois', we can in fact absorb most of the subsidiary comedy into the main trend. For much comedy from a bourgeois viewpoint is none the less attempting to improve the crude bourgeoisie.

The social evolution of England can be seen as a movement from a feudal to a managerial society, from a culture local, agrarian, and aristocratic to one nationwide, industrial and democratic. The chief force in that movement has been the ever-increasing influence of the commercial and industrial classes and their values. From the time of the Reformation—and more emphatically after Tudors gave way to Stuarts—those values seem to have been connected with Protestant individualism: an attitude that led insensibly to economic laissez-faire* and the repression of bodily pleasures. To this emotional

* This is not to suggest that Protestantism was the *cause* of capitalism or the sole reason for its development. There was capitalism without Protestantism in Italy as early as the fourteenth century. But Tawney is surely right to emphasise the connection in the post-Reformation period.

divorce of body and spirit, Descartes gave philosophical authority in a vital transition period.

The Protestant attitude despite its many virtues tended, at least as much as the Catholic, to gravitate emotionally towards the severe and puritanical, while practically it gravitated rather more easily than Catholicism towards a morality that interfered little with sharp business but much with harmless pleasures—particularly sensual ones. Such an attitude is not naturally clement to comedy, and is itself the preordained comic target both of the more sophisticated, the more pagan or the more tolerant, and of the unprivileged or the over-privileged. In short, one sees why the main line of English comedy, between the Reformation and the twentieth century, should be describable as an attempt to civilise the middle-class: whether by flattering it like Addison, attacking its assumptions like Fielding, its social effects like Dickens, or like Shaw and Butler, its morality and ideas. (Modern man, feeling dehumanised in his vast and necessarily complex social machine, is perhaps more apt to locate absurdity in 'the system' than in class-personalities).

This does not mean that all, or even most English comedy is conserving and tolerant. Jonson attacks in the cause of a past ideal, but Shaw is forward-looking; Fielding opposes to resistive narrowness an attitude of tolerance; Byron and Butler, however, while not being resistive are not tolerant either. And, of course, there are some major exceptions to the rule. Pope, for instance, while neither Protestant nor Puritan is sometimes spokesman of the laissez-faire optimism that is their direct (if illegitimate) descendant.

Before the Reformation, the picture is naturally different. Recent neo-Catholic admiration for the Middle Ages under-emphasises perhaps their more repellent aspects: cruelty, heavy and inequitable taxation, serfdom, clerical interference with private life and personal pleasures, and so on. At any rate it is significant that parallel to, and often parodying the aristocratic literature of heroic romance, courtly love and dream allegory, is a popular literature which is mock-heroic, sensual and earthy. Indeed, the divorce of 'higher' and 'lower' faculties noted by Professor Knights as an affliction of the post-Renaissance world is equally evident in the pre-Renaissance world; moments of integration are rare. He writes (in his essay on W. B. Yeats, in *Explorations*, London 1946, p. 174) as follows:

> In a passage on 'The Thinking of the Body' that deserves to be famous he wrote: 'Art bids us touch and taste and hear and see the world, and shrinks from what Blake calls mathematical form, from every abstract

thing, from all that is of the brain only, from all that is not a fountain jetting from the entire hopes, memories, and sensations of the body'. But it is 'the personality as a whole', not merely 'the tumult of the blood' that informs the greatest poetry. He saw clearly that the divorce between 'higher' and 'lower' faculties was a symptom of the disease which had afflicted the post-Renaissance world, so that by the beginning of the nineteenth century, 'the highest faculties had faded, taking the sense of beauty with them, into some sort of vague heaven and left the lower to lumber where they best could'. In literature, therefore (and Yeats touches here the now familiar contrast between the poetry of the seventeenth and the poetry of the nineteenth century), 'partly from the lack of that spoken word which knits us to normal man, we have lost in personality, in our delight in the whole man—blood, imagination, intellect, running together'.

This is true, but there is as little literature of such quality before Chaucer as there is after Shakespeare. Of the comparatively small amount of comedy or farce in the vernacular surviving from the medieval period the twelfth/thirteenth-Century French work, the *Roman de Renart*, is perhaps the best. In method, a parody of the heroic *chansons de geste*, it shares with English folksongs and *fabliaux* a critical irreverence, in mood, toward the Faith and Chivalry that were already becoming shibboleths of the higher orders, clerical and lay. But more mature and personal comedy is to be found in the Latin writings of the Goliards; witness the Archpoet's *Confessio*, which Helen Waddell calls 'the first articulate reasoned rebellion against the denying of the body' (*Mediaeval Latin Lyrics*, London 1952. The poem and its translation appear on pp. 182-91).

Most of this, however, is not comedy of innovation (where it is comedy at all and not simply farce); it is comedy of release, a literary equivalent of the Feast of Fools; a moral and emotional holiday, comparable to some of Aristophanes' comedies. There is rarely evidence of a desire for *permanent* change of values or attitudes. In Chaucer the feudal and popular attitudes coexist (in, say, the *Knight's Tale* and the *Miller's*) without much uneasiness.

Even by this time, however, the feudal order was rapidly breaking up under the stress of the after effects of the Black Death of 1348-9, and the wars with France; and the break-up was permitting the rise of a new élite. Chaucer's Knight is already an outmoded type, and most of his clerics are clearly due for supersession.

Anti-clericalism was, indeed, widespread in the fourteenth and fifteenth centuries. The exclusiveness and rigidity of the old order—

of which the Church was an integral part—aroused hostility in bustling and ambitious members of the commons. Ribald satire appears in urban street ballads, which eventually began to oust the traditional ballads and heroic romances. It appears, too, in the secular Interludes and Moralities that were replacing the biblical Miracle plays. At a higher level, Chaucer and Dunbar also criticise both Church and chivalry, courtly love and idealism. The *Tua Mariit Wemen and the Wedo* is as great a satirical attack on pastoral idealism and courtly love, as the *Pardoner's Prologue* is on clerical corruption. And the zestful realism of Skelton's *Tunning of Elinor Rumming* is complementary to his satires on the falseness of court life. All this comedy is innovating in tendency, though all three authors at other times may themselves display the attitudes or use the diction they attack.

The effects of the Reformation were so drastic that for almost the whole of the reign of Elizabeth order was preferred to innovation. The new aristocracy, the new bourgeoisie, and the new class of lay intellectuals needed to consolidate their gains, from the monastic estates, the new world of the Americas, and the old literature of Greece and Rome. In Shakespeare's lifetime there is a brief 'Athenian' period in which stability and freedom are so balanced as to allow of a richly humanist comedy, inquiring and varied rather than tendentious and onesided; a comedy that seems to express an achieved integration rather than a striving for conditions propitious to integration. By Jonson's time, however, the Elizabethan attempt to arrest the flux that followed the breaking of the medieval framework was failing; and the forces of change provoke again a comedy of more specific social purpose—then, and often thenceforth, usually written from an anti-commercial viewpoint.

Inevitably, after the Reformation, the already halfhearted influence of the Church on economic ethics waned. Moneymaking, so the new belief ran, was good or bad not in itself but according to the character of the moneymaker. A similar change of outlook affects the treatment of love in literature. Like money, love becomes good or bad not in itself but according to the end in view. The shift of erotic ideal from the adulterous love of the Courtly Code, and the free pagan love of the folk-song, to love in marriage is completed by the Puritans in the seventeenth century and vulgarised by such descendants as Richardson (who provoked the comedy of Fielding) in the eighteenth. At the end of the sixteenth century, however, Jonson was using comedy to attack on a wider front the new bourgeois combination of moral self-righteousness and economic *laissez-faire*.

Ironically enough, the artistic individualism necessary for the attack could hardly have existed without the economic and social individualism attacked. Both reflected the spirit of the age; whereas medieval writing was typically anonymous. Donne was neither Puritan nor bourgeois but his reaction against the affectation and artifice of the courtly literature of his time was akin to the Puritan's reaction from frivolity and falseness. Both were after a personal subjective 'truth'.

That neither the older nor the newer outlook can be described from any viewpoint as wholly right or wholly wrong becomes painfully apparent in the Civil War, when broadly speaking, social progressiveness was with the Roundheads, humanism with the Royalists. Most of the writers were of the King's party, often not so much because they were unprogressive as because that party did not discourage the arts. Puritanism, on the other hand, frowned on entertainment; its energies were practical. Moreover, it was on the offensive during the sixteenth and seventeenth centuries and had no time for distraction. Not until the early eighteenth century was it victorious and comparatively tolerant. For one thing, tolerance was good for trade; for another, the Restoration had resulted in a balance of power that rendered force useless.

In the seventeenth century, Puritan comedy consists of little more than a few street ballads (some of them by Andrew Marvell), whereas the bulk of anti-Puritan comedy, in the form of plays, verse satires and street ballads, is enormous. Puritanism is typically patristic in kind, and the patrist, as was noted (p. 29), is not attuned to the mode of comedy. On the other hand, as Potts cogently points out:

> The world of Restoration comedy, small and never very important historically, soon melted away. In the Eighteenth Century English civilisation broke up into innumerable units centred in the home.

> (*Comedy*, p. 62)

As the court became dull and Germanic, the coffee-house replaced it as a centre for the intelligentsia—but the coffee-house was primarily the territory of the middle-class merchant. Satire *for* bourgeois values replaced satire *against* them, and sentimental comedy supplanted the Restoration drama of wit that had tried to sustain a society of rational gallantry and gaiety. When Pope concluded the *Essay on Man* with the reflection

> That REASON, PASSION, answer one great aim,
> That true SELF-LOVE and SOCIAL are the same

he was expressing the optimism of the rising class of his period, the merchants and traders now at one in principle—and often by marriage—with the improving and enclosing landed aristocracy. Pope's greatness, it need hardly be added, lies elsewhere, in verse which deepened, qualified and subtilised those values. Very rarely is his view so typical of that individualism for the prosperous then customary in practice, and soon to be embodied in economic theory.

With the growing dominance of the commercial element in the nation the middle-class outlook lost its initial vitality and intelligence, as well as its fervour, and became the legitimate target for comedy of several types. The more mercenary a class becomes, the more inclined is it to be over-severe in those branches of morality that do not interfere with trade, in order to compensate for some laxity in those that do. A phenomenon early observed by Butler: such men

> Compound for sins they are inclined to
> By damning those they have no mind to. *(Hudibras*, Pt. I)

By the middle of the eighteenth century (and still in the nineteenth, despite Fielding) 'morality' was almost exclusively sexual and resistive. The mere description of *one* of the seven deadly sins in operation—no matter to what end—was, as it often still is, condemned as 'immoral'.

At this point, the main line of comedy almost meets the most important and influential undercurrent, the street ballad. For comedy of release did not die after the Reformation. Right up the twentieth century, though with a sad decline in quality after Victoria's accession, street ballads show the releasing elements noted in Aristophanes: degradation of the high, mighty or respectable, vitality, and controlled licence. They are racy, bacchic, irreverent, unpuritanical: the opposite of all that is smug, genteel, oppressive or high-faluting. They share at least the temper of Fielding's comedy, and are not completely unlike some of Sterne. Indeed, from the Elizabethan to the Romantic period the street-ballad is not only a source of releasing comedy in itself—opposing the common-sensual to the insensible—but also a source of strength to higher forms. When the two streams are widely separated both lose vitality, tending to become crude and sentimental respectively.

Very little comedy between *The Way of the World* and *The Way of All Flesh* is free from sentimentality: feelings *manufactured* instead of *discovered*. Even in Sheridan it is to be found, and in Dickens there is so much that his books, though they contain comic sections, cannot be considered as comedies in the sense given in the previous chapter. This unevenness appears to result from his having no coherent attitude to life, to morality, or to the social problems of his age, so that on certain stubborn rocks the tide of his comedy breaks in a froth of rhetoric. He presents a piecemeal world, where patches of comic illumination are intermingled with farce, cant, sentimentality, and indignation.

Society itself, of course, was more piecemeal than it had been, and was changing so rapidly that not even the freest minds could compass an appropriate moral, emotional and intellectual evolution that might have served to *guide* the change. No nineteenth-century writer of comedy before Shaw had a guiding coherence of outlook to give unity to his comedy; and Shaw seems to have managed it only by freezing his emotional assets, thus ignoring that expansion (effected by the Romantics) in the inner world, which countered the industrial expansion in the outer. Even today, in an age of more dispassionate thought and much deeper knowledge of psychology, it is difficult to maintain a coherent attitude which will remain self-consistent, though unfettered by any rigid system. For a writer in the nineteenth century 'the central effort of a living being to remain an integrated whole . . .' was almost impossible without drastic limitation. Jane Austen achieved it by limiting herself to a comic microcosm of 'three or four families in a country village' and excluding most of the aspects of life which the street-ballad emphasised; Dickens achieved it, on rare occasions, by limiting himself to one social abuse; Carroll achieved it by withdrawal.

Blake, Byron and Shelley had been able to satirise, say, the evangelical attitude fundamentally, for it was then clearly anti-revolutionary and restraining. Religion and morality, as they saw them, were being exploited by the middle and upper classes to sustain and justify inequity. The mid-Victorian writer, on the other hand, had no wish to revolt; he was himself emotionally committed to many values inseparable from the abuses he disliked; and he had evidence of philanthropic action by evangelicalism. If he saw that such action, while ameliorating its effects, promoted an outlook complementary to that of utilitarianism, he saw it unclearly. Moreover, Darwinism seemed to confirm the necessity of ruthless competition, and inhuman indifference to the unfit or unlucky. Hence, agnostics were little readier than evangelicals or anglo-Catholics to challenge the ethics of their age. On the whole they limited themselves to its dogmas. Only with Arnold's *Literature and Dogma* (1873)—which clarifies out of the confused liberal outlook of his day something of the humanism latent in it—did a coherent and comprehensive comic approach become remotely possible. But by that time the liberal impulse was becoming exhausted. Already in France the naturalist movement was more icily probing the bourgeois mode of life. In England, a hint of the same hardness marks Butler's satiric comedy. For the first time in the Victorian age a comic work is partially concerned with underlying causes as well as symptomatic abuses. Shaw's comedy is similarly fundamental in kind; and he is intent on undermining a much wider area of the system than Butler. But such an intention is necessarily isolating. Both Shaw and Butler, for this reason, become slightly cranky, lacking in the warmth and richness that comes from a tentacular rootedness within one's society. Henry James, too, who writes the most refined comedy of the age is far removed from the robust popular strain—which, indeed, by this time had little in it to tempt any sort of artist.

Only with the Irishman, James Joyce, do the intellectual and popular strains unite: in a union firmer and more inclusive than any since Rabelais and Shakespeare. In Joyce the 'humanist' tradition of comedy reaches its culmination. On the eve of the modern slow disintegration of the society and values painfully evolved, with many setbacks, from the time of the Reformation, or earlier, appears *Ulysses*. In this great comic epic, as in some of Shakespeare, the insinuation of humane values seems to be not deliberate but simply the natural by-product of a zestful exploration of the full human situation—by a personality that has achieved integration and understanding with pain and effort, but without embitterment. Both see life whole; in both, body and mind are equally accepted, not only in theory but in the texture of the writing: in the verbal fabric of their creation. In both, compassion and wisdom rule over distaste, and neither makes order by exclusion or expurgation.

Accepting the richness of human nature Joyce comes to a unified comprehension of life, from which he may forge 'the uncreated conscience' of the race in 'unfettered freedom'—freedom from the bitterness of nationalism, the arbitrary unity of Irish Catholicism, or the narrowing rigidity of English nonconformity. Such an achievement would hardly have been possible had Joyce not lived in Ireland —and left it—at a time when Freud and Darwin, Ibsen, Shaw and the French naturalists had stimulated an intellectual Reformation in the nineteenth-century milieu; a milieu where, as in that of the fifteenth century, patristic authoritarianism, a rigid class-system, and fossil conventions had damned back natural human impulses towards fullness of life and thought.

Since Joyce's time, comedy has contracted, in part because there is no going beyond *Ulysses*, but perhaps chiefly because the main obstacles to humane integration and fulfilment—totalitarianism, technology, and bureaucracy—seem beyond the reach of ridicule and, in an overpopulated world, almost inevitable. Comedy may protest, but despairs of altering. It therefore tends to be mithridatic whether scathingly as in Orwell's *Animal Farm* and Heller's *Catch-22*, or philosophically as in Beckett's *Waiting for Godot* and Stoppard's *Jumpers*.

For the rest, there is much good farce and divertisement. But these are not modes of attack by laughter on those thick-skinned giants of our day. They are ways of temporary escape by laughter.

In the foregoing outline perhaps too much has been implied, and certainly too little has been amplified. A writer's personal circumstances may play as big a part in the nature of his writing as the circumstances of his age—though if his work is to last as comedy it must transcend the limits of person as well as period. Again, since comedy is chiefly a demonstration of absurdity, and since the absurd involves an idea of disjunction (of personal ideals and the facts of human nature, of social ideals and the facts of society, of profession and action, and so forth), comedy surely *must* imply some sort of integration. When we adopt 'integration' as a touchstone, then, are we letting ourselves be trapped in a circular definition? No, for a bad comedy, or one of purely temporary use in its own day, may tend to an illusory integration based on an artificial absurdity. Lasting comedy must be demonstrating a genuine absurdity. Unless it symbolises something real even the most technically accomplished comedy will not work for long. Technical quality, however, is undoubtedly another touchstone of merit.

It is obviously time to turn from the general to the particular—bearing in mind (to sum up) three questions:

'Is it comedy at all?' Is the work, that is to say, a mode of art working purposively in a detached yet genial, accommodating way through laughter?

'What sort of comedy is it?' Humorous, cynical, satirical, or celebratory? Is it using the right methods? Using them well?

'Is it good comedy?' Technically? Socially, in its own day? Personally, for our day? Or both?

The answers will not be simple, for these matters are not ultimately separable, and the work of art is a continuum.

PART II

5

Medieval *c.*1350-1530

A. *General*   B. *Chaucer, Dunbar*

A. GENERAL

That the Middle Ages were not suddenly reformed out of existence by Henry VIII has become a truism. Nevertheless the Reformation marks a real turning-point.

> Henceforth medieval ideas and forms and institutions were either relics or legacies; the way of life which had given them birth was dead. If an Englishman of the 13th century could have visited England in 1520 he would have found much to excite his wonder, yet all the old landmarks would still have been there. Fifty years later he would have encountered many familiar features, but they would have been mere survivals in a world beyond his comprehension, a way of life separated from his by a revolution.
>
> (Myers, A. R. *England in the Late Middle Ages*, London 1952, p. 192)

That revolution—and its connection with comedy—is aptly symbolised in the transfer to Thomas Cromwell, a layman-secretary, of the authority of Cardinal Wolsey, last of the line of clerical chancellors, and target of Skelton's most pungent satire.

In contrast to medieval Christianity, the Renaissance laid emphasis on self-reliance and completeness of personality rather than abnegation and submission. It is perhaps natural enough, therefore, that nearly all medieval comedy in English is found after 1350—in the pre-Renaissance period, so to speak—for it seems to be largely the expression of men finding medieval forms and ideals no longer adequate to the economic facts or to their own ambitions. More rarely, it is the expression of men who resent the growing wealth and bumptiousness of such yeomen, tradesmen and other lower-class members of the bourgeoisie.

Generalisations are always suspect, particularly so when they concern a period as long and varied, as the Middle Ages. None the less, it does seem true to say that, with increased prosperity, security and opportunity, certain institutions once accepted for the sake of security after the collapse of Roman civilisation became increasingly irksome. Hence, their abuses came to be viewed with less tolerant feelings.

Insofar as such feelings crystallise in comedy they generally bear on what has come to seem 'unnatural' in the Church and the Feudal system (or occasionally, the Commons)—namely, corruption, commercialisation, and courtly love. The abuses, perhaps, were really greater, the inconsistencies more glaring in the fourteenth and fifteenth centuries, as both orders felt obliged to compromise to retain power, and thereby became corrupted with what they condemned.*
But it is difficult not to believe that the mainspring of criticism was natural hostility to orders concerned with preserving the *status quo*, when men felt no longer fear, but opportunity in a changing world.

The contrast between clerical or chivalric pretensions and practice offered a ready target. The Church was in principle opposed to sensuality and capitalism. In practice, its personnel was often notoriously sensual, its management increasingly ran it as an ecclesiastical bank (offering spiritual credit, or cancelling moral bad debts in exchange for cash), and its operations were those of big business. Chivalry would spare the nobility (who could be held to ransom) but slew the citizenry without compunction. Gradually, too, the long bow and better training of infantry diminished the value of horse-power—the basis of chivalry—and therefore lessened the prestige of knighthood amongst unknightly men. Latterly, even those within the 'orders' of chivalry (modelled on the religious orders) felt that the chivalric ideal had become a game too remote from reality, and at times mocked it. The Code of Courtly Love appeared to some similarly fictitious, and was subjected, probably, to more mockery, usually in the form of parody, even than the friars. The most important source book†
shows not only differences from modern views on love, but also the Code's internal inconsistencies. It was constitutionally susceptible to

* A significant straw in the wind, in the pre-Renaissance period, is provided by Colet, who left the foundation of Paul's Grammar School to the care neither of the clergy, bishop, nor Chapter of the Cathedral, nor of a Minister at Court, but to that of the Company of Mercers, since he found 'less corruption in such a body of citizens than in any other order of mankind'.

† *The Art of Courtly Love*, Andreas Capellanus (Andrew the Chaplain), for Countess Marie of Champagne, late twelfth century. Edited, in translation, by G. G. Parry, New York 1941.

comedy, even had there been no contrast between the refining idealism (which linked it in theory to Chivalry) and the facts of life.

Love, it holds to be impossible within marriage. A not unnatural assumption in view of the almost universal practice in wealthy families of 'arranged' marriage; but marriage is regarded as fatal even for those already in love. One's duty was to fall in love after, and outside marriage (before marriage it's too risky. Even if a woman avoids pregnancy she won't be able to conceal the loss of her virginity from her husband when she does marry. This will cause jealousy—a bad thing for marriage, but *essential* for love). Certain queer court rulings follow logically from these premises. For example, a woman reveals her *bad* character if after marriage (to someone else) she continues to refuse her 'solaces' to a pleading lover (Case V I I).

Love is alleged to be the source of all knightly virtues, but women are regarded as 'higher' than men, creatures to be treated with exaggerated courtesy and respect—though the degree of exaggeration varies according to their status. Unfaithfulness to a lover is considered criminal unless merely 'with a strumpet or somebody's servant girl'. Peasants are not considered fit to be instructed in the theory of love at all,

> lest while they are devoting themselves to conduct which is not natural to them the kindly farms which are usually made fruitful by their efforts may through lack of cultivation prove useless to us. And if you should, by some chance, fall in love with some of their women, be careful to puff them up with lots of praise and then, when you find a convenient place do not hesitate to take what you seek by force.

Andreas's book gives little support for the common assumption that Courtly Love was simply the effect of Mariolatry on the relation of the sexes, and therefore purely spiritual and platonic, or else a conventional game. That was probably true of Italy (witness Dante and Beatrice, Petrarch and Laura), and partly true of Catalan and Provence, where the husband's permission was often sought before the troubadour paid court. But Provence also developed a technique of 'pure' love, which permitted naked caresses but stopped short of the final 'solaces'. There was probably an indirect connection with the Cathar heresy, stamped out by the Albigensian crusade that put an end to Provençal civilisation (Taylor, *Sex in History*, Chap. 5). In France and England, however, a less idealistic, and perhaps healthier, 'mixed' love was the rule. The Code, in fact, formalised and refined a technique of adultery—in which a severely practical element mingled with the high-faluting. 'We are separated by too wide and too rough an expanse of country to be able to offer each other love's solaces or to find proper opportunities for meeting' is one reason given by a woman of the simple nobility for rejecting an offer of love. Similarly, although the only permissible cause of love is supposed to be good character, and its only justification the furthering of virtuous endeavour, impotence is stated to be as fatal to its continuance as marriage itself. Again, love is impossible in marriage, but it is not proper to love a woman one would be ashamed to marry. Adultery is a sin, but 'mixed' love should be reserved for married women, only 'pure' love being appropriate for maidens.

There are, however, more radical inconsistencies. Love is said to be the source of all good, yet it cannot subsist without jealousy and apprehension. Again, love is an almost sacramental virtue, yet reputation is lost if it should become public knowledge—a contradiction reflected in the very structure of Andreas's work, in which two long books on the virtues and technique of love are followed by one short book urging its damnable wickedness (though with the caveat that passion within marriage would be still more reprehensible).

Obviously little was needed for the development of an attacking comedy save a certain degree of freedom, a cracking of the moulds that shaped men's lives and minds—which came, as it was bound to, with the passage of time. The only surprising thing about the advent of such comedy is that there was not more of it (though the high mortality-rate of all secular MSS, together with the medieval disposition to stomach incompatibles without complaint, no doubt largely accounts for that). But why so little comedy from the orthodox side, despite the legitimate targets that arose almost as soon as the middle-class itself?

The short answer is, probably, that holders of power do not need comedy. Certainly the Church preferred to counter-attack by denunciation and, latterly, the use of the Inquisition. Moreover, as a patristic body it was not naturally adapted to comedy, and it disapproved of laughter almost as much as it disapproved of dancing and sex. Had not Chrysostom said 'Christ is crucified, and dost thou laugh?'? Again, both clerical and feudal powers spent much energy on internecine rivalries: between monks and friars, barons and king, and finally (suicidally indeed) Yorkists and Lancastrians. Furthermore if comedy really is rather the expression of human flexibility than human will (v. Pt. I, p. 22) then 'moulds' would necessarily be alien to it.

The typically medieval moulds—hierarchic dogmatism, manorialism, and monasticism—grew from the desire for protection, in the period of chaos and despair that followed the collapse of the Roman Empire; all three institutions began by filling a need, but ended by provoking profound dissatisfaction with their systematic rigidity; particularly among men with less power and more ambition than those of the classes which thwarted them.

Of the first of these institutions, Dr Coulton writes:

> By William's time the Western branch of this Church, the Ecclesia Romana . . . had become one of the completest examples of a Totalitarian State that history records. It claimed to swallow up and standardize all important variations, so that there should be only one Party, that of the State, For this end almost all means were employed; and for many generations at least, they were employed with success. Yet before 1500, for all her greatness, this Church was in many ways out of touch with the 'modern' world.
>
> (Coulton, G. G. *Medieval Panorama*, Cambridge 1949, p. 5)

The second, he writes, enforced rigid class divisions, and inequitable distinctions, both social and legal. He adds, 'no orthodox Churchman protested against the principle of serfdom; that was left to the heretic Wyclif' (Ibid, p. 56). The Black Death (1348-9), of course, not only hastened the evolution of a money economy, which undermined the feudal system, but also led to that violent expression of dissatisfaction, the Peasants' Revolt of 1381.

The reason for comic attacks on the third institution is clearly implicit in the concluding sentence of the following quotation—the whole of which, however, is generally relevant:

> It is often asserted that the Reformation was a plunder of the poor; that it dispossessed them of their heritage in favour of a squirearchy. The fact is that the Mediaeval Church, on its financial side, was a squirearchy richer and more jealous of its possessions than any which has existed since the Reformation. What that revolution did was to transfer enormous wealth from one squirearchy to another; from a squirearchy which, in its very nature, was intensely conservative and seldom let go anything of its possessions to another which lived far more among the people, and whose very extravagances often led to the division of land; so that there grew up in Elizabethan and Jacobean times a whole class of small yeomen farmers.
>
> The mediaeval Church was no doubt more friendly to the poor than any state institution of those days would have been. But it was far from that Christian fraternity and generous beneficence which is often claimed for it, and which the earliest Christians had actually displayed. It was deeply feudalized. . . . Popes were the most absolute

sovereigns of their day, and sometimes the most luxurious. . . . Bishops and abbots had enormous wealth, and lived too often in ostentation and luxury. Archdeacons and rural deans were notorious takers of bribes. Among the parish clergy, even those who wanted to give generous doles had little power. The monasteries, which drew two-thirds of their income from nearly one-third of the English parishes, were, it is true, the main distributors of such charities as could be counted upon by the mediaeval poor: but we have irrefragable evidence that they thus gave back far less than they took.

(Ibid. p. 723)

It is significant that English Vernacular comedy of an anti-clerical kind should have developed in the fourteenth century: a century of growing nationalism (and therefore anti-feudalism and anti-papalism) in all fields: religion, politics, trade and war, when the Commons took the constitutional lead abandoned by the Peers—the king needing the Commons to grant taxes for the 100 Years' War (1337/1453)—and industry and towns grew apace. Inevitably anti-feudal, since feudalism represented the landed interest, the free towns had in any case always been a refuge for escaped serfs, many of whom rose to become prominent burghers and perhaps the fathers of educated professional men. This period, too, was the time of the Pope's Babylonish captivity at Avignon, which led to the great Schism, when two—and later three—popes claimed to be sole arbiters of revealed truth. Most important of all, it was the period of the Black Death, whose mass execution hastened not only the decay of the manorial system (largely through shortage of labour) but also the rise of Lollardy: by revealing—where priests had fled or died—the competence of laymen to manage without them, even in sacramental matters. Moreover, this was the period just after Ockham (d.1350) had scrutinised the arguments of traditional philosophy and demonstrated that there could be no rational basis for religious faith, the sole justification for which, therefore, must be authority. Ockham drew the conclusion that blind obedience was to be required of the flock; the Church, that reasoning should be limited (thus encouraging both resistance and a more rapid growth of discreditable superstitions); but some of the flock inferred that if faith meant the acceptance of authority it might as well be the authority of one's conscience or the Bible.

So many social solvents at work provided a soil in which comedy could take root—to be written, if French example is any guide, not only by bourgeois and clerical malcontents but also by cynical courtiers

alive to new trends. In addition, with the gradual emergence of a class
of wealthy and educated laymen, English gained in prestige. Chaucer
made it fit for Court, and eventually Skelton used it to write the
first Morality play of secular values, in order to influence royal policy.
His *Magnyfycence* not only appealed to human judgement of an
Aristotelian sort (Measure) instead of to revelation or authority,
but also it gave 'a morality of rule, which says that kings *ought*
to refrain from prodigality, and look after publike wele or welth
(felicity): i.e. this world's goods (contrast *Everyman*!)' (A. P. Rossiter,
English Drama from Early Times to the Elizabethans, London 1950,
p. 117). A bourgeois attitude, though Skelton was in Orders and
at court.

During the medieval period, like Don Quixote and Sancho Panza,
courtly romances and dream allegories existed alongside those earthly
fabliaux and folk-songs which were often the expression of Europe's
ineradicable paganism. This latter quality appears even in miracle
plays, as a sort of fifth-column grotesquerie:

> It derives from that opposite and authentic world of the diabolical, in
> which the shadows of primitive paganism survived; where an unholy
> zest . . . readily turns to a positive *zest-for-unholiness* in which the
> Spirit of Negation almost speaks out loud and bold. Cain's back-
> chatting the Almighty with 'God's out of his wit' and bidding him
> go to hell to look for Abel is one with the prophanities of the Chester
> Joseph consoling himself with the thought that there have been (as
> Leontes remarks) 'cuckolds ere now' and with the N-town Summoner
> and the backbiters. In all, the legacy of Joculator and Jongleur has
> become one with the spirit of the comic rejoicings of the folk, as a
> kind of opposite to or negation of their nominal religion.

(Ibid. p. 74)

Such comic patches do not make a comedy, but they do prepare the
way for comedy (of a sort) in later Interludes, or in such ballads as
Jacke Jugeler (E. K. Chambers and F. Sidgwick, *Early English
Lyrics*, London 1947, p. 251).

Although probably intended primarily as a subtle attack on the
Catholic Church, during Mary's reign, this ballad displays in some
degree most of the typical aspects of medieval comedy. Even if, in
this case, they are all simply the result of envy by a Have-Not for the
Haves, the final product is much less crude than usual.

Firstly, it appears to parody the romance ballad; secondly, to express
the bawdy reaction of human nature to doctrinal severity (note the

innuendo in stanza 5); thirdly, it is indirectly satirical of Courtly
Love; fourthly, it is more directly anti-feudal in its hostility to snobbery
of wealth and position; and fifthly, it is probably anti-Catholic and
anti-clerical insofar as the baron's daughter is taken in by one apparently 'an angel come from hevene towre' but actually a mere vulgar
miracle-monger, a beguiling conjurer.

Outside Chaucer, there is little extant medieval comedy of comparable quality, though much indication—in places ranging from
mystery plays to romances—of comic potential. Exception might be
made, however, for *The Land of Cockayne*, which parodies with a
Gallic lightness of touch the medieval conception of Paradise (In the
praer is a tree Swithe likful to se. . . .) and denigrates the medieval
idea of heavenly bliss: drinking water in company with old Encoh and
Elijah; though as a whole it is comedy-farce of release, in the form of
nonsensical wishfulfilment. The two 'Shepherds' plays by the Wake-
field master,* too, succeed in making comedy by fusing pagan fertility
feelings with a Christian story, so as to embody an outlook on life at
once tender, vigorous and humorous (and, incidentally, socially
critical). And just a little later, Henryson skilfully adapts Aesop's
fables for comic satire on the clergy and the nobility. But most comic
writing is crude and elementary—or turns out on inspection to be
really farce or nonsense verse. Moreover, what may seem mocking is
often not so. Thus, the Interlude *De Clerico et Puella* (available in
Early English Texts, ed. Bruce Dickins and R. M. Wilson, Cambridge 1951) is a farce, and the song of the same name turns out to be
an amorous ballad rather than a satirical one. Similarly, *Jolly Jankin*
(*Secular Lyrics of the XIVth and XVth Centuries*, ed. R. H. Robbins,
London 1952, No. 27) brings love-making and the Mass into close
relationship—typified, for example, by the pun on 'Alison' in the
refrain, 'Kyrieleyson'—but without any intention of blasphemous
mockery. The poet is simply using a familiar form and vocabulary,
in much the same way as devotional writers used the form and vocabulary of love-lyrics to praise the Virgin. In the next poem, however,
(No. 28) we are probably just over the imaginary boundary that
separates comedy from farce. The writer does seem to be consciously
embodying feelings once associated with midsummer fertility rites,
as a relief from the asceticism of orthodoxy. The irony of making the
male protagonist 'our holy water clerk' can hardly have been quite

---

* Critical assessments of these plays are available in Rossiter, *op. cit.*, and John
Speirs' essay in *The Pelican Guide to English Literature* (ed. Ford) Vol. 1, London
1954.

unintentional, though it may have become more striking with the passage of time:

> Led I the dance a midsummer day,
> I made smale trippus sooth for to say
> Jack our holy water clerk came by the way,
> And he looked me upon; he thought that I was gay.
> > Though I on no guile. . . .
> > > smale trippus, *fine steps*

And so on to bed:

> He priked and he pranced, nolde he never lynne
> It was the merriest night that ever I came in
> > Thought I on no guile
>
> When Jack had done, then he rang the bell;
> All night there he made me to dwell;
> Oft, I trow, we haddun served the reaggeth devil of helle*
> Of other small burdus kep I not to telle
> > Thought I on no guile.

lynne, *cease*; reaggeth, *shaggy*; burdus, *frivolities*; kep I not, *care I not*

The tone of the conclusion is at most that of a resigned recognition of natural process; certainly not of moral warning:

> . . . . my girdle aros, my wombe wax out;
> 'Evil-spun yarn ever it will out'—
> > Thought I on no guile.

But in poems like *Silver White* or *In My Lady's Chamber* (to be found in the same collection) we pass definitely over to farce. There is no purpose other than that of arousing laughter, by hearty and far from clean fun.

Anti-clerical satire, however, is fairly common. *A Freyer's Compleynt* (*Cambridge Middle English Lyrics*, ed. H. A. Person, Washington 1953, p. 42), despite its rather blatant irony , is one of the better examples, but Robbins (No. 110) provides a more unusual kind. Its mode of irony is crude though ingenious, for it requires two readings —by dot and stroke—in order to make its point:

PRIESTS

Trusty. seldom/ to their friends unjust/.
Glad for to help. no Cristen creature/

---

* For a gloss, on this phrase *v.* Boccaccio's *Decameron*, Novel X, Third Day. But is there not also an oblique recognition in this line of the pagan Gods 'served' in Midsummer rites? Their reality was never questioned, though their status was reduced to that of 'devils'—allegedly served as such by the witches' covens.

c

Willing to grieve/. setting all their joy and lust
Only in the pleasure / of god. having no cure/
Who is most riche. with them they will be sure/
Where need is. giving neither reward nor fee/
Unreasonably. thus live priests/. pardee.

lust, *wish, desire*; cure, *care*; sure, *reliable*

Straightforward anti-feminist writing tends to elephantine irony or to invective. The first type derives from the courtly attitude, giving to women in a disbelieving way, the attributes the Courtly Code gallantly credited them with. The second type derives from the Church's traditional denunciation of the sex that had brought about the Fall; this satire is likely to be better, but not comic (for examples, compare Robbins 38 and 211). Only where anti-feminism is subordinated to more general mockery of Courtly Love—often by humorous parody—is there even the most distant approach to Chaucer's finesse. Two stanzas from representative courtly-love and comic-love poems sufficiently illustrate the point.

(a) When other men sleep
Then do I sigh and weep
All Ragius in my bed,
As one for pains near dead
That unkindnesse have killed me
And put me to this pain;
Alas, what Remedy
That I cannot refreyne!

(Robbins, No. 206)

(b) Though love do me so mikell woe,
I love you best, I make a vow,
That my shoe bindeth my little toe,
And all my smart it is for you.
Forsothe, me thinketh it will me slo
But ye somewhat my sorow slake,
That barefoot to my bedde I go,
An when I sleep I may not wake

slo, *slay*

(Chambers and Sidgwick, No. 126)

A few poems, of halting rhythm and uninspired fantasy attempt to satirise the rising middle-class. This often involves indirect satire of the commercialisation of the feudal system, or the Church. Witness *Sir Penny II* (Robbins 58):

Dukes, Erles and ilk baroune
to serve him they are ful boun. . . .

He may buy both heaven and hell
and ilke thing that is to sell,
in erth he has swilk grace. . . .

boun, *bound*; swilk, *such*

The period background explains the existence of most of this work, and perhaps even justifies it, as something which filled a need in its own day, but it is apparent that most English medieval comedy can have little permanent appeal. However, inferior though this literature may be to that of France, it does at least help to substantiate the impression that Chaucer's milieu was fluid enough to permit, in a genius, the creation of comedy both sceptical and complex. In addition, of course, Chaucer was in touch with cosmopolitan ideas, both bourgeois (as the son of a vintner trading with foreign merchants) and courtly (as a royal official and emissary). His capacity for comic writing is intermittently displayed from the beginning, though most obviously in the eagle of *The House of Fame*, some of the birds in *The Parliament of Fowles*, and that other flighty character, Pandarus, in *Troilus and Criseyde*. But only in some of *The Canterbury Tales* does it issue in complete comedies.

B. CHAUCER: *The Miller's Tale. The Reeve's Tale, The Wife of Bath's Prologue*

Chaucer's superiority to his contemporaries was probably furthered by the fact that he was less committed to any class or party. Like Shakespeare's, his seems to be comedy rather of judicial discrimination than partisan propaganda: the product of a rare integration which 'places' the shortcomings of less integrated men of all kinds, without prejudice. To be sure, there is a great deal of anti-clericalism in Chaucer; so much, indeed, that it is not difficult to credit the account of his two-shilling fine for beating a friar in Fleet Street. And some of it is bitingly ironical: as in the Pardoner's *Prologue*, or the Wife of Bath's aside on the comparative safety of times when there are no evil 'fayeryes'—only the 'lymytours':

Wommen may go now saufly up and down
In every bussh or under every tree;
Ther is noon oother incubus but he
And he wol doon hem but dishonour

(*The Wife of Bath's Tale, The Complete Works of Geoffrey Chaucer*, ed. F. N. Robinson, London 1957, Fragment I ll. 879/881.)

Significantly, the *Tale* shows her to be on the side of the 'fayerye'—
the pagan nature gods. It also contains anti-feudal implications: in the
Knight's unchivalrous behaviour:

> He saugh a mayde walkinge him biforn,
> Of which mayde anon, maugree hir heed,
> By verray force, he rafte hire maydenhed
>
> (ll. 886/8)

and in the later lines against the pretensions of lineage. Against these
examples, however, may be set the *Knight's Tale*, the quality of the
poor Parson (which leads the Host to accuse him of Lollardy), and
the fine behaviour of the Knight in the *Franklin's Tale*. Discrimination comes by contrast and comparison.

On the other hand, it might be inferred from the prologues and
tales of the Miller and Reeve that Chaucer was anti-bourgeois, in
principle. But his apparent opposition to 'sovereignty' in marriage (by
either partner) would seem to align him with bourgeois commonsense,
and therefore with the tendency to reject other traditional ideas. And
it is a Franklin whose tale points the way to acceptable compromise.
What Chaucer's final *intention* might have been we cannot certainly
tell, but the final *impression* left by the *Tales* as a whole is that of a
neutral observer—a bourgeois in court service, pro-Christian, but
anti-clerical—making discriminations among groups from all three
Estates. The general effect of the various particular attitudes is that
of an appreciative though critical tolerance underlying them all.
So where the mode of discrimination is that of comedy, Chaucer's
great gift, is not so much a flair for satire as the ability to convey
zestfully a three-dimensional world. The reader (or more properly
hearer) experiences it as a sequence of events rather than a pattern of
symbols, yet he is not *en soi*, not submerged in it. For though he may
not be buoyed by abstract ideas, his head is just kept above water by a
pervasive quizzical tone and frequent shifts of viewpoint.

In general, then, there is a balance between tales, so that one acts
as foil to another (the *Knight's Tale*, for instance, giving a complementary exaggeration to that of the *Miller*). There is also a balance
within tales, characters being neither entirely individuals nor entirely
types. And there is a balance of perspectives, the reader seeing the
story sometimes from afar and sometimes in close-up, sometimes as an
expression of the teller's view of life, and sometimes—through inter-
spersed ironies and comments—of Chaucer's (a view of a view, in
that case). The result of this funambulism is a complex 'Human'
Comedy of Dantean scale though, as it stands, less careful structure.

To examine the *Canterbury Tales* as a whole, however, is beyond the scope of this work. But a brief examination of three of the best pieces of comedy in it, by those robust members of the lower bourgeoisie, the Miller, the Reeve and the Wife of Bath, will serve to reveal Chaucer's intrinsic merit and his superiority to his contempories. So much more is taken into account, so much less taken for granted.

To some degree, these three tales are by their very nature implicitly satirical of bourgeois churlishness. A satirical element enhanced by the prologues to each tale: both tellers show themselves choleric and touchy; the Miller is drunk (in the morning too) and lacking in decorum; and the Reeve turns out to be a hypocritical prig, for his high moral tone in the Miller's *Prologue* is discredited not only by his talk but by the uncharitable prayer concluding his own prologue, 'I pray to God his nekke may to-breke'. Furthermore, each one's portrait of the other in their tales is so convincingly done that no-one could doubt the existence of such people, or doubt that they got their just deserts. Scattered satire of other kinds is also to be found, for neither tale is strictly in character (though both at first appear to be). Thus, the Miller might well have been the man to have made mocking asides on courtly love, but hardly to have shown the sophistication his tale reveals about astrology. He is just the man to have hated a dandified clerk like Absolon, and to have despised him for such contemptible refinements as being 'somdeel squamous of fartyng'* (squeamish); it is out of question, however, that he should have had the subtlety to make him talk in parody. There, Chaucer is speaking; the Miller is merely a mouthpiece.

In this brilliant portrait of Absolon, then, we get a vivid impression of the provincial gallant, given with malicious economy beyond the scope of the Miller at his most imaginably articulate, yet not out of keeping with his nature—and this malice places him while he is placing Absolon. By such means the reader is prevented from being drawn into an 'objective' world, though the portrait itself is lifelike. He is therefore able to appreciate with comic detachment that parody and burlesque of courtly love (for instance) which culminates in Absolon's request for 'thy grace, and sweete bryd, thyne oore!' (favour)—the request, of course, being granted in a way *fundamentally* destructive of the artificial manner. The destructive impulse may

---

* Presumably Chaucer's audience were expected to see in this an ironic reflection on the Miller himself, since the Reeve explicitly acquits *his* Miller of this refinement —an innocence that arouses no approval in the two Cambridge undergraduates of his Tale. (Robinson, *op. cit.* Fragment I. ll. 4162/72.)

plausibly be the Miller's, but the parody is Chaucer's, and the resultant comic distance is the reader's. Despite the incident's being slapstick, he need not be farcically *en soi*.

Similarly, there is ironical satire centred on astrology. The aged reeve is taken in by it, notwithstanding his folksy sageness on the subject (ll. 3450/60). This is credulity to the n-th degree, and he is deservedly cuckolded for it. Nicholas, who *uses* his astrology, rather like a Restoration rogue, for his own ends, is not satirised but rewarded (his punishment coming when his wit overreaches itself and falls into folly). Since ability, not virtue, is used as a touchstone most approval goes to the clerk (though, like the other characters, he gets his deserts) —and this again is not quite what might be expected of a man like the Miller, though it is plausible enough in the total context. Finally, the tale ends with a condemnation of jealousy. This fits in well with the Miller's philosophical complaisance in his *Prologue*:

> An housbonde shall nat been inquisityf
> Of Goddes pryvetee, nor of his wyf.
> So he may fynde Goddes foyson there,
> Of the remenant nedeth nat enquere.
>
> (ll. 3163/6)

However, the condemnation of jealousy must also represent Chaucer's view: witness the end of the *Knight's Tale*, and the tales of the 'Marriage Group' passim.

Yet all this evidence of local satire, shifting viewpoints, and shrugging detachment, does not warrant our styling *The Miller's Tale* as a whole anything other than 'releasing' comedy—as the pilgrims take it to be:

> —they lough and pleyde
> Ne at this tale I saugh no man him greve,
> But it were only Osewald the Reve.
>
> (ll. 3858/60)

For all its refinement of technique, its alchemical blending of mood, scene and action, it remains in essence a *fabliau*, giving rein to sensual vitality and vigorous ribaldry—though a *fabliau* giving far greater attention to character-building than any other. However, its great achievement is its creation of an experiential world. Alison's pitiful situation, for example, is plainly suggested in two lines—and richly too, for the image with which they end is rich in implication though plain in expression:

> Of eighteene yeere she was of age
> Jalous he was, and heeld hire narwe in cage

But how much it is enriched by the description of her that follows!
Not relying, like most medieval writers, only on visual description,
Chaucer presents Alison to all the senses, so that the reader not only
understands, but feels why her inadequate husband is possessive—
and why Nicholas should want to be. Her freshness is reflected in her
dress, her liveliness in her singing 'as yerne as any swalwe syttynge on a
berne', her youth and gaiety in the fact that

> Thereto she koude skippe and make game
> As any kyde or calf folwynge his dame.

Her kissableness is given by images of taste and smell—which permit
the attentive reader to know what Absolon expects:

> Her mouth was sweete as bragot or the meeth
> Or hoord of apples leyd in hey or heeth.

> bragot or the meeth, *honey and ale; mead*

Her untamed slenderness is given by the image of a weasel, her
unbroken quality—with a hinted promise, too, of spirited riding—
by the line 'Wynsynge she was, as is a joly colt', with its image of
muscular tension. No wonder the writer, with artistic spontaneity,
is impelled to interjection:

> There nys no man so wys that koude thenche
> So gay a popelote or swiche a wenche. . . .
> She was a prymerole, a piggesnye
> For any lord to leggen in his bedde
> Or yet for any good yeman to wedde

> thenche, *imagine*;   leggen, *lay*

Technical mastery of other kinds, however, is also evident. There
is subtlety in the handling of thematic detail, as in the humorous wit
of Nicholas's choice of song, *Angelus ad virginem*, or of his turning the
doctrine on the sinfulness of conjugal relations into an aid to adultery
(by getting the reeve to sleep apart from his wife). Or there is the
functional use of rhyme. When Absolon cries

> My faire bryd, my sweete cynamome
> Awaketh, leman myn, and speketh to me

the double-rhyme acts on the sentiment like a ludicrous slip of the
tongue. How well, too, speech is made to reflect character! Alison's
reply to Absolon conveys the impression of an utterly different mood
and personality.

The *Reeve's Tale* displays similar artistry. There is, for instance a particularly fine use of rhyme in ll. 4225/8 where the Miller's 'hast?' alone at the end of the line, clinches the dramatic reversal with a shock like that of the solitary foot-print in *Robinson Crusoe*. And one brilliant touch of tenderness guarantees, so to speak, the genuineness of the whole account, even more than the rounded characters. Up to the moment when Aleyn leaves her bed Malyne could be the stock-figure of any revenge *fabliau*. But the parting—particularly her final words—gives an inescapable effect of life:

> 'And, goode leman, God thee save and keepe!'
> And with that word almost she gan to wepe.

For, after all, the *fabliau's* usual world of uncomplicated sensuality is as illusory in its way as the realm of courtly love.

Yet such technical similarity is superficial, the difference fundamental. Whereas the *Miller's Tale* is essentially a celebration of natural life, the Reeve's is essentially a comic satire on vulgar pride and aggressive roguery. However, so much of the effect needed is obtained, and with such economy, in the opening sequence that the comedy as a whole is almost capsized by the bedroom farce that follows it. Funny though it may be in its own right, it is really too big for the boat. But the miller and his wife are so vividly and ironically created that they remain in mind, so that the farce is felt as an expanded postscript, reminding the reader that such absurd pride leads to a fall. Both have been seen strutting in family procession to church, pert and overdressed, and as proud as if the one were not a cheating lout, the other the parson's illegitimate daughter. Indeed, it is *because* she was somewhat besmirched that she was 'ful of hoker and of bisemare' (disdain, scorn). A nice psychological touch, and one beyond the sensibility of a man such as the Reeve.

Anti-clerical satire comes in as background only. Similarly, the few lines of sardonic commonsense by the miller to the clerks serve merely as a reminder that Chaucer purports to be unbiassed:

> My hous is streit, but ye han lerned art;
> Ye konne by argumentes make a place
> A myle brood of twenty foot of space.
> Lat se now if this place may suffise,
> Or make it rowm with speche, as is your gise.

> streit, *cramped, small*;   rowm, *roomy*

In any case no impression of pro-clerkly bias could have survived the *Wife of Bath's Prologue*, in which clerks of divers kinds are routed by that embattled bourgeoise.

Insofar as she opposes 'experience' to 'auctoritee', she represents the new outlook—and apparently she represents it under an aspect more favourably regarded by Chaucer than that represented by the reeve and miller, for he gives her not only as much sensuous vitality as Alison and Nicholas combined, but also the intellectual energy to meet and beat the schoolmen on their own ground. This latter quality makes it impossible to take her not as something new but merely something old—simply the embodiment of a different, pagan tradition—as Dunbar's widow might be taken. She has a genuine intellectual case, as well as an instinctive attitude.

However, even in the innovatory comedy of the first part of the *Prologue*, her quality is conveyed not merely by the incontrovertibility of her arguments but also (and mainly) by the texture of her speech. For example:

> Virginitee is great perfection,
> And continence eek with devocion

she says—and with what dutiful lack of conviction the lines could be uttered!—continuing:

> But Crist, that of perfection is welle,
> Bad nat every wight he sholde go selle
> Al that he had, and give it to the poore
> And in swich wise folwe hym and his foore.
> He spak to hem that wolde lyve parfitly;
> And lordynges, by your leve, that am nat I.
>
> (ll. 105/12 Fragment III)
>
> foore, *path*

The argument contains a neat scholastic distinction, and is crisp to the point of curtness, for she is subduing herself to her medium. Her natural style is hinted at in the inflection invited by line 108 which can hardly be read metrically at all but goes well with a heavy sardonic stress on 'every'. It is even more evident in the emphatic conclusion. The first part of the last line is light and alliterative, encouraging a quick delivery so that the last words can all be stressed—in preparation for the idea that there are reasons of temperament as well as logic:

> —I nam nat precious
> In wyfhod I wol use myn instrument
> As frely as my makere hath it sent.
> If I be daungerous, God yeve me sorwe!
> Myn housbonde shal it have bothe eve and morwe.
>
> (ll. 148/52)
>
> daungerous, *niggardly and standoffish*

Energy of character is here enacted: in the bold breaking of metre, the pounding spondees (*nam nat*, *God yeve*), in the mock-humility passing instantly into self-assertion (*I wol*) and scorn (danger being a ladylike quality), and in the defiant promise of the conclusion—or is it a threat?

Such indications of temperamental opposition to orthodoxy, added to opposition of the intellect, prepare the way for the unorthodoxy of her lament for lost youth, a moving *ubi sunt* passage. It is secular, not religious; regretful, not repentant:

> But, Lord Crist! whan that it remembreth me
> Upon my yowthe, and on my jolitee,
> It tickleth me aboute myn herte roote.
> Unto this day it doth myn herte boote
> That I have had my world as in my tyme.
> But age, allas! that al wole envenyme
> Hath me biraft my beautee and my pith.
> Lat go, farewel! the devil go therwith!
> The flour is goon, ther is namoore to telle;
> The bren, as I best kan, now moste I selle.

(ll. 469/78)

> boote, *good*

Remembering life rather than mortality, and bent on persistence not repentance, it is as unexpected, natural and characteristic as Malyne's farewell, or the Wife's own heartfelt cry 'Allas! Allas! that evere love was synne!' Nor is there any sign of an intention to stigmatise her 'worldliness', in this part of the poem. On the contrary, it makes a direct appeal to universal human experience, bypassing the inculcated responses of period convention; and the last lines express an indomitable resilience that could not today be considered other than admirable.

Elsewhere, however, the case is different. For most of the latter part of the Wife's *Prologue* though it enacts her character, is not 'in character;' it is plausible, but not realistic. We pass from a naturalistic character to a more typically medieval symbolic one. Like the Pardoner, the Wyf of Bath has a double nature. For the period auditor, accustomed to the very human portrayal of various Deadly Sins, the transition from sympathetic individual to censurable type, would be unlikely to jar. For the modern reader, both she and the Pardoner, brazen though they are, may seem characters too wily to have exposed themselves as wholeheartedly as they are made to do. In each case, they say what might have been plausibly said to a tavern crony but hardly to the pilgrimage at large. However, the naturalistic style (and in the Wife's case the cogent preliminaries to her life-story) go far, even for a non-medievalist modern reader towards creating a willing suspension of disbelief. Thereafter, the fact that they are condemned out of their own mouths makes the satire more piquant and more convincing, by raising its status from allegation to admission.

The *Prologue*, then, in the course of its winding garrulity, changes from toughly humorous comedy of an innovating and anti-patristic kind, to satirical comedy of a conserving sort, disclosing woman's traditional 'deceite, wepying, synnyng' (l. 401). The three 'good' husbands turn out to be styled so only because they are rich and old, and therefore easily governed and cheated. Yet the goodness of their fond generosity and submission does not save them:

> O Lord! the peyne I dide hem and the wo,
> Ful giltelees, by Goddes sweete pyne!
> For as an hors I koude byte and whyne.
> I koude pleyne, and yit was in the gilt,
> Or elles often tyme hadde I been spilt.

(ll. 384/8)

The Wife is shown to be as domineering as she is indomitable. Similarly, against her resource is set her cunning; against her courage, her ruthlessness; against her commonsense, her greed. In short, the vitality of her love of life is matched by the vulgarity of her life of love; and the reader is presented not with a judgement but a summing up.

DUNBAR: *The Tua Mariit Wemen and the Wedo*

Dunbar's world and Chaucer's were not radically dissimilar; and he too was a royal official and therefore also inclined to satirise nobles less than clerics or commoners. But his work lacks Chaucer's comic poise, its smiling abstention (or apparent abstention) from personal involvement. What is worse is that his personal involvement seems at times merely professional. He carries to excess medieval insouciance about inconsistency, so that in his work as a whole the only unity is that of literary zeal. His Muse turns to any subject with whorish readiness; the energy and enthusiasm, the verbal virtuosity, therefore, come at last to seem factitious. Moreover, his aureate diction comes directly from Latin sources, not largely *via* France like Chaucer's, while his vernacular diction and forms are more primitive than Chaucer's in proportion as Edinburgh was culturally more peripheral than London.

All this makes for a more extreme manner—which, like the rhetoric of a barrister with a bad case, usually does not quite hide the comparative naïvety of the matter, and sometimes enhances it. Hence, Dunbar has much farce and flyting but very little comedy. Even his satires, such as those on the merchants or the sessions of Edinburgh, rely on invective and are, therefore, not comic by the standards defined in Part I. Only in *The Tua Mariit Wemen and the Wedo* has Dunbar written comedy comparable in quality—and indeed in theme —with *The Wife of Bath's Prologue*. The differences, however, are as significant as the similarities.

Dunbar takes his theme of the *mal mariée* at a more primitive and pagan level; his women do not *argue* against the prohibitive morality of the Church; they take its inadequacy for granted, and go on to something more radical than questioning the value of virginity: namely, the 'unnaturalness' of the marriage-system as a whole:

> It is againe the law of luf, of kynd, and of nature,
> Togidder hairtis to strene, that stryveis with uther:
> Birdis has ane better law na bernis be meikill
>
> That ilk yeir with new joy, joyis ane maik
> And fangis thame ane freshe feyr, unfulyeit and constant
> And lattis thair fulyeit feiris flie quhair thai pleis
>
> (ll. 49/53)
>
> na bernis be meikill, *than men by far*;   ilk, *each*;   fangis, *take*;
>   feyr, *mate*;   unfulyeit, *unwearied*;   quhair, *where*
>   (*Poems of William Dunbar*, ed. W. M. Mackenzie, Edinburgh 1932)

The old alliterative measure suits the content. Unfitted for subtle characterisation, it is ideal for forceful statement. Chaucer's description of January, in the savage comedy of *The Merchant's Tale*, may be more effective in portraying an individual character, but Dunbar's verse probably fulfils somewhat better the simpler function of conveying the frustration and disgust of Young Girl married perforce to Impotent Elder. The technique of exaggeration necessarily involves some sacrifice of nuance, but eventually hammers home an indelible impression—not of the relationship of two people, but of a stock primitive passion made articulate:

> But quhen that glowrand gaist grippis me about,
> Then think I hiddows Mahoune has me in armes;
> Thair ma na sanye me save fra that auld Sathane
> For, thocht I croce me all cleine, fra the croun doun
> He wil my corse all beclip, and clasp me to his breist.

Quhen schaiffyne is that old schalk with a sharp resour
He schowis me his schevill mouth and schedis my lippis
And with his hurcheone skyn sa heklis he my chekis
That as a glemand gleyd glows my chaftis
I schrenk for the sharp stound, bot schout dare I nought
For schore of that auld schraw, schame him betide!

(ll. 100/10)

ma na sanye, *may no blessing*; thocht I croce me, *though I cross myself*;
schalk, *churl*; schowis, *shoves*; schevill, *wry*; schedis, *parts*;
hurcheone, *hedgehog*; heklis, *rasps*; gleyd, *embers*; chaftis, *jaws*;
stound, *pain*; schore, *the threatening*

Though the effect of such verse is cumulative, even so short a
sample must raise doubt about the satirical nature of the poem.
Patrick Cruttwell has said that 'Dunbar shows no sympathy for the
attitude he is dramatically rendering: much less than Chaucer shows
for *his* young girl who is married to a dotard, in *The Marchauntes Tale*.
Chaucer is Shakespearean in his balancing of irony and sympathy;
Dunbar, who is a real Scot, fiercer, narrower, more doctrinaire,
degrades his women's 'naturalness' to utter 'animalism' (*The Pelican
Guide to English Literature*, ed. Ford, Vol. I, London 1954). But it
is quite obvious that the woman has a good case—and very ably
Dunbar presents it! In this poem, surely, if in few others, he is not
doctrinaire. Were he so, it would be just another example of invective
satire, pure and simple; whereas it is in fact neither simple nor pure.

To begin with (as Cruttwell himself points out) there is the careful
framing of the poem within the pastoral pastiche of its introduction
and conclusion. This has the dual effect of linking the women with the
Spring so that they become at times almost natural forces—and of
mocking conventional idealisations of nature, womanly or earthly.
It also 'distances' the reader—as does the occasional mockery of
Courtly Love, or the widow's parody of a preacher's opening gambit:

God my spreit now inspir and my speche quykkin,
And send me sentence to say substantious and noble;
Sa that my preching may pers your perverst hertis,
And mak yow mekar to men in maneris and conditiouns.

(ll. 247/50)

Now there may be an implicit attack on the widow here, but not for
*un*conscious hypocrisy. And in that her irony is quite conscious, the
passage links this part of the poem with earlier parts (despite the
fact that the widow is in a different comic category from the wives),
by recapitulating the theme of opposition, by the representatives of

Nature's law, to that of the Church. This point is finally enforced by her further ironic parody, towards the end of the poem, which opposes to both Courtly and Churchly 'Love' that of a bountiful nature-goddess:

> That is no liffand leid so law of degree
> That sall me luf unluffit, I am so loik hertit;
> And gif his lust so be lent into my lynge quhit,
> That he be lost or with me lig, his lif sall nocht danger
> I am so merciful in mynd, and menys all wichtis
> My sely saull salbe saif, quhen sa bot all jugis

> leid, *person*;   loik hertit, *warm hearted*;   gif, *if*;   lynge quhit,
> *white body*;   lig, *lie*;   sall, *shall*;   menys all wichtis, *pity all wights*;
> quhen sa bot all jugis, *when all are judged*

That such generosity is not quite in keeping with her grasping nature makes it but the more obvious that the main purpose of the poem is not to satirise a type of woman. The satire is subordinate.

The wives indeed are hardly individualised sufficiently to be satirised, and as types of sexually defrauded womanhood they are shown to have a legitimate complaint. Any satirical effect must be partly at the expense of the current system of arranged marriage and the hypocrisy demanded of women subjected to it. For both are afflicted with husbands almost impotent, by reason of excessive age and debauchery respectively. However, Dunbar's general attitude is not satirical, and his net—and rather gross—effect is of riotous Rabelaisian release. Under the combined effect of the scene, the season, and the wine they are bibbing, the women let themselves go in an orgy of words, sweeping aside accumulated frustrations and restraints. Dunbar, far from being fiercely condemnatory, revels in it—though as in a Feast of Fools rather than a meeting for Women's Suffrage. The pastiche, the parody, and the obtrusive technical exaggeration prevent us however from being completely involved in releasing *farce*. That slight detachment does, moreover, allow the poem's subordinate satirical element to be gradually increased—as in the *Wife of Bath's Prologue*—when the widow takes over from the young wives.

In her the reverse side of 'nature' shows itself: not vitality and desire, but self-preservation and greed, so that she becomes self-satirising—at least until her final apotheosis as a sort of Celtic Aphrodite.

The fact that she shares at least one basic quality with the wives (together, on the other hand, with one or two satirical touches in their portrayal) helps to preserve the poem from disruption. Yet

Dunbar's seems more of a merely technical unity than Chaucer's, relying rather on alliteration than other forms of amalgamation. Having more gusto but less finesse, his comedy is the less integrative. His satirical and his releasing comedy do not fuse as complementary parts of an integrated whole. The binding ingredient of 'character' is missing. Again, insofar as Dunbar's widow is less a created character than Chaucer's her self-satire is less effective. If no real self seems to exist why heed warnings about it? The releasing comedy, in any case, is by its very nature not directly integrative. It is the sort of comedy which is nearest to farce, and is intended only for temporary relief, not permanent change.

The Tua Mariit Wemen and the Wedo, however, still satisfies a recurrent need, and is likely to go on doing so till Scotland takes after Tahiti.

Much else in the medieval period appears to have been potentially capable of offering lasting satisfaction like the works of Chaucer and Dunbar, but seems to have needed a more favourable environment in order to develop from an isolated comic cell in some larger whole to a whole comedy. So Langland's Avarice (Passus V, B Text) must wait on Jonson's society to develop its full comic potentialities; while those implicit in the tempting of Gawain in bed had to attend on the advent of Methodism. Even then, Fielding could not keep up his irony about the virtue of Joseph Andrews. The author of *Gawain and the Green Knight*, however, could not be ironic at all. No Richardson was provoking him to suspect the morality of such virtue; he admired it, while obviously also seeing it as rather funny and unnatural. *Autre temps, autre moeurs....*

6

Renaissance *c.*1560-1640

A. *General* B. *Shakespeare, Jonson, and other Dramatists*

A. GENERAL

For present purposes the Renaissance may be taken to extend from the accession of Elizabeth I (1558) to the outbreak of the Civil War and the closing of the theatres (1642). As its conclusion implies, a period of conflict and change, much of it reflected in comedy (though often in confused and indirect ways).

The most notable change *not* specifically the subject of comedy is the replacement of medieval scholasticism by primitive scientific attitudes. But increasing scepticism in general, and increasing economic individualism, *are* reflected in comedy—usually in the form of ostensible opposition and uneasy attraction to both. Another change and source of conflict was the recent arrival on the social scene both of a wealthy bourgeoisie and a jumped-up aristocracy—to say nothing of a classical new learning and an old pagan English subculture, somewhat at odds with each other yet both equally opposed to the foreign menace of Catholicism and the internal menace of Puritanism: legitimate targets for comedy.

The post-Reformation hierarchy was far from being fossilised in tradition; yet hierarchy and tradition were still largely taken to be 'natural', and the natural to be preferable to the artificial. Other, more innovatory ideas of the natural, however, were not unknown. *Lear* reflects them in tragedy. Was 'Nature' inherent in Edgar's legitimacy or Edmund's innate ability? In the Order and 'degree' of the planets and the seasons or in animal instinct and selfseeking enterprise? In comedy, such uncertainties about the nature of Nature fuse with uncertainties about economic individualism (rightly associated with the Puritans, but known also not to be foreign to the new aristocracy), and are further complicated by uncertainties as to the nature of artificiality. Where does one draw the line between poise and pose, urbanity and affectation? Anyway, if an 'unnatural' citizen upstart has made his pile by the sweat of his brow and without forfeiting honest worth, how is he to be evaluated, in an expansionist age, as against a courtier whose culture is 'natural'—to the manor born—but dronelike?

The closing of the theatres supports the established opinion that drama was the dominant literary form of this period (so much so that it seems legitimate, as space is precious, to restrict this chapter to dramatic comedy). That they were closed by the Puritans indicates that the rising bourgeoisie of the late medieval period had at last become dominant. And these two facts together certainly suggest that comic drama should confirm the broad hypothesis that if comedy before the Reformation was predominantly anti-feudal and anti-clerical, comedy afterwards would be predominantly anti-bourgeois, or at least concerned to civilise the bourgeoisie by showing up its short-comings. Indeed Renaissance comedy does confirm the hypothesis, but only 'as through a glass darkly'.

If the period is looked at backwards from the Civil War, a tidal movement is discernible, in comic literature as in sombre history. In each case, however—apart from the matters already mentioned—there is the complication of multifarious cross-currents. Seen panorami-cally, the clash of (predominantly) aristocratic Royalists and (pre-dominantly) squirearchical and mercantile Roundheads, of State religion and sect religion, authoritarian Order and authoritarian Con-science, seems the inevitable culmination of the period, the medieval situation having been slowly twisted to a final violent reversal. There really is a constant class tension, of economics and attitudes. But within the evolution that eventually turned to revolution there is as much change as continuity, and more complication than simplicity.

Whereas medieval Europe had tended to divide horizontally into Estates and corporations of clergy, nobles, villeins and burghers, governed locally, Renaissance Europe tended to divide vertically into States in which a national idea overshadowed that of class, and the conception of individual enterprise and freedom could more hope-fully challenge that of social and ideological conformity. Moreover, the Reformation, the discovery of the New World, and the growth of individualism led to a more unfixed state of mind that affected *all* classes. 'We are living in a new world today,' said Luther, 'and things are done differently.' And then, as if to exemplify complication, he was horrified when the peasants revolted; that was doing things too differently.

In general, then, we may agree with L. C. Knights (*Drama and Society in the Age of Jonson*, London 1937) in finding most comedy to be based on a clash between the old values of 'degree' and the new commercial values—especially when these terms are widened to include an opposition of public and private, social and individual values:

> Or to put it another way, the dramatic treatment of economic problems showed them as moral and individual problems—which in the last analysis they are.

(p. 176)

But even from a panoramic viewpoint the literary picture is not quite so clear (as we might expect from the social picture). For one thing, the dramatists' sympathies were not unmixed—and rightly so. For if one result of individualism and mercantilism was instability and social irresponsibility another was release and daring:

> an uprush of the libido, an intensification of the senses, an introduction of the mind to its own labyrinth, expansion of every activity that promoted animation, joy, bodily exuberance.

(Lewis Mumford, The Condition of Man, London 1944, p. 196)

Even Jonson is really something of an exception to Knights's rule, and he is unusual in the definiteness of his opinions on content and theme as well as form—though admittedly that definiteness is at the heart of his merits: those qualities that tend to justify Enright s claim that Jonson is the greatest of English comic dramatists:

> Overreach and Shylock are powerful creations—what is missing is the key to their characters; poetry and plot are at odds. Whereas the figure of Volpone is a *finished* creation, all the questions which his character raises are answered in the play itself: he is constructed and then demolished, while the other two linger on in some vague limbo of the imagination. . . . These remarks are no denigration of Shakespeare's comedies; of their kind they are obviously the finest we possess. But I think it should be suggested that a more serious kind of comedy exists, even though Jonson is the only English genius of the first rank who employed it. Romantic comedy in Shakespeare's hands took on Shakespearean stature, but his comedies, for all their inimitable beauties, are continually raising issues they do not finally resolve.

('Elizabethan and Jacobean Comedy', Pelican Guide to English Literature,
2, London 1955, pp. 416-7)

Certainly Jonson has had much more influence on later comic drama right through to Shaw. Writers of his own day, even if influenced by him, found it difficult to be even as relatively unambiguous as Jonson. On the one hand, the very pace of change—new religion, new world, new learning, new science, new ways—predisposed writers to hanker after stability; on the other hand, there were new opportunities, new ideas, the excitement of discovery, and the frustration of finding privilege still often usurping the place of talent. If the dramatist tended to support the aristocracy, it was perhaps largely because the aristocracy supported him against the enmity of Puritan citizens (who controlled the City council); so his support of 'degree' was often qualified by some questioning of its basis (witness Falstaff on the concept of 'Honour' and on the general pretensions of the squabbling feudal nobility). However, the Elizabethan and Jacobean nobility had itself moved far from feudalism, and was often more innovatory than the Puritans, who became increasingly negative and sour as the period wore on. Moreover, these opposed classes, despite their differences, had much in common:

> The new class [*of post-Reformation landed gentry: the Dudleys, Cecils, Cavendishes, Greshams*] inevitably supported the reformed religion, since in many cases the fortunes of its members had been founded on the spoils of the old Church. As the successors of the old nobility, they had little respect for the conception of feudal loyalty, and having risen in the social hierarchy by means of the sober realities of dynastic marriage, they were equally contemptuous of the traditions of Courtly Love and of the extremes of neo-Platonism.
>
> (Maurice Evans, *English Poetry in the Sixteenth Century*, London 1959, p. 21)

One oddity produced by hostility to Puritanism was an unaristocratic leaning towards rogues: free men preferring dangerous fun to painful sobriety; another, a leaning towards paganism. Moreover, war-weariness in the 1590s, high prices, and taxation caused discontent with the ruling class, yet the players were driven to increasing dependence on the Court as the Puritans became stronger and more hostile to the theatre. Reasons, equally, for complexity in comedy, or for incoherence.

Again, though all the middle-class lacked some of the qualities of high degree not all could be classed as sour and hypocritical Puritans; so Heywood and Dekker and, in *The City Madam* at least, Massinger, were able to write comedies—perhaps significantly rather bad ones—for a middle-class audience, with the implication that the unpolished virtues of industriousness outweighed a lack of courtly ideals and refinements; while many writers who held more firmly to the values associated with 'degree' set against certain of its corruptions some sturdy and honest (if slightly patronised) bourgeois. On this, one of the main topics of comedy, the dramatists in fact often seem mixed up, unsure whether or not privilege and extravagance in the landed gentry outweighed rank, wit and polish, unsure therefore whether the crude, moneyminded bourgeoisie was best improved by marriage into the aristocracy to refine money with manners, or by the cultivation of its own best traits to promote honest, unartificial worth.

The pattern is further complicated by a concern shown throughout the Renaissance for language itself, which leads to a good deal of rather inbred literary comedy. Finally, all social dissatisfactions are partially cancelled by an enormous pride in England, the English (defenders of the faith, defeaters of the Armada) and the English language—a pride still persisting to some degree even in the cynical sophisticated years of the drama's last stand, at Court. All this blurs lines of division. In a sense, one could say that almost every creative writer was on the side of the 'Renaissance' as against the 'Reformation', and therefore something or other was shared by even the most divergent.

The famous war of the theatres, between Jonsonians and Shakespearians, was about contemporary literary, rather than social or moral principles, and seems pretty remote now—though it shows a healthy critical concern for literary qualities. Shakespeare is technically at the opposite pole from Jonson, as a comic dramatist; yet he is not fundamentally opposed to him. He is certainly *not*, for example, firmly on the side of puritan individualism, and he certainly *is*, with reservations, on the side of degree and Order. But his comedies are varied in matter and rather Chaucerian in manner. There is a relished recognition of duality, of the alternatives inherent in human nature, of the shifts men are put to in adjusting the claims of the outer and inner worlds. His comedy tends to be neither socially innovatory nor (like Jonson's) conserving, but in the quite different category of the psychologically releasing. In his *Essai sur les Idées dans l'œuvre de Shakespeare* (Paris 1947) Paul Reyher finds underlying the varied topics of his comedy a constant opposition of the Natural and the Artificial. But, even allowing 'the natural' to include whatever has come to be taken for granted it is not quite straightforward, since Shakespeare's idea of 'the artificial' includes both medieval and renaissance elements (for instance Courtly Love as well as the School of Night); his values are not wholly retrospective, and in any case are rarely *directly* related to the issues of his own day.

With Puritans self-barred from the field, then, we find in comedy a great variey of attitudes—middle-class and courtly, innovatory and conserving, releasing and restraining—often conflicting, but rarely *diametrically* opposed. In technique, too, the spectrum runs from highly classical forms to traditional English ones—but again in every major play there is invariably some degree of admixture, and thus something in common.

Most of the comedies that deal with the artificial and the natural in love use the issue of the arranged marriage, and in almost all cases they are on the side of young love, or perhaps more accurately, against the *commercialism* of parents or others in authority. In other matters Elizabethan dramatists are usually conserving, for Order; in this, partially innovatory. Thus, in Field's *A Woman is a Weathercock* (*c.*1612), Bellafront, the weathercock, is blamed, because she has 'unnaturally' not resisted the pressures of family, convention and money. His *Amends for Ladies* (*c.*1618) makes the same point about the dominance of money values:

> BOLD But see what thought the bridegroom takes,
> My conscience knows, now, this is
> A most preposterous match; yet for the commodity
> We wink at all inconveniency.
>
> (v. i)

This common concern of different kinds of comic dramatist inevitably often involves other aspects of the clash of public and private values.

Similarly, on the other side, whatever their degree of inclination to authority, urbanity, nobility or idealism, writers show some awareness of the inherent dangers of tyranny, public posing, or self-deception (something clearly relatable to the themes of Traditional versus New, Natural versus Artificial, and the alleged life-denial and hypocrisy of Puritanism). In nearly all cases, it is a matter not of *whether*, but of *how far*, or *how much of*, the new bourgeois values are to be condemned or accepted, to *what extent* the traditional ones are to be qualified or questioned.

Besides these period, social reasons for difference-in-sameness, sameness-in-difference, there may well be permanent psychological ones. Harding (quoted on pp. 24 and 25) indicated that 'the central effort of a living being to remain an integrated whole'—a major criterion for comedy—was a matter not only of conflicts in the self but also of conflicts with society, the two indeed not being entirely separable. This effort, in so disturbed a period, may account for what is superficially a surprising thing about Elizabethan drama:

namely, the strength of the element related to the ritual origins of comedy: 'the drama of the green world', whose underlying theme is 'the triumph of life over the waste land, the death and revival of the year impersonated by figures still human and once divine as well'. ('The Argument of Comedy' by Northrop Frye, *Shakespeare's Comedies*, ed. Lerner, London 1967, p. 321). The 'natural', in this sort of celebratory comedy, is what is felt to be psychologically integrative, in the sense of 'life-giving', 'expansive', rather than what is 'natural' because in accordance with established convention, decorum or law. Indeed many of these comedies begin with some accepted but irrational law or convention (its absurdity being more emphasised than its inhumanity), and end less with moral judgement or conventional reform than a dance or other celebration expressive of co-operative harmony combined with freedom—as we see so often in Shakespeare, the chief exemplar of this kind. However, just as the psychologically integrative is not necessarily inconsistent with a concern for social norms, so in the comedy of manners—where realism replaces romance—there may well be in the implied ideas of 'natural' and 'artificial' an admixture of the psychologically integrative with the social or moral norms that usually get more emphasis. In this line of country Jonson is clearly king, and Matthew Hodgart's remarks on him seem apropos to the present argument:

> Apart from the ending, *Volpone* is the greatest of all satiric comedies, a triumphant combination of moral realism with creative fantasy. Since a famous study by L. C. Knights, there has been much discussion about the moral basis of Jonson's satire: is it social in direction and concerned with the new acquisitive ethos of growing capitalism, or is it simply an expression of the classical ethos of the golden mean, and of avoiding excess? My own view is that Jonson held the Renaissance ideal of the all-round man, who should fulfil his potentialities in action in every noble pursuit: anything that hinders man's self-expression, whether capitalistic greed or restrictive puritanism, is an offence against the vitality of the human spirit.
>
> (*Satire*, London 1961, p. 192)

Though the ideal of the all-round man was no doubt meant to encourage an outward style of living more than an inward one, the two are by no means inconsistent with each other, or, as Hodgart's concluding phrase indicates, with the idea of an umbilical link to the ritual origins of comedy. Nor is any of this completely inconsistent with Knights's view, since the 'acquisitive ethos of growing capitalism' could well be felt to be unnatural by limiting human potentiality and offending against the vitality of the human spirit *as well as* by being different from the established, orthodox Christian ethos which Jonson had grown up with, and to which society still paid lip-service.

In short, all the differences, sizable though some of them are in principle, are in practice differences of emphasis. For Shakespeare and his like, one might say, all the world's a stage, full of role-players who need to find their true selves in order to be fulfilled as human beings. For 'the tribe of Ben', all the world's a fair, full of cheats and gulls. But theatre and fair have something in common.

B. SHAKESPEARE, JONSON, AND OTHERS

To avoid taking Shakespeare and Jonson as the representatives of the two main streams of renaissance comedy would be perverse. Orthodoxy here is irreproachable. With all due allowance made for Nashe's ebullient prose satire in the anti-bourgeois *Pierce Penniless*, the witty pro-Puritan Marprelate pamphlets, of Marston's and Donne's narrative verse satires, there remains no doubt that in this period drama is dominant, and Shakespeare and Jonson clearly outstanding in dramatic comedy. Furthermore, they complement each other well as representatives of different aspects of their dramatic inheritance.

The gradual accumulation of a comic tradition in English theatre is by now common knowledge; only the chief landmarks need to be recalled: *Mankind* (*c.*1475) is still a religious Morality play, but it marks a shift towards entertainment; Skelton's *Magnificence* (*c.*1516) is more edificatory, but marks a shift—in a period of social unrest— towards secular morality; thenceforward writers deal with almost any topic.

Heywood's Interludes (1533), *The Pardoner and the Friar* and *John, Tib and Sir John* (or *Johan, Johan*), insofar as they are anti-clerical are still very much in the medieval tradition, but insofar as they are self-contained dramatic farces for popular entertainment they mark a step towards the richness of late-renaissance comedy, which gathered up *significance* (to make it comedy), *farce* and *entertainment* (to make it funny and popular), and various *forms* (to make it suitable for variety, and indeed complexity of content).

Certain elements of form, from ballads, songs, processions and May-games have already been mentioned. The morality element imposes others, notably a ready acceptance of symbolic characters and a non-realistic diction: one not merely reflecting reality but shining a light on it. Surrey's blank verse provides a more flexible and manageable medium than the inherited metres. Udall's *Ralph Roister Doister* (*c.*1553) combines short rhymed doggerel verse with a larger structural form derived from Plautus; it observes the unities, in an unEnglish way. *Gammer Gurton's Needle* (*c.*1566) is English farce, for the first time expanded to five acts, using verse form and having a unified Plautine action. In terms of textural form, oddly enough, classical influence cuts both ways. The emphasis on decorum tended to support the saxonisers (Ascham, Cheke and others) as against the inkhornists, in the Elizabethan debate on diction. On the other hand, it naturally encouraged the acceptance of Grecian and Latinate—i.e. inkhorn— terms and, mainly through Italian, a stylistic elegance and balance that might be appropriate to a unified and balanced plot-structure, but would obviously inhibit characterisation and be inappropriate for low life.

From about 1580, then, any blend of texture, structure and content was possible; and practically every conceivable blend is to be found.* Few, if any, achieved comedies, however, survive from before the 1590s, and the great period comes in the next decade. This could be merely a matter of literary development, but since comedy requires a certain detachment, it is probably not unconnected with the growth of a critical spirit as conflicts within the nation sharpened. No doubt several factors combined to cause this change of mood: the rise of Puritanism perhaps encouraged a shift from gaiety to wit (as a means of safely expressing 'immoral' opposition); the opening of indoor theatres and the ban on non-dramatic satire at the end of the 1590s must also have helped to alter the nature of drama; and there was growing dissatisfaction with the government. But judging from the comedies themselves it seems that the chief factor—connected with the others of course—was the growing dominance of commercial values. All the fanfares, had after all ushered in an unheroic age. So while the amusing, but rarely *comic* drama of the period before the turn of the century seems to reflect the upward movement of a prospering society with a belief in brave new worlds, the comic drama following is more critical or, in the case of the romance kind, more shadowed. 'Mid- summer Night's Dream,' so to speak, becomes 'Twelfth Night' as the festive season draws to a close. After that, a decadence of increasing cynicism and empty frivolity.

To this rule there are exceptions, the most notable being Marlowe's *Jew of Malta* (*c.*1589): not quite Eliot's 'savage farce' but a savage

* It is at this time that the first permanent theatres were established, *The Theatre* (1576) and *The Curtain* (1577). In 1576, too, the Children of the Chapel began public performances in a room in the dismantled Blackfriars Abbey.

farci-comedy, a socially innovatory, psychologically releasing attempt at 'scuttling the old hulk' of society—the comedy concerning the disparity between society's ostensible moral and religious ideals and the substantial realities. But Marlowe is ten years before his time, and it is more than coincidental that Ben Jonson does not make his successful appearance on the scene till the end of the century, and that Shakespeare's mood changes at the same time.

Lyly's *Endimion* (c.1591) almost seems to qualify as another exception: a rare example of a comedy in favour of artifice. Its language is elaborately, sometimes charmingly, often tediously, artificial, and its action far from natural. But if it is a comedy at all, it is an antirational one, extolling Royalist virtues; chastity, selfless adoration, blind obedience:

> CYNTHIA Come, my lords, let us in. You, Gyptes and Pythagoras, if you cannot content yourselves in our court to fall from the vain follies of philosophers to such virtues as are here practised, you shall be entertained according to your deserts: for Cynthia is no step-mother to strangers.
>
> PYTHAGORAS I had rather in Cynthia's court spend ten years, than in Greece one hour.
>
> GYPTES And I choose rather to live by the sight of Cynthia than by possessing all Egypt
>
> (v. iii)

However, the high proportion of irrelevant farce and the linguistic patterning as the only comic methods suggest a divertisement paying elegant court to Queen Elizabeth—a suggestion confirmed by the concluding lines of the Prologue and of the Epilogue:

> We present neither comedy, nor tragedy, nor story, nor anything, but that whosoever heareth may say this, Why, here is a tale of the Man in the Moon.

> Dread Sovereign, the malicious that seek to overthrow us with threats, do but stiffen our thoughts, and make them sturdier in storms: but if your Highness vouchsafe with your favourable beams to glance upon us, we shall not only stoop, but with all humility, lay both our hands and hearts at your Majesty's feet.

Peele's *Old Wives' Tale* (1595) is a gallimaufry of narrative, lyric, and dramatic types of writing; it has the texture of divertisement, a romance structure, and in its content a mixture of realism, folklore, and burlesque of old romances. The framing technique by which old Madge's tale modulates into the drama proper is highly sophisticated

—more so than Shakespeare's in *The Taming of the Shrew*—and there are many other incidental merits, but, again, it is not an achieved comedy; rather, a farcical romance: not exactly a burlesque of romance, but something that points towards such comedy (especially Beaumont and Fletcher's *Knight of the Burning Pestle*). And Greene's *Famous History of Friar Bacon* (1584) is not dissimilar. These are plays that seem to have influenced Shakespeare later on in his career; at the start of it, he is producing the super-Plautine farce, *The Comedy of Errors*, and that harlequin comedy against affectation, the shimmering-surfaced, masquelike *Love's Labour's Lost*. All these prepare the way; and towards the turn of the century, and thereafter, Dekker and Heywood write pro-bourgeois, Massinger pro- *and* anti-bourgeois comedy, Marston, Middleton and Jonson comedies of social unrest,* while Shakespeare contributes the symbolic, romance-comedies of *As You Like It* and *Twelfth Night* (along with the tragi-comedies; and then the final romances).

Dekker's *Shoemaker's Holiday* (*c.*1599) is probably the best of the not very distinguished group of pro-bourgeois comedies; and it seems to mark the end of the expansive Elizabethan strain. Dekker begins by reversing the usual situation, emphasising approvingly the *citizen's* objection to the marriage of his daughter with an aristocrat, and he ends by having his shoemaker, now Lord Mayor of London, outbrave the Earl of Lincoln. However, the play survives rather for its Rabelaisian texture than for anything in the structure or theme. In so far as Simon Eyre and his men impress us with the worth of the bourgeoisie it is not by virtue of what they say but how they say it. We are left less impressed with a sense of right values than of natural energy and vitality. In fact, the sensibility revealed is vulgar; here, unsatirically, we witness untrammelled joy in money, status and ostentation—the guiltless bourgeois ecstacy of the first flush of capitalism:

> EYRE Go, vanish, vanish! Avannt I say! By the Lord of Ludgate, it's mad life to be a lord mayor; it's a stirring life, a fine life, a velvet life, a careful life. Well, Simon Eyre, yet set a good face on it, in honour of Saint Hugh. Soft, the king this day comes to dine with me, to see my new buildings; his majesty is welcome, he shall have good cheer, delicate cheer, gentlemanlike cheer . . .
>
> (v. i)

---

* These categories—bourgeois comedy and comedy of social unrest—are taken from Allardyce Nicoll, *World Drama*, Vol. I, London 1949. They are not, of course, mutually exclusive.

But the zing and zest of the language carries the crudity and infuses citizen propaganda with something of the 'green world' energies of celebration comedy—as, for example in these random samples:

> Sybil Will I, quoth a? At whose suit? By my troth, yes I'll go. A cambric apron, gloves, a pair of purple stockings and a stomacher! I'll sweat in purple, mistress, for you; I'll take anything that comes a God's name. O rich! a cambric apron! Faith, then have at 'Up tails all.' I'll go jiggy-joggy to London, and be here in a trice, young mistress.
>
> (II. i)

> Eyre Where be these boys, these girls, these drabs, these scoundrels? They wallow in the fat brewiss of my bounty, and lick up the crumbs of my table, yet will not rise to see my walks cleansed. Come out, you powderbeef queans! What, Nan! What, Madge Mumblecrust! Come out, you fat midriff-swag-belly whores, and sweep me these kennels that the noisome stench offend not the noses of my neighbouts.
>
> (II. iii)

The suspect element in the bourgeois traits celebrated by Dekker, and others, becomes glaringly apparent in *Eastward Ho* (*c.*1605), a product of the combined talents of Chapman, Jonson and Marston that shows three heads not to be better than one. Perhaps it is a parody of earlier citizen comedies as Miss Bradbrook plausibly argues in her *Growth and Structure of Elizabethan Comedy* (London 1955). If so, it is not nearly so good a parody as Beaumont and Fletcher's *Knight of the Burning Pestle* (1609) which brilliantly adapts Peele's framing-technique to ridicule gallimaufry romances like his *Old Wives' Tale*, and uses the literary naïvety of bumptious citizens (who cannot distinguish between stage action and life: e.g. iii. i) to satirise their general vulgarity, stupidity and homebased martial ardour, at the same time parodying a variety of high faluting styles. *Eastward Ho* is crude enough to be a parody, but not consistent enough to be a good one (and in this it is typical of other comedies, by Marston anyway, that certainly do not purport to be parodies). Parody or not, it is revealing. The Morality inheritance is clear:

> Touchstone To make up the match with my eldest daughter, my wive's dilling, whom she longs to call Madam. He shall find me unwillingly readie Boy. Ther's another affliction too. As I have two Prentises: the one of a boundless prodigalitie, the other of a most hopeful industrie. So have I onely two daughters: the eldest, of a proud ambition and nice wantonness: the other of a modest humilitie and comely sobernesse. The one must be ladified forsooth: and be attir'd just to the Court-cut, and long tayle. So far is she ill naturde

to the place and meanes of my preferment and fortune that she
throwes all the contempt and dispight, hatred itself can cast upon it.
Well, a peece of Land she has, 'twas her grandmother's gift: let her
and Sir Petronel flash out that. But as for my substance, shee that
scornes mee, as I am a Citizen and Tradesman, shall never pamper
her pride with my Industrie.

(I. i)

This motif raises the question, latent in Dekker, overt in many
later dramatists, as to whether the bourgeoisie (admittedly rough
diamond, if diamond at all) should be polished by intermarrying with
impoverished aristocrats or improved in sterling worth by developing
its own code—a question over which Elizabethan dramatists seem to
have been deeply indecisive, to the detriment of their comedy. In this
particular comedy the fact that pro-bourgeois material is counter-
balanced (II. i) by a wide-ranging attack on all kinds of *greedy* commercialism suggests that the play was basically a somewhat confused
attempt to civilise the bourgeoisie rather than to be wholly for or
against it. Elsewhere there are odds and ends of mockery on wives,
maids, modern nobility, romances, and, of course, Puritans. These
give some sparkle to the surface, contributing to a humorous tone, but
are not thematic: arabesques, not motifs.

What You Will (*c.*1607) written by Marston alone, is also pro-
bourgeois in so far as it makes the usual attack on spendthrift gentry,
anti-bourgeois in its condemnation of citizen women eager to wed
them. Since it supports 'natural' rather than fashionable marriage, it is
innovatory, restraining and integrative in kind. Certain parts, too,
indicate some perception of the shortcomings of citizen worthies.
But the whole is again marred by a smothering of sauces: snippets of
satire on pedantry, clothes, affected speech and so on—all the usual
topics of preachers, and non-dramatic satirists, till satires were banned
—a variety that could be esthetically integrated into an atmospheric
unity only by a greater genius for style than Marston possessed. *The
Dutch Courtezan* (*c.*1605) promises to be more interesting. It takes
the issue of Nature versus Artificiality in a specifically *sexual*, instead
of a primarily *monetary* way, and announces a clear-cut theme at the
end of Act I:

> Of all the fooles that would all man outthrust,
> He that 'gainst Nature would seem wise is worst

True, it soon becomes apparent that the argument in support of the
morality of prostitution in the opening scene is Donnelike, rhetorical
play, to make puns rather than a case. But the first scene of Act II

does seem seriously to question accepted sexual *mores* (which in effect limited young men to whores or married women):

> MALHEUREUS ... harke how the free born birdes
> Caroll their unaffected passions,
> Now sing they sonnets, thus they cry, we love;
> O breath of heaven! thus they harmless soules
> Give intertaine to mutuall affects.
> They have no Baudes: no mercenary bedds
> No politike restraints: no artificial heats,
> No faint dissemblings, no custome makes them blush,
> No shame afflicts their name, O you happy beasts
> In whome an inborne heat is not held sinne,
> How far transcend you wretched, wretched man
> Whom nationall custome, Tyrannous respects
> Of slavish order, fetters, lames his power
> Calling that sinne in us, which in all things else
> Is nature's highest virtue ...

In the same scene this is intelligently related to the Puritans' narrowing of the idea of vice:

> MALHEUREUS ... lying, malice, envy are held but slydnyngs,
> Errors of rage, when custom and the world
> Calls lust a crime spotted with blackest terrors.

However, nothing comes of this; plot takes over from theme, the sympathetic courtesan suddenly changes her nature and becomes a villainess, unlawful love is censured and, worst of all, the irrelevant, criminal and unfunny japes of Cocledemoy are approved—presumably because his victim, the vintner Mulligrub, is a Puritan, though (unlike Malvolio) he neither does nor says anything to warrant punishment. And again we are left not with complexity but confusion.

In much drama of the period uncertainty of aim is accompanied by formal flaws: main plots and subplots are ill-matched, verse and prose are often mixed randomly, neither action nor verbal texture always indicates which parts are important for characterisation or theme, which are merely tonal play. Such works could not be integrative in the substantial way proper to works of art. It is in this, formal, respect that Shakespeare and Jonson are most obviously the summits of their respective kinds:

> Shakespeare finally evolved a stable form of Elizabethan comedy, first modelling himself with some strictness upon learned example, and then rejecting the over-ingenious and over-planned pattern of his

earliest attempts for a more popular style. His strength alone was capable of welding the two traditions [i.e. *learned and popular*] firmly together, and his rejection of simple learning in favour of complex nature was a decisive step . . . [*in a*] development . . . from prescribed formula towards organic growth.

(M. C. Bradbrook, *Growth and Structure*, p. 5)

Jonson's art was more imitable than Shakespeare's; it did not depend so much upon special insight as upon general standards of decorum, order, and hard work. Nevertheless, Jonson was bold in his readiness to modify classical precept, he admired the native tradition, and the form he evolved was as far removed from the pedantic as it was from the spontaneous.

(Ibid. p. 6)

The Knight of the Burning Pestle is reminiscent of the Pyramus-and-Thisbe scenes of *A Midsummer Night's Dream*, and the verse-quality of Day's *Parliament of Bees* (*c.*1607) is comparable to that of Shakespeare's fairy world (but Day's masque is rather a series of poems than a play). Day's *Humour Out of Breath* (*c.*1608), whose title probably comes from a line in *The Comedy of Errors*, has something of the verbal sparkle of *Love's Labour's Lost*, but is a divertisement not a comedy, its action being neither educative nor purposive but downright silly. Apart from these, practically nothing of note is of the Shakespearian kind.

Of the multitude, on the other hand, who found Jonson's critical comedy 'imitable', the best is undoubtedly Middleton, a playwright once praised for realism and blamed for cynicism, and now praised for skilful conventionalism infused with ironic morality, and blamed only for the occasional impertinent set speeches of repentance that are apt to mar his works. There is in fact some justice in all these points. His actions are realistically set in London, his language is mostly a racy prose (and like his verse, Jonsonian, rather than Shakespearian, in its unmetaphorical quality). On the other hand, the subject is usually conventional. His three best comedies, *A Mad World My Masters* (*c.*1606), *A Trick to Catch the Old One* (*c.*1606), and *A Chaste Maid in Cheapside* (*c.*1612), are all concerned with the subject of scores of comedies, commercial marriage and the opportunity it gives for gulling the greedy. Whether these comedies are amoral or, contrariwise, provide a 'silent judgement' by 'weight of irony—by all that is left unsaid' (M. C. Bradbrook, *Growth and Structure*, p. 157) is a moot point. The trouble with silent irony is that it may be imaginary irony. G. J. Watson, the most recent editor of *A Trick*, argues for a structural irony: 'the formal nature of the intrigue makes the thematic point' (*New Mermaids*, London 1968, p. xxvi). This, however, does not prove the moral case; since all Middleton's characters are knaves, any intrigue-plot is bound to catch some of them out, thus reversing their expectations in an apparently ironic way. For those who are thus caught out it is true that Middleton sometimes provides beforehand touches of dramatic irony in their dialogue (that we recognise them as such at the time indicates that we expect *these* characters to be punished). The witty, profligate, knavish gentry, however, usually escape punishment, and are indeed often rewarded. The *action* of these comedies, therefore, implies an anti-bourgeois theme (the money-men to be melted down not merely refined). And the *tone*—a not uncommon one in the Renaissance—implies a theme of celebration, of the energy and enterprise of successful tricksters—a tone not seriously affected by perfunctory moral speeches towards the finale. Certain *statements* do indeed imply that Middleton's purported subject was the greedy cunning way of the world:

> MOTHER Every part of the world shoots up daily into more subtlety.
> The very spider weaves her cauls with more art and cunning to
>   entrap the fly.
> The shallow plowman can distinguish now
> 'Twixt simple truth and a dissembling brow,
> Your base mechanic fellow can spy out
> A weakness in a lord, and learns to flout,
> How does't behoove us then that live by sleight
> To have our wits wound up to their stretch'd height.

> (1. i)

Tone and action, however, combine to give this theme a class bias. Middleton seems to be amoral about wits, 'structurally' or 'silently' or 'dramatically' ironic about grasping cits. He is structurally conserving (tending to preserve the status quo in values), tonally releasing (revelling in knavish ingenuity) and thematically innovatory (implying the need for different social norms). But these elements are not quite integrated, despite the intelligence of style and structure. This hint of uncertainty, slightly marring his dead-pan comedies, in which the gags come sick and fast, foreshadows the catchpenny amoral cynicism that ruins so much of Beaumont and Fletcher and such dramatists as Brome and Shirley, who try to have their moral cake and eat it, by being restraining and releasing as convenient.

Massinger's *A New Way to Pay Old Debts* (*c*.1625), which is based on *A Trick*, illustrates the decline. Though it has much merit, the dialogue is not so funny as Middleton's; though the verse often

brilliantly reflects different moods of Overreach, the diction of the
favoured characters, Lovell and Alworth (unlike that of Witgood in
A Trick) is too often sentimental and thus out of keeping with the rest;
and the subplot, anyway, is too prominent. Moreover, Overreach
dominates the play, perhaps to the detriment of a potentially greater
whole, yet his character remains unsufficiently accounted for. Above
all, the play purports to be one of compromise, integrative in so far
as it adjusts the innovatory to the conserving with the idea that
marriage with the bourgeoisie was all right if the gains had been
well-gotten:

> LADY I dare then say thus;
>   As you are noble (howe'er common men
>   Make sordid wealth the object and sole end
>   Of their industrious aime) 'twill not agree
>   With those of eminent blood (who are engag'd
>   More to prefer their honours, than to increase
>   The state left to 'em by their ancestors)
>   To study large additions to their fortunes
>   And quite neglect their births: though I must grant
>   Riches well got to be a useful servant,
>   But a bad master
> LOVELL Madam, 'tis confess'd;
>   But what infer you from it?
> LADY This my lord;
>   That as all wrong, though thrust into one scale
>   Slide of themselves off, when right fills the other,
>   And cannot bide the trial: so all wealth
>   (I mean if ill acquired), cemented to honour
>   By virtuous ways achiev'd and bravely purchas'd,
>   Is but as rubbish pour'd into a river
>   (Howe'er intended to make a good bank)
>   Rendering the water that was pure before,
>   Polluted, and unwholesome.
>   (IV. ii)

The turgid style alone betrays a lack of conviction—pity the actress
faced with these speeches!—and in fact both in tone and action the
play comes down heavily on the side of the nobility. Overreach himself exemplifies inner confusion—as much the dramatist's as his own
one feels. He speaks of

> . . . there ever having been
> More than a feud, a strange antipathy
>
> Between us and true gentry.
>   (II. i)

Yet nothing is made of the irony of his longing to join them, by marrying off his daughter:

> All my ambition is to have my daughter
> Right honourable, which my lord can make her.
> And might I live to dance upon my knee
> A young Lord Lovell, borne by her unto you,
> I write *nil ultra* to my proudest hopes.
>
> (IV. i)

Finally, as this great capitalist villain, gulled, falls into instant madness, there is the botched-up ending, with a moral that in no way follows from the action:

> LOVELL Here is a precedent to teach wicked men
> That when they leave religion, and turn atheists
> Their own abilities leave 'em.
>
> (V. i)

All these, however, are plays that at least *attempt* to expose vice to laughter or to ridicule absurdities coherently. In the Caroline drama that succeeds them moral standards and characterisation are usually non-existent (characters simply behaving in accordance with the needs of 'theatre'), apparently daring scenes work out innocently, and an empty smartness pervades the dialogue. Shirley, Brome, Killigrew, among the best, are lethally tedious to read in any quantity. Insofar as theirs are intrigue comedies they derive from Jonson or anticipate Etherege, Congreve and Wycherley but have none of their virtues. Only William Davenant seems to have any talent, and that is purely textural. Thus *The Wits* (1636), his best comedy, opens with a brilliantly debunking comment by the returning soldier:

> PERT Faith, we have been to kill we know not whom
> Nor why, led on to break a commandment
> With the consent of custom and the laws.
>
> (I. i)

But nothing whatever is developed from this; it rests as an isolated aphorism. The play contains some bravura passages comparable with the best of Congreve, but the action is both pointless and incredible, witness the end, where Pallatine the elder ('richly landed, and a wit'!) after suffering various frauds, nevertheless acts as follows:

> AMPLE If sir your nature be so excellent
> As your kind brother hath confirmed to Luce
> And me, follow, and I'll present you straight
> With certain writings you shall seal to, hoodwink'd,

D

> And purely ignorant of what they are.
> This is the swiftest and easiest test
> That I can make of your bold love. Do this,
> Perhaps I may vouchsafe to marry you.
> The writings are within.
> ELDER PALL Lead me to trial! Come!

This sort of silly *coup de théâtre* had become endemic in the drama by the time the Puritans mercifully finished it off. But here and there in these irritating divertisements is to be discerned the fag-end of the major theme of the earlier drama, that of the natural in relation to the artificial, especially in the context of commercial values and marriage. Killigrew, for instance, here writes as powerfully and bitterly as Jonson in *Volpone*—but this is a single speech in a play without any coherent comic theme or tone:

> JOLLY The lady has reason; for being allowed but one, who would choose such weasels as we see daily married, that are all head and tail, crooked, dirty, sold vermin, predestined for cuckolds, painted snails with houses on their backs and horns as big as Dutch cows? Would any woman marry such? Nay, can any woman be honest that lets such hodmandods crawl o'er her virgin breast and belly and suffer 'em to leave their slimy paths upon their bodies, only for jointures? Out, 'tis mercenary and base! The generous heart has only the laws of nature and kindness in her view ...
>
> (*The Parson's Wedding*, v. iv)

To go back to Jonson himself, and to Shakespeare, is to enter a meaningful comic world. They till their respective fields responsibly, where Beaumont and Fletcher and the Caroline dramatists are usually mere sharecroppers getting what they can before winter comes.

Apart from the overlapping already mentioned, Shakespeare and Jonson are complementary comic playwrights in various ways. Generally speaking, Shakespeare seems to promote integration with nature, Jonson with society. In the one a *sharing* is offered, in the other a *warning*. Shakespeare relies not on one comic view, but on a comic sense of relativity. Consequently he creates characters whom one may laugh *with*, who are funny in themselves, like Beatrice and Benedick, or Falstaff. In Jonson, the characters are to be laughed *at*, and are funny only as parts of an all-embracing design. It is significant that contemporaries should have been ready to buy a playbook made up of the Falstaffian parts of separate Histories. They *can* be excerpted, although in each play they are parts of a whole.

Falstaff is in the Rabelaisian, Aristophanic tradition that does not reappear in English till Joyce (though it is glimpsed in Sterne). It depends on vigour, speed, zest for living, which overwhelm our resistance and allow us to indulge repressed tendencies. There is no one completely satirical, or completely Falstaffian comedy in Shakespeare; his comedies blend the innovatory and the conserving, the restraining and the releasing. Jonson's tend to be conserving and mithridatic; a clear idea, a bizarre central symbol, sections that mirror each other, all contribute to a unified exemplary effect. Shakespeare, on the other hand, is often too magnanimous, sacrificing dramatic pattern for human interest, allowing characters like Shylock and Malvolio to outgrow the comic idea, so as to be as much pitiable as mockable. Of course, romance comedy can afford much more botchery and implausibility than comedy of manners, since it makes no pretence to realism; moreover, some of the 'servant-monster' plays that Jonson derided, though ill-formed as stories are shapely enough if seen as dynamic constellations of moods and personalities. In such plays, as A. P. Rossiter puts it, 'tone-contrast means conflict of *values*. That conflict is the real *plot*, as distinct from mere story' (*Angel with Horns*, ed. Graham Storey, London 1961, p. 278). They mingle elements of ritual, revel and masque, working towards clarification, where Jonson works by diagnostic demonstration, in the manner of one graphically plotting the development of a dire disease, as a first step towards prevention or cure. As elements in a demonstration, Jonson's characters are inflexible, their action ludicrously repetitive; that is their tragedy and our comedy. Shakespeare's are adaptable:

> One way to explore the question in Shakespeare's comedies is to ask why only likable girls engage in transvestism. Julia (*Two Gentlemen of Verona*), Portia, Rosalind, Celia, Viola, Imogen, all prove their resourcefulness, their suppleness, their courageous willingness to change roles by changing clothes and sexes ... One of the first comedies, *Love's Labour's Lost*, makes game of men who are maladroit at shifting roles and disguises, and so throughout most of the rest, the palm goes to the quicksilver wit, the alert, the volatile, the adroit improvisor, the *débrouillard*—not only the Puck, the Autolycus, but the Petruchio, the Maria (*Twelfth Night*), the Rosalind, the Prince Hal. The tragedies, on the other hand, dramatize typically a stubborn rigidity, heroically or blindly tardy in its adaptations, dooming the protagonist to an agonizing and belated evolution upward to tragic wisdom.

(Thomas Greene, 'The Self in Renaissance Literature', *The Disciplines of Criticism*, ed. Demetz, Greene and Lowry, New Haven and London 1969, p. 263)

In Jonson, however, disguise furthers plot, not characterisation. His, one might say, are teaching comedies, Shakespeare's, comedies of research. Of the tragi-comedies we should have to speak differently; nothing in Jonson is more severe than the contempt for Cressida, and indeed for other characters in *Troilus and Cressida* (for she 'is only the feminine of the rest of them. They all fancy or pretend they are being or doing one thing, whereas they are shown up as something quite different: something which egoism, or lack of moral insight, prevents their recognising'. Rossiter, *Angel with Horns*, p. 134). The pure comedies, however, are gentler and rowdier; in danger, more than Jonson's, of falling into divertisement or farce, but in less danger of dying with the age that brought them forth.

A Midsummer Night's Dream (*c*.1595), which uses the common comic subject of forced marriage only as a starting-mechanism, its real subject being something other, exemplifies most of the essentially Shakespearian qualities, in a slight but highly successful form. The fact that the play has seemed to so many commentators to have been for a wedding celebration indicates the reason for calling it 'slight'; it is rather a wish-fulfilment dream; nothing goes seriously wrong, and what does is put right by magic. True, the darker aspect of life is glanced at, but only very delicately:

> LYSANDER Or if there were a sympathy in choice,
> War, death, or sickness did lay siege to it,
> Making it momentany as a sound,
> Swift as a shadow, short as any dream,
> Brief as the lightning in the collied night,
> That in a spleen unfolds both heaven and earth,
> And ere a man hath power to say 'Behold!'
> The jaws of darkness do devour it up.
> So quick bright things come to confusion.

(I. i)

The double meaning of 'quick'—*alive* and *lively*—acts as a reminder that it is not only the vitality of love, but life itself, that is doomed. Certain other images keep this idea tactfully in mind. But in general, error and misbehaviour are smiled at, and from the beginning it is evident that all will painlessly come right in the end. Moreover, the element of farce is so large that the play as a whole might well be supposed hardly to be a comedy at all in the strict sense. However, a serious theme is to be discerned in the fantastic action: namely that an imbalance of body, mind and emotions (or anything analogous to these) is undesirable. What is 'natural' to mankind, it is implied, is to be *fully* human. To put it another way: since human experience is complex neither the natural nor the artificial is fully adequate—or rather, for man the artificial *is* natural. The point is perfectly made in *The Winter's Tale*:

> PERDITA ... streak'd gillyvors,
> Which some call nature's bastards; of that kind
> Our rustic garden's barren, and I care not
> To get slips of them.
> POLIXENES Wherefore, gentle maiden,
> Do you neglect them?
> PERDITA For I have heard it said
> There is an art which in their piedness shares
> With great creating nature.
> POLIXENES Say there be;
> Yet nature is made better by no mean
> But nature makes that mean: so, over that art,
> Which you say adds to nature, is an art
> That nature makes. You see, sweet maid, we marry
> A gentler scion to the wildest stock,
> And make conceive a bark of baser kind
> By bud of nobler race; this is an art
> Which does mend nature, change it rather, but
> The art itself is nature.
> PERDITA So it is.

(IV. iii)

In *A Midsummer Night's Dream*, unlike the *Winter's Tale*, disproportion leads only to absurdity, not disaster; it is light humorous comedy, as much delighting in the follies it touches on as reproving them. Naturally, such comedy cannot go deeply into human nature, or concern itself with actions that affect society importantly. To that extent, romance comedy may be considered, as Enright maintains, a weaker *kind* than satiric or critical comedy.

Within this kind, however (of which *As You Like It* and *Twelfth Night* are even better examples), *A Midsummer Night's Dream* is in the first rank. In this comedy of love and folly, dream and reality, Shakespeare weaves into one symbolic pattern the disparate worlds of court, commons and incorporeity, in a triumph of style.

Usually prose is given to the rude mechanicals (who have the most individual characters and are closest to reality), an easy but majestic blank verse for Theseus and the courtiers (who inhabit Athens, symbol of urbane sanity), blank verse of varying elegance for the less unrealistic, less absurd, or more important speeches of the fairies and the lovers (in the bewitching wood), and rhyme for the ethereal, the parodic, or the *apparently* serious. Crudely speaking, the style furthest removed from common speech tends here—as elsewhere in Shakespeare —to be used for the content furthest from common life, or content not to be taken at quite its face value; and vice versa.

That the play should be taken symbolically—though not as a detailed allegory—is abundantly evident, if not from the title, the handling of style, the contrast of city and wood, the co-presence of homely English mechanicals with fairies in a Greek wood, or Titania's rapture over Bottom turned outwardly into the ass he inwardly is, then from the ending:

> PUCK (*to the audience*) If we shadows have offended,
>   Think but this, and all is mended:
>   That you have but slumbered here
>   While these visions did appear.
>   And this weak and idle theme,
>   No more yielding but a dream,
>   Gentles do not reprehend.
>   If you pardon we will mend.
>
> (v. i)

These lines from the epilogue make almost explicit the metaphorical and symbolical nature of the play—but not fully explicit. The words 'shadows', 'visions', 'theme', 'dream' strongly suggest that the audience is in the same position as the lovers, having had a significant experience that seems to hover between outer and inner realities, the plain and the ungraspable ('Methinks I see with parted eye,/When everything seems double' IV. i). But *what* the experience signifies precisely we are left to ponder, like the lovers, Bottom, and indeed all dreamers.

Do the disparate worlds symbolise mankind's interacting emotions, body, and spirit, as our blunt statement of the theme seems to imply— and as, respectively, the lovers, the names Bottom, Snout and Starveling, and the sprites, seem to hint? Perhaps not quite so bluntly that, and certainly not that only; for this is a play of shifting symbolic suggestions and promptings rather than definite allegorical commitments. The characters tend to be types; especially the lovers, who are never more obviously indistinguishable from each other than when they think themselves, in their passion, most individual. The dancelike structure —epitomised in the ritual revel at the end—with its changing formations, has a formal, patterned quality about it. So there is some encouragement to allegorise. But 'to generalise' or 'seek significances' would be apter phrases; for the suave interplay of styles creates a

moonlit, not to say moonstruck atmosphere. And within that prevailing mood, the elements of sentiment, of buffoonery, and of spritely
plotting are sufficiently indeterminate (if only because not directly
reflecting real life, and therefore capable of more than one relationship
with it) to be appropriate for such other areas of experience, besides
those of emotions, body and spirit, as these three fictional worlds
might suggest. For instance, the romantic, the commonsensical, and
the esthetic—all benevolently mocked. There is, then, no *fixed*
symbolic significance, nor is any one character a model of the balance
and harmony exemplified by the play itself; yet as a whole it has the
effect of most dreams in being often experientially meaningful,
though sometimes merely pleasurable.

As You Like It (*c.*1600) is neither more mimetic nor better struc-
tured, as an action in time. After a clumsy delivery of necessary
information for the audience, the characters are hustled off to the
forest of Arden—another symbolic wood—in Act I, and in Act V
they are hustled back, improved in self-knowledge (and hastily married)
to a reformed civilisation. In between, the structure is again like a
masque or piece of music, a matter of variations on a theme. The
plot-botchery is unimportant in a work that does not purport to have
much direct relationship with real life or current abuses. Shakespeare
was concerned mainly with that in human nature which might be
'for all time'.*

This is a comedy of human ecology, dealing with the balance of
nature, and the need for common sense (in its primary meaning of a
unifying quality). Of this, Rosalind, not Touchstone, is the great
exemplar. He is well-named in that he is basic; every affectation is
wrecked on the rocks of his cynicism, its weakness revealed. But she
is the norm, set in the middle of the spectrum of tonal values, midway
between cynicism and pastoralism. So she is given some of the liveliest
prose in the language. At the other extreme from her characteristic
speech is the parody of artificial pastoral verse given to Silvius and
Phebe. Appropriately enough, then, they get the most down-to-earth
rebuke (in one of Rosalind's rare passages of verse—very natural

---

* The danger of using a metaphoric, rather than a mimetic world for this
concern is that you may seem to purvey what is for no time. If you mix in some
realism with the symbolic fantasy, there is the danger of producing incoherence
instead of anchoring the whole to reality and, ideally, achieving an esthetic variety-in-
unity. Only stylistic genius can get away with this sort of comedy—which is no
doubt why every major comic dramatist down to the present day has preferred to
follow Jonson.

verse, contrasting strongly with the artificiality of Silvius's and
Phebe's):

> ROSALIND You foolish shepheard, wherefore do you follow her,
>   Like foggy south, puffing with wind and rain?
>   You are a thousand times a properer man
>   Than she a woman: 'tis such fools as you
>   That makes the world full of ill-favour'd children:
>   'Tis not her glass but you that flatters her;
>   And out of you she sees herself more proper
>   Than any of her lineaments can show her.
>   But, mistress, know yourself: down on your knees,
>   And thank heaven, fasting, for a good man's love:
>   For I must tell you friendly in your ear,
>   Sell when you can: you are not for all markets:
>   Cry the man mercy; love him; take his offer:
>   Foul is most foul, being foul, to be a scoffer.

(III. v)

Jaques's affected melancholy, another form of humanly artificial
imbalance, expressed in a rather Lylian prose, is also brilliantly placed
by Rosalind.

> JAQUES I have neither the scholar's melancholy, which is emulation,
>   nor the musician's, which is fantastical, nor the courtier's, which is
>   proud, nor the soldier's, which is ambitious, nor the lawyer's, which
>   is politic, nor the lover's, which is all these: but it is a melancholy
>   of mine own, compounded of many simples, extracted from many
>   objects, and indeed the sundry contemplation of my travels, in
>   which my often rumination wraps me in a most humorous sadness.
> ROSALIND A traveller! By my faith, you have great reason to be sad;
>   I fear you have sold your own lands to see other mens; then to have
>   seen much and to have nothing, is to have rich eyes and poor hands.
> JAQUES Yes, I have gained my experience.
> ROSALIND And your experience makes you sad: I had rather have a
>   fool to make me merry than experience to make me sad; and to
>   travel for it too!

(IV. i)

The reference to a fool links up with II. vii, where Jaques reveals
something of his own limitations while mocking Touchstone ('A fool,
a fool! I met a fool i' the forest'). Yet Jaques, like other characters,
functions positively as well as negatively. By contrast, every pose
highlights its complement. So Jaques's satirical melancholy spots
flaws in the Duke's pastoralism.

Once the contrast of Court and Country has been effected—in favour of the latter—the main body of the action consists of changing confrontations, wit combats, that test varieties of pastoral—and find them not empty, but less than fully adequate. This is Peele's golden world seen sceptically. Even the *jeune premier*, Orlando, has to be tried by a disguised Rosalind and prodded into a sane passion instead of an artificial fire before he is acceptable. Despite the testings and touches of satire, however, the general mood is celebratory: reconcile-ments, reforms and resurrections are shown to be achievable. Never-theless, a serious moral seems to be implicit.

When Jaques says 'All the world's a stage/And all the men and women merely players' he is bringing out a truth suggested by the play scenes in *A Midsummer Night's Dream*, explicit in many other stage references in Shakespeare, and enacted in the 'play' scene (IV. i) of *As You Like It* (where the audience is aware of the disguised Rosalind as a boy actor playing a girl playing a boy, Ganymede, playing a girl): namely, that finding natural reality, or one's 'true' self, is like peeling an onion. A balanced society, a harmonious humane-ness, the reconciliation of the practical and the ideal, is not something given but something to be learnt, like a dance, with others.

In *Timber, or Discoveries*, Jonson assigns a low place in comedy to laughter:

> Nor is the moving of laughter always the end of comedy; that is rather a fowling for the people's delight, or their fooling. For, as Aristotle says rightly, the moving of laughter is a fault in comedy.

A comment certainly relevant to *Volpone*, which approaches the border of tragi-comedy, provoking not laughter but a grim inward smile of intellectual appreciation. It is also relevant to *Twelfth Night* (*c.*1601) which borders on serious romance. Despite the gusto of the subplot, the farcical action against Malvolio, the verbal vigour of the resistance to him ('Go shake your ears,' 'Go rub your chain with crumbs,' 'Dost thou think, because thou art virtuous, there shall be no more cakes and ale?'), despite the happy ending, where again every Jack gets his Jill, despite the fact that nothing violent or wicked happens, a tonal sadness suffuses the whole, a sense that the age of cakes and ale is in fact drawing to a close, that Malvolio's unrelenting threat, 'I'll be revenged on the whole pack of you', should not be taken lightly. If 'the whirligig of time' brought in the 'revenges', it will do so again.

Time, indeed, is less unimportant in this comedy than in the previous ones. It is not that the plot more nearly approaches the regular intrigue kind—though it does—but rather that the tone is more wry than in the earlier comedies. The theme is similar: self-deception, illusion, *mauvaise foi*; and, again, there is irony of discrepant awareness as a comic means, with the audience at the top level, knowing all, Viola next, and the rest absurd in varying degrees of blindness. A related comic irony comes from the juxtaposition of 'broad' scenes in the subplot with illusorily 'deep' scenes in the main one. But the sense of time passing now bleaches out the colourful 'Dream' element, makes this less 'As You Like It' than As It Is. The opening music has 'a dying fall' and the play ends, in falling rain, with the lonely Feste, alone, singing a folk song that opens up endless vistas of *l'Absurde*:

> When that I was and a little tiny boy
>   With hey ho, the wind and the rain,
> A foolish thing was but a toy,
>   For the rain it raineth every day
> ....
> A great while ago the world begun,
>   With hey ho the wind and the rain.
> But that's all one, our play is done,
>   And we'll strive to please you every day.

Much else tinges the 'fertility' comedy with touches of shadow. 'Present mirth hath present laughter' but 'Youth's a stuff will not endure'—a point sharp enough for the audience of that song, Sir Toby Belch and Sir Andrew Aguecheek. Viola, like Rosalind, finds the truth of her lover through disguise, but is far less happy about it, and with good reason:

> ... She never told her love
> But let concealment, like a worm i' the bud,
> Feed on her damask cheek; she pin'd in thought,
> And with a green and yellow melancholy
> She sat like patience on a monument,
> Smiling at grief. Was not this love indeed?

(II. iv)

Any sense of integration results not from what happens, but from the quality of what is. Nothing leads one to feel that the instant switching of the Duke's love, and Olivia's, indicates a reformation of character as well as a change of object. These marriages seem emblematic, not symbolic, of unity; in personal terms, very much open to the swift corrosion of time. Integration is a matter of structure and style; more subtly than *A Midsummer Night's Dream* or *As You Like It*, *Twelfth Night* weaves varied strands into one web, varied shades into one pattern. If it is concerned, as they are, with the proper blending of art and nature, dream and reality, it is less optimistic in tone, less celebratory. The cocktail of ritual, revel and romance is qualified with a strong dash of bitters, so that this is the least releasing of Shakespeare's pure comedies, and the most mithridatic, preparing the audience for that thirteenth night when the revels are ended.

Jonson's are systematic comedies in which folly is to be contemplated and condemned rather than experienced and pardoned (on promise of improvement). They operate by creating a recognisable social context; and the intricate action follows logically from character and circumstance, not from the demands of theatrical or symbolical convenience. As J. B. Bamborough says of their structure:

> No praise can be too high for the construction of his comedies. Nothing in them happens by chance and no 'loose ends' are ever left dangling . . . Alongside the plays of his contemporaries, which often seem like heaps of broken parts, Jonson's plays resemble well-oiled, smoothly-running machines.
> (*Ben Jonson*, Writers and their Works No. 112, London 1959, pp. 12-13)

However, what Bamborough says of their texture is also true: it is the subject that gives force to the verse, not the verse to the subject:

> We may doubt whether Jonson could through his language alone make something poetry about which we previously have felt indifferent . . . and it is not an accident that the two emotions, desire and scorn, which Jonson found it easiest to communicate, demand the actual presence of people or things in themselves desirable or contemptible. Jonson, that is, is a poet of the actual, the real solid world about us, and not often of the inner world of hopes and ideals, velleities and doubts.
> (Ibid., p. 35)

Shakespeare's work, then, provides more esthesis of condensation (disinterested delight from scattered spangles, as it were); Jonson's, of composition (from the matching of parts to whole, and structural form with general content). For the purpose of critical comedy even his one weakness, the verbal restriction, is a strength, as it contributes to clarity.

Volpone (1605) is the diagnostic of greed. Not necessarily greed as one might actually meet it, but greed as it would become if it were allowed to run its full course. With clinical ruthlessness, like one demonstrating the ravages of syphilis through to the tertiary stage, Jonson anatomises his characters.

The symbolic heart of the action is the scene (II. i) in which Volpone, disguised as a quack doctor, is hypocritically damning rival quacks: a charlatan playing charlatan about charlatans; and the point is reinforced in various other ways—the name Volpone, the fox, the action, in which he and Mosca (the fly), so succeed in multiple deception that nothing is left but to deceive each other, to their mutual destruction, and the use of symbolic properties, especially the dwarf, hermaphrodite and eunuch, who clearly signify Volpone's false, twisted nature.

> CORVINO Has he children?
> MOSCA Bastards,
> Some dozen or more, that he begot on beggars,
> Gypsies, and Jews, and blackmoors, when he was drunk.
> Knew you not that sir? 'tis the common fable.
> He's the true father of his family,
> In all save me.
>
> (I. i)

There is also the diction; witness that of the opening where (as elsewhere) religious terminology, classical reference, and the language of love are all debased by being used about 'Riches, the dumb god'. E. B. Partridge (*The Broken Compass*, London 1958) also cites many passages suggesting that the love of gold in Volpone and Mosca is a form of sexual substitution.

Yet, for all this, they are not the least favoured characters. Indeed, if Jonson's comedies ever had heroes,* they would be the heroes of this one. They gain some stature, though ironically, by their use as moral commentators on the greedy birds of prey, Corvino, Corbaccio, and Voltore. Furthermore, they are greedy *and* intelligent, and therefore less subhuman than their dupes, who are stupidly greedy. And then there is the fact that Volpone does have standards; he is an aristocrat among villains. True, he adds nothing to the world's wealth (a virtue, anyway, that might involve grinding men); neither, though,

---

* One of the two slight weaknesses in *Volpone*, in fact, is the presence—not found in his other three masterpieces, *The Alchemist*, *Bartholomew Fair*, and *The Silent Woman* (a brilliant farce)—of a pseudo-hero and pseudo-heroine, Bonaria and Celia, two good and very dull characters. The other weakness is the unnecessary provision, in a subplot, of an ironic parallel to Celia in Lady Would-Be, and to the real Machiavellian, Volpone, in the bumbling English one, Sir Politick Would-Be.

does he swindle the weak: his victims must be worthy of his steel, gentry, lawyers, merchants:

> ... I use no trade, no venture;
> I wound no earth with ploughshares, fat no beasts
> To feed the shambles; have no mills for iron,
> Oil, corn, or men, to grind them into powder;
> I blow no subtle glass, expose no ships
> To threat'nings of the furrow-faced sea;
> I turn no monies in the public bank,
> Nor usure private.
>
> Mosca No, sir, nor devour
> Soft prodigals. You shall have some will swallow
> A melting heir as glibly as your Dutch
> Will pills of butter, and ne'er purge for it;
> Tear forth the fathers of poor families
> Out of their beds, and coffin them alive
> In some kind clasping prison, where their bones
> May be forthcoming when the flesh is rotten;
> You loathe the widow's or the orphan's tears
> Should wash your pavements, or their piteous cries
> Ring in your roofs and beat the air for vengeance.

(I. i)

But most telling of all is their zest for roguery. Volpone is telling the truth when he says 'I glory/More in the cunning purchase of my wealth/Than in the glad possession' (i. i) or 'The pleasure of all woman-kind's not like it' (v. i). It is the life-force perverted, but still the life-force; whereas the dupes are mere money-grubbing machines. Were it not for the harsh ending, sometimes censured, this comedy would be at once socially conserving (by blaming rogues) and psychologically releasing (by admiring them): i.e. it would be in part a moral cheat. However, it is this very zest that is made to bring about not merely the downfall, but the doom of Volpone and Mosca, so that the element of immoral psychological release is safely contained within the social warning. When they have reached the ultimate peak of trickery and fraud, they still cannot be content to retire, but must go on self-destructively to *inevitable* disaster. It is one's sense of this inevitability, together with the diabolic stature of Volpone, that brings this comedy within hailing distance of tragedy.

The Alchemist (1610), probably Jonson's most flawless comedy, starts where *Volpone* left off—with the two tricksters, Face and Subtle, prepared to destroy each other. But they are saved by the mercenary love of a bad woman:

DOL ....
Have you together cozen'd all this while,
And all the world, and shall it now be said,
You've made the most courteous shift to cozen yourselves?
You will accuse him! You will 'bring him in the statute!' . . .
Fall to your couples again, and cozen kindly
And heartily and lovingly, as you should.

(I. i)

From this point they go on to operate a dazzling series of gulling devices, unpunished and almost unblamed (even the sensible, honest Surly is more discomfited than they are, as punishment for the snarling immoderation of his virtue). But they are *exposed*, self-exposed by their speech, in which high-faluting epithets of state, religion, war and big business are counterpointed by low-faluting animal and sexual references; and dignifying euphemisms jostle gross vulgarities, to give repeated effects of complementary ironies. Ironies of character, too, are used as comic means to a satiric mood, particularly in the devastating scenes with the Puritans Ananias and Tribulation Wholesome, which parody sectarian jargon with great accuracy, and by ironic context reveal it as hypocritical cant:

SUBTLE ....
And with a tincture make you as good Dutch dollars
As any are in Holland.

TRIBULATION Can you so?

SUBTLE Ay, and shall bide the third examination.

ANANIAS And it will be joyful tidings to the brethren.

SUBTLE But you must carry it secret.

TRIBULATION Ay: but stay.
This act of coining, is it lawful?

ANANIAS Lawful!
We know no magistrate, or, if we did,
This is foreign coin.

SUBTLE It is no coining, sir, but casting.

TRIBULATION Ha! You distinguish well:
Casting of money may be lawful.

ANANIAS 'Tis, sir.

TRIBULATION Truly, I take it so.

SUBTLE There is no scruple,
Sir, to be made of it; believe Ananias:
This case of conscience he is studied in.

TRIBULATION I'll make a question of it to the brethren.

ANANIAS The brethren shall approve it lawful, doubt not. Where shall it be done?

(III. ii)

Similarly alchemy itself is damned, not only by Subtle's assumption of confraternity with sectarianism, but also by its transmutation of religious terms into 'scientific' jargon.

Jonson's, we have said, is not the language of reverberation. His method is accumulation and varied repetition—very appropriate for his limited, obsessive automatons, whose repetitive behaviour acts as an awful warning. His is the gift of plenitudinous invention, register after register piling up, and within each, example after example, epithet after epithet—the effect coming to a climax in Sir Epicure Mammon's great fantasies of earthly felicity.

This sort of texture, of course, is in keeping with the inventive accumulation of the plot, which manipulates eight intrigues—of Mammon, Surly, Drugger, Dapper, Kastril, Dame Pliant, the Puritans, and finally, in reminiscence of the beginning, of the rogues against each other—with incomparable skill, observing all the unities, yet achieving variety of mood and pace. Gifford is surely right when he observes in his edition of 1816:

> [*The action*] occupies no more time than the representation demands; and the plot, notwithstanding the amazing vigour and variety of the action, is confined to a single spot, without the slightest sacrifice of probability. . . . In a word, if a model be sought of all that is regular in design and perfect in execution in the English drama, it will be found (if found at all) in the ALCHEMIST.

Gifford also remarks that the play committed a sort of suicide, in being so successful in putting down alchemy (where the law had failed) that people came to suppose it no longer relevant. However, the fraudulent pretensions of alchemy is only its ostensible theme (the subject of no more than two of the intrigues). The explosion—which comes at the textural climax, when Sir Epicure's verbal balloon is overblown—is only the *symbolic* climax of the action. In fact, the tricky triumvirate operate magical and divinatory frauds as well; and all demonstrate the effects of superstition and gullibility.

Those who exploit the 'humorous' (men dominated animal-like by one trait or obsession) are no doubt themselves unvirtuous, but, being unwitting agents of virtue by revealing these effects, are nevertheless to be pardoned—almost, indeed, to be admired. In this way—

since Face and Subtle are neither as villainous nor as dangerous as
Volpone and Mosca—*The Alchemist* manages to be almost equally
socially conserving and psychologically releasing without moral confusion, and to exemplify esthetically the complex integration implicit
in this escape from the horns of a looming moral dilemma.

In *Bartholomew Fair* (1614) the process is carried farther. In an
atmosphere of holiday—a sort of Feast of Misrule—the cutpurse,
Edgeworth, and the gamester, Quarlous, turn out to be the most
heroic figures; and the grave Justice, Adam Overdo, is as much
censured as the hypocritical Puritan, Zeal-of-the-Land Busy:

> QUARLOUS Nay, sir, stand you not fixed like a stake at Finsbury,
> to be shot at, or the whipping post in the Fair, but get your wife
> out o' the air, it will make her worse else: and remember you are but
> Adam, flesh and blood! you have your frailty, forget your other
> name of Overdo, and invite us all to supper.
>
> (v. iii)

Overweening pride, self-righteousness and hypocrisy, in the persons
of the Puritans, properly ride to a fall; Overdo acts with the best of
intentions, for justice and fairness, and is the *deus ex machina* who
exposes the others—yet in the very act of doing so he is made to expose
himself as one who has taken pains to be a serious ass. There are
several minor instances of such wit of situation, notably that in which
Nokes is gulled of his purse through an anti-cutpurse ballad. The
rogues escape.

> Jonson was becoming increasingly susceptible to rogues. Intellectual
> ability always captivated him, but he gradually warmed to the human
> qualities of roguery; here the delicate balance between admiration and
> contempt for the rogues, delight and contempt in the fools, makes it
> impossible to regard them as improving moral studies. The rogues
> frequently get off scot-free, and virtue's reward is a chilly disregard.
> The general mixture of farce and irony is here almost Chaucerian.
>
> (M. C. Bradbrook, *Growth and Structure*, p. 146)

Or, one might equally well say, almost Shakespearean. This is
Jonson's most genial comedy, verging not on tragedy, like *Volpone*,
but on farce. True, the Fair is Vanity Fair, an image of the world,
and within it in the grotesque puppet-show of Littlewit's pop-version
of 'Hero and Leander' we have an image of its debasement, its utter
divorce from the ideal, Moreover, certain common targets of comic
satire are aimed at besides the Puritans: in particular, the law and
commercial marriage—but only in passing: poor Grace Wellborn is

being forced by her guardian, Overdo, to marry the silly youth Nokes (who bit by bit loses not only his two purses in the fair but also his clothes, the most stupid character thus, realistically, coming off worst, not the most wicked one). But the point is not emphasised, and she escapes almost incidentally in the general bustle of cheating and gulling that goes on. In any case, moral satire tends to be overwhelmed by the Falstaffian gusto that characterises the texture of this rich broth of prose. Take only part of Quarlous's reproof to his friend Winwife:

> Well, I will forbear, sir; but i'faith, would thou wouldst leave thy exercise of widow-hunting once; this drawing after an old reverend smock by the splay-foot! There cannot be an ancient tripe or trillibub in the town, but thou art straight nosing it, and 'tis a fine occupation thou'lt confine thyself to when thous hast got one; scrubbing a piece of buff, as if thou hadst the perpetuity of Pannier-alley to stink in; or perhaps worse, currying a carcase that thou hast bound thyself to alive. I'll be sworn, some of them that thou art or hast been a suitor to, are so old as no chaste or married pleasure can ever become them; the honest instrument of procreation has forty years since left to belong to them; thou must visit them as thou wouldst do a tomb, with a torch or three handfuls of link, flaming hot, and so thou mayst hap to make them feel thee, and after come to inherit according to thy inches. A sweet course, for a man to waste the brand of life for, to be still raking himself a fortune in an old woman's embers
>
> (I. i)

Strong words. A bit too strong, unless considered as the relish rather than the meat of the matter; so it is with more admiration than surprise that we find Quarlous himself marrying this same widow, while Grace is saved from Nokes by Winwife. Indeed, in the maze of dupery everyone, though none more than the wise Justice, is revealed in a light quite contrary to his or her pretensions. All come to know themselves, but as to whether they will reform, we are given little inkling. Since the parts are so imbued with the gusto of the whole, in fact, we are left feeling it would rather spoil the fun of the fair if they did. This is a comedy whose texture is in general releasing, though the action adumbrates restraint. Any warning it gives seems to be mithridatic rather than exhortatory. It aims to vaccinate the public since the disease appears to be ineradicable. Jonson almost seems to revel even in the Puritans' hypocrisy. At any rate this drama is less harsh with them than they were to be with the drama. But that is the difference between comic and fanatic condemnation.

7

Augustan c.1660-1760

A. *General*   B. *Etherege, Wycherley, Congreve, Farquhar;
Dryden, Pope; Swift, Fielding, Sterne*

A. GENERAL

The century from the restoration of Charles II to the accession
of George III constitutes a Golden Age of English comedy. In the
periods previously considered, one kind of comic literature pre-
dominated sufficiently to be taken as representative: narrative poem
in the 'medieval' period, play in the 'Renaissance'. The equally
loosely styled 'Augustan' period, however, presents no possibility of
such economy. Poets as good as Prior, Butler, Gay, and even Marvell
might go unconsidered, but not giants like Dryden and Pope. Of the
dramatists, many during the first fifty years, and all during the next,
might well be left aside, but still Etherege, Wycherley and Congreve
at least would demand attention. And who would dare omit the
narrative prose of Swift, Fielding, and Sterne from any account of
English comedy?

Perhaps a century covering six reigns, and including not only such
literary variety but also the Plague, the Great Fire, the Agricultural
Revolution, the Glorious Revolution, the introduction of the party
system and Cabinet government, to say nothing of several wars,
should not be styled, however loosly, a 'period'. Certainly the Augus-
tanism of the beginning is different in many ways from that of the end.
Yet it is difficult to know where to make a division. Etherege and
Congreve do not seem different in *kind*, but Congreve was not born
when Etherege's first play appeared. Dryden and Pope—conjoined
as 'classics of our prose' in Matthew Arnold's dismissive phrase—
seem in our post-romantic period to be fundamentally more alike
than different, but Dryden was dead long before Pope's first publication. Even Swift and Sterne, widely separated as they are in date and
style, could never be mistaken for renaissance or romantic writers.
What, though, justifies the particular umbrella-appellation of
'Augustan'? Surely this: the period from 1660 to 1760 was in some

sense what the Romantics condemned it as, an age deeply influenced first by Hobbes's materialism, then by science and Blake's bogymen Newton and Locke, an 'age of reason'.

Restoration 'reason,' of course, was not the same as Georgian 'reason'; nor did either go unquestioned at the time—indeed much of the comedy from Rochester to Sterne consists in just such questioning—yet one thing is sure: it was not an age of romanticism. After the chaos and bloodshed of the Civil War, and the fanaticism of the succeeding Reign of the Saints, what people most valued were social stability and personal urbanity. Reason, of any sort, came to be preferred to emotionalism. Enthusiasm, the mainspring of the aptly named 'romantic *revival*,' was for a hundred years anathema to the literate.

> After the triumph of the Parliamentary armies came the 'rule of the saints,' with their canting piety used as shibboleth to obtain the favour of the dominant party; their interference with the lives of ordinary people; their closing of the theatres and suppressing of customary sport; Anti-clericalism, thus provoked, reacted so violently as to become one of the chief causes of the anti-Romanist Revolution of 1688. For many generations to come, hatred of Puritanism took its place beside hatred of Romanism in the instincts and traditions of the chapel-burning mobs, as well as that of the great majority of the upper class.
>
> (G. M. Trevelyan, *English Social History*, London 1942, p. 233)

Nothing, it might seem, had changed; the Restoration had indeed restored the status quo, leaving Puritans and Romanists again as the chief objects, respectively, of scorn and fear. There seems, also to be the same cross-current of concern about the value of older aristocratic codes as against those of bourgeois *parvenus*:

> "I ever abominated that scheme of politicks,' Swift wrote, '(now about thirty years old) of setting up the mony'd Interest in opposition to the landed. For, I conceiv'd, there could not be a truer maxim in our government than this, That the possessors of the soil are the best judges of what is for the advantage of the kingdom.' A conservative by settled conviction, in social instincts as in literary texts, he states comprehensively in his political writings of the last years of Queen Anne the political philosophy underlying the conservative position. It is unnecessary to mention other writers preoccupied with the conflict between the landed and the moneyed interests; almost all of them were.
>
> (J. Loftis, *Comedy and Society from Congreve to Fielding*, Stanford 1959, p. 2)

In reality, nothing had been restored unchanged. Puritans were no longer a vocal minority within the Anglican Church; they were a once-ruling majority now excluded from it by law and choice. So whereas Renaissance comedy directed at them had been conserving and restraining, that of the Restoration was innovatory and releasing: the attempt of a courtly avant-garde group, representing a precariously-held power, to substitute a courtly hedonist ideal of the Wit for the bourgeois puritan ideal of the Saint. The conflicts were of real values, not mere snobbery. Moreover, they had become idealogically deepened:

> The Civil War was not therefore a social war, but a struggle in which the parties divided on political and religious issues, along a line of cleavage that answered, roughly and with many personal exceptions, to certain divisions of social type.

> (Trevelyan, p. 242)

This ideological element, persisting into the Restoration, is what makes its comedy distinctively different from that of the Renaissance despite a certain similarity in theme and the influence of Jonson in style. The background of linked political and religious principles sharpened comedy of all kinds—as it sharpened differences of economic views. Satiric comedy, therefore, was the norm—shading off at one side into non-comic satire, at the other into purposeful persiflage. Perhaps not till Sterne do we get any fully celebratory, or 'free' festive comedy—though by definition some degree of this quality, or of qualities closely akin to it, is to be found in all works counting as *comedy*.

Gradually, however, opinion, formed into official parties; not much like modern ones perhaps; but still, people began to think of themselves as Whigs or Tories, and called themselves such. The Whigs were effectively led by a group of big landowners prepared to join 'the mony'd Interest': ex-Puritans, latitudinarians, or, later, deists, ready for change and able to afford it, and therefore willing to associate themselves with finance, with science—especially as it affected agriculture—and with the big merchants; Tories tended to be the small country squires, the rural majority, who had been Royalists in the war, and were still High Anglican, anti-mercantilist (therefore anti-urban) and anti-scientific: Fielding's Squire Western, with his hatred of lords, as Whigs and 'Hanover rats', is an archetypal son of such men. These divisions, however, and the party names associated with them do not become established until the 1680s; and their establishment marks an important stage in the evolution of Augustan society and Augustan comedy.

Crudely speaking, that evolution consists in pragmatism's coming to take precedence over principle as the Civil War recedes into the past, and culture moves from the Court, now a court of foreigner-Kings, to the coffee-house, from aristocratic to middle-class writers. Argument and questioning give way to ridicule and irony from a basis of common assumption. The later comedy of the period, therefore, is paradoxically more conserving though less aristocratic—a fact made plain enough if Rochester's *Satire Against Mankind* is compared with Pope's *Essay on Man*, or any aristocratic Restoration comedy with any of the so-called sentimental comedies of Steele or Cibber. By the eighteenth century, Whig puritanism was in effect victorious—and enjoyed a long reign in office under Walpole, from the death of Queen Anne to 1742. Being victorious it was more tolerant (tolerance, too, being good for trade); and anyway the struggles of the Restoration period had revealed, or perhaps established, a balance of power. Stalemate leads to consensus, and ideological satire against bourgeois standards consequently comes to be replaced by more conventional satire on behalf of the new moral consensus. From this basis, Pope attacks deviators of all classes and both parties—though not quite impartially: the satire tends to be comic for Tory and bourgeois backsliders, bitter for Whig and aristocratic (and, of course, for his many personal enemies). Conflict *between* value-systems gradually merges into conflict *within* a compromise value-system.

More importantly, perhaps, what might be called innovatory comedy (when seen against the background of the Commonwealth) is replaced by conserving comedy. In short, comedy gradually comes to be concerned less with the establishment of an acceptable life-style, or the ridiculing of the opposition's unacceptable one, than with correcting the corruption that resulted from a consensus based on the fear that reform, change, might bring back the bad old days of bitterness and violence—though, as the Whig lords and money-men are in control it still tends sometimes to have a strong political element in it.

The earlier Augustan 'reason' is *rationalist*, the later *reasonable*; the one is allied with philosophy and struggle, the other with common-sense and consensus. As an age of fundamental dispute evolves into the age of the Enlightenment, cits once satirised mainly for their puritanism come to be satirised for their mammonism in the more materialistic, middle-class period—and even that does not matter fundamentally, for a convenient conservatism

> Shew'd erring Pride, WHATEVER IS, IS RIGHT;
> That REASON, PASSION, answer one great aim;
> That true SELF-LOVE and SOCIAL are the same;

That VIRTUE only makes our Bliss below;
And all our Knowledge is, OURSELVES TO KNOW.

(Pope, *Essay on Man*, 394-8)

One wonders on what grounds Pope could consistently justify the practice of satire. However, the *Essay* is not comic—or at any rate not intentionally—so there would be little point in anatomising its global weaknesses or local felicities. Sufficient to say that its ostensibly philosophic purport is misleading; Pope finds what he wanted to find, pursues assurance rather than truth. He is right in claiming the merit of compromise, not philosophic impartiality:

> If I could flatter myself that this Essay has any merit, it is in steering betwixt the extremes of doctrines seemingly opposite, in passing over terms utterly unintelligible, and in forming a *temperate* yet not *inconsistent*, and a *short* yet not *imperfect* system of ethics.
>
> ('The Design' prefaced to the *Essay*)

Rochester, writing earlier, is less temperate in his *Satire Against Mankind*; this gives the work a verbal zest that shifts it further from the didactic, nearer to the comic—but it is nevertheless more genuinely philosophic (insofar as a poem can be so without perverting its form). He seems to look for what is the case, not what he wants to be the case.*

From Newton's discovery that matter is governed by simple mechanical principles, for instance, Pope drew only the heartening conclusion that mind too might be reduced to a simple system: 'The science of Human Nature is, like all other sciences, reduced to a *few clear points*' (*The Design*). A conclusion that later provided him with the satirically and comically useful idea that each person is governed by a ruling passion, a sort of psychological force of gravity, that underlies all his apparent variety. Rochester, writing before Newton's *Principia* was published, is tougher minded, sees less palatable implications in current ideas. Suppose, as Hobbes had suggested, that mind *is* matter, in the brain and nervous system? Why then, man is just a thinking machine that breaks down and becomes useless:

> Huddl'd in dirt the reasoning engine lies,
> Who was so proud, so witty, and so wise.
>
> (ll. 29-30)

During the course of his attack on the pretensions of human reason, he justifies his paradoxical thesis as to the superiority of animals, by

---

* Swift (b.1667) is an apparent exception who tends to prove the rule. He is in fact of an earlier generation than Pope (b.1683), and his satires come somewhere between the *Essay on Man* and the *Satire Against Mankind*, being emotionally less accepting than the one but less philosophically questioning than the other.

a witty and intellectually lucid distinction between theological reason
(deducing 'whimsies' from unverifiable axioms) and 'right reason'
(based, like science, on the evidence of the senses). In doing so, he
provides a philosophic justification for hedonism—the so-called
'libertinism' of the tradition of Rabelais and Montaigne—as against
the prohibitions of Christianity, deduced from *a priori* dogmas:

> Our *Sphere* of Action is lifes happiness,
> And he who thinks beyond thinks like an *Ass*.
> Thus, whilst 'gainst false reas'ning I inveigh
> I own right *Reason*, which I would obey,
> That *Reason* that distinguishes by sense,
> And gives us *Rules* of good, and ill, from thence:
> That bounds desires with a reforming Will,
> To keep 'em more in Vigour, not to Kill.
> Your *Reason* hinders, mine helps t'enjoy,
> Renewing Appetites, yours would destroy.
>
> (ll. 96-105)

But the pursuit of this idea leads him to attack also the *aristocratic*
ideals of honour and glory, and without pulling the punches:

> *Birds*, feed on *Birds*, *Beasts* on each other prey,
> But savage *Man* alone, does *Man*, betray:
> Prest by necessity, they Kill for Food,
> *Man*, undoes *Man*, to do himself no good . . .
> For hunger, or for Love, they fight, or tear,
> Whilst wretch'd *Man* is still in arms for fear;
> For feare he armes and is of Armes afraid,
> By fear, to fear, successively betray'd.
> Base fear, the source whence his best passions came,
> His boasted Honour, and his dear bought Fame . . .
> Merely for safety, after Fame we thirst,
> For all Men, wou'd be cowards if they durst.
>
> (ll. 129-158)

The same tendency, for the earlier work to be more probing, is to
be found in fully comic writing. Naturally it makes assumptions, and
uses ridicule, but rather less complacently; it more often backs
assumption with argument. Witness, for instance, the demolition of
Pinchwife's proprietorial attitude to wives, which concludes as
follows:

> PINCHWIFE Well, gentleman, you may laugh at me; but you shall
>   never lie with my wife: I know the town.
>
> HORNER But prithee was not the way you were in better? Is not keep-
>   ing better than marriage?

PINCHWIFE A pox on 't! The jades would jilt me, I could never keep a whore to myself.

HORNER So, then you only married to keep a whore to yourself. Well, let me tell you, women, as you say, are like soldiers; made constant and loyal by good pay rather than by oaths and covenants.

(Wycherley, *The Country Wife*, I. i)

Witness also the rational, and unconventional, contract between Mirabell and Millamant in Congreve's *Way of the World*, and the greater element of argument in Dryden's *Absalom and Achitophel* than any of Pope's satires.

Even Samuel Butler's *Hudibras*, which seems to run its unpremeditated way much as one would expect from a man who proclaimed Beer to be his Muse, can cut unexpectedly deep. For example, his attack on the Presbyterians—the most authoritarian of the sects— by-passed theology altogether for underlying questions of philosophy and psychology. What is the basis of faith, the validity of forced belief, the nature of religious truth? Do traits of character determine which system a man chooses to believe? Beneath the clatter of metre and the rapid fire of rhyme, in fact, some independent thinking is going —comically revealed in paradox, wit, and humorous incongruity:

> ... That stubborn crew
> Of errant saints whom all men grant
> To be the true Church Militant.
> Such as do base their faith upon
> The holy text of pike and gun;
> Decide all controversies by
> Infallible artillery;
> And prove their doctrine orthodox
> With apostolic blows and knocks;
> Call fire and sword and desolation
> A godly thorough Reformation,
> Which always must be going on,
> And still be doing, never done,
> As if Religion were intended
> For nothing else but to be mended.
> A sect whose chief devotion lies
> In odd perverse antipathies,
> In falling out with that or this
> And finding somewhat still amiss;
> More peevish, cross and splenetic
> Than dog distract or monkey sick:

That with more care keep holyday
The wrong, than others the right way;
Compound for sins they are inclined to
By damning those they have no mind to.
Still so perverse and opposite
As if they worshipped God for spite,
The self-same thing they will abhor
One way and long another for;
Freewill they one way disavow,
Another, nothing else allow;
All piety consists therein
In them, in other men all sin.
Rather than fail they will defy
That which they love most tenderly;
Quarrel with mincepies, and disparage
Their best and dearest friend plum-porridge;
Fat pig, and goose itself oppose,
And blaspheme custard through the nose.

(1. ll. 190-228)

There is another strain that also becomes diluted when middle-
class men take over; a comedy of style. The Cavalier poets created
'a style from a despair'; they had braved out hard times by emphasising
all the unpuritan qualities: elegance, ease, polish, flippancy. Regardless
of content, these formal qualities were themselves an assertion, a
defiance even, and in the circumstances a virtue. When Addison
tries to take them over to civilise the squirearchy, the result is merely
a muddling of manners and morality, which Fielding clears up—
with a heavier-handed comic moralism than that of the Cavaliers
and their successors. In the days of victory, however, the manner
developed by Cavalier poets could be used for subtle comic aggression:
to oppose without preaching, to *exemplify* a style of life—one deriving
from the assumptions of an unpuritanical aristocracy based on landed
inheritance—whose contrary by implication was barbarous and
absurd. Take the following poem, *To Phyllis*, by Sedley:

Phyllis, for shame, let us improve
    A thousand several ways
These few short minutes stol'n by love
    From many tedious days.

Whilst you want courage to despise
    The censure of the grave,
For all the tyrants in your eyes,
    Your heart is but a slave.

> My love is full of noble pride,
>   And never will submit
> To let that Fop, discretion, ride
>   In triumph over wit.
>
> False friends I have, as well as you,
>   That daily counsel me
> Vain frivolous trifles to pursue
>   And leave off loving thee.
>
> When I the least belief bestow
>   On what such fools advise
> May I be dull enough to grow
>   Most miserably wise.

Thematically, a love-poem, or rather a poem of seduction, these verses work rhetorically against the Puritan way of life—not by actually saying anything against it, but by opposing to it a radically different life-style. What ought to seem outrageous paradox, by conventional standards, is casually taken for granted, as self-evident. 'Shame' is *not* to make love 'A thousand several ways,' the censure of grave people is despicable, pride noble; discretion far from being sensible is foppery—which, as most Restoration plays indicate, is clearly inferior to 'wit' (Rochester's 'right Reason'). What would traditionally have been called 'true' friends, are taken to be 'false'—the 'vain frivolous trifles' they urge being presumably such things as work, money, respectability. And so, cumulatively, to the last stanza, which most wittily completes the inversion. All this could be, and should be, taken as a lover's complimentary hyperbole. But the fact that Sedley uses just *this* form of hyperbole, and with such formal suavity, gives an extra implication to the stance.

Puritan comedy is almost non-existent, largely for reasons of ideology and temperament (though, of course, certain parts of that very earnest work *The Pilgrim's Progress* could be excerpted as self-contained comic vignettes). After 1663, no doubt, the first Licensing Act, against the publication of seditious and heretical works, especially by Roundheads, must have helped; but little change is to be found after it lapsed in 1696. Yet the masterpiece of this kind of poem is by a Puritan—an exceptional Puritan, however, who had been a Royalist, and briefly even a Catholic. It is, too, a fairly early poem. What it seems to show is the gain in density and human depth that comes from a less confrontatory stance. Marvell's address 'To his Coy Mistress', just like Sedley's to Phyllis, is certainly anti-Puritan in its effect, both in style and content (the more surprisingly so if 'quaint' is supposed to be a Chaucerian pun—a supposition not altogether ruled out by the *O.E.D.*):

> Thy beauty shall no more be found:
> Nor in thy marble vault shall sound
> My echoing song; then worms shall try
> That long-preserved virginity;
> And your quaint honour turn to dust,
> And into ashes all my lust.
> The grave's a fine and private place
> But none, I think, do there embrace.

Like Sedley's, the writing itself is emblematic of an unconstipated life-style; but this poem is releasing in a bigger way than his. It is *more* innovatory, since it allows a Saturnalian or hedonistic attitude to sex to come through without having to reduce textural density and emotion as Sedley does to sustain the confrontatory pose. Indeed, this is not confrontatory. It works in a different way: by starting off with a humorous parody of courtly love in the first section, ('Had we but world enough and time . . .'), teasingly hyperbolical, passing into a more needling irony in the second ('But at my back I always hear. . .'), and finally, with a change of rhythm, into a section of metaphysical wit, whose ambiguities develop urgency of feeling within the elegance of form:

> Now, let us sport us while we may;
> And now, like amorous birds of prey
> Rather at once our time devour.
> Than languish in his slow-chapt power.
> Let us roll all our strength, and all
> Our sweetness up into one ball;
> And tear our pleasures with rough strife
> Thorough the iron gates of life.

Birds of *prey* . . . devour . . . tear . . . *rough* strife. There is little suavity about this sexual encounter—and sexual it is; strength and sweetness are man and woman, the ball the two of them embraced, as well as the cannonball of the primary image; the gates, surely, anatomical as well as fortificatory and abstract. In short, something of Puritan seriousness and roughness has developed from the Cavalier comedy of the earlier lines, to make the whole a love-poem in which emotional seriousness fuses with libertine suggestion, both being kept in hand—just within the bounds of comedy—by a logical structure and a varying comic texture of parodic, ironic and metaphysical wit. These qualities are to be found separately elsewhere but not in combination. Were Restoration comic plays what many have accused them of being, thoroughly libertine, they might have provided a dramatic equivalent. But a more appropriate criticism seems to be that they are not libertine enough, (only just enough to shock the bourgeoisie); that they compromise with anti-sensual standards they don't really believe in; do not so much fuse, as muddle oldfashioned and newfangled moralities, by adopting 'right Reason' (that of the Wit) as their standard, but insinuating it under cover of attacking hypocrisy, folly, and affectation rather than openly exploring its consequences. However, the best of these plays are better than any dramatic comedy since, and may well serve as a starting point for concentrating generalisation into particular literary appreciations.

B. i. Etherege, Wycherley, Congreve, Farquhar

Superficially, Restoration Comedy looks very Jonsonian; the names of characters and the titles often suggest distant kinship with the Morality tradition, and when plots are taken—not infrequently—from Molière they are usually given a typically Jonsonian complication. The essential difference is that these plays are indeed comedy of manners: the type-characters and the action itself are supposed to exhibit not 'humours', eccentricities, but normal, if formalised representatives of the society in question (hence the constant endeavour of contemporaries to associate key characters with real personages). One difficulty in writing about this comedy is that so many critics have said so many different things about it, all of them true. It must be allowed thinness and grossness, libertinism and conventionality, trivial realism and artificiality, excessive wittiness and dullness, frivolity and seriousness, cloud-cuckoldry and moral criticism.

Harrington Smith, in *The Gay Couple in Restoration Comedy* (Cambridge, Mass. 1948), sees an evolution from gay comedy (1660-75), through cynical comedy (1675-87), to exemplary comedy gradually petering out in sentimentality as the playwrights give in to various pressures: 'the Ladies' of the boxes, the increased number of citizens and their wives in the audience, the cessation of court patronage with the accession of William IV, and the attacks of Collier and others. Bonamy Dobrée (*Restoration Comedy*, Oxford 1924) sees the attempt to rationalise, i.e. paganise, the relations of the sexes as having failed and been replaced, when Congreve wrote, by a more traditional outlook; love and sincerity replacing untied permissiveness. Potts (*Comedy*, 1948) and Kenneth Muir (*The Comedy of Manners*, London

1970) discern a similar trend. Within such an evolution there is
clearly room for a variety of characteristics. Etherege certainly has
something of Sedley's thinness; Congreve something of Marvell's
feeling (with the consequent risk of a frivolous structure's sinking by
force of textural gravity); Wycherley is both cynical and socially
critical; Farquhar gross and also sentimental. All adopt certain
conventions of form (from Jonson and Molière) and content (from
'the Town'—Westminster, Whitehall and their environs), and all in
so far as they reflect a society trying to establish a French stylishness,
to set against the uncouth, pushing bourgeoisie, are both realistic and
artificial. The replies to Collier (1698), however, indicate how soon
the serious ideological challenge to bourgeois Puritan values faded.
Most of them defensively excuse the dramatists on the grounds that
they were satirising what Collier assumed them to be advocating.
Even the strongly worded 'Letter to A. H. Esq.; Concerning the
Stage', in the same year, does not positively support the implicit revisionist affirmations lying behind the early Restoration drama's experimental denials but rather negatively concentrates on the initial
provocation:

> It would be happy if the World had learnt no more irreligion from the
> Pulpit than it has from the Stage; at least the Consequence of the first
> has been more fatal. What dismal Effect has the holy Cant had upon
> the Multitude: What Rebellion, Bloodshed and Mischief have been
> encouraged under the name of *Sanctity*, *Religion*, and the *Good Old
> Cause*. Who ever learnt to cut a King's Throat by seeing of Plays?
> But by going to Church the People were instructed *to bind the King in
> Chains, and his Nobles in fetters of Iron, That the Kingdom ought to be
> taken away and given to the Saints*; And who would not be a Saint for
> such an Inheritance? . . . But when Men of debauch'd Principles shall
> become the Teachers of the Nation, what may we not expect from
> their Industry and Sedition.
> (Augustan Reprint Society, Series Three, No. 1, *Essays on the Stage*, Ann
> Arbor 1946)

By the turn of the century players were being successfully prosecuted
for 'prophanely using the Name of God upon the Stage', and businessmen were being treated respectfully on the stage. Congreve was no
sentimentalist, and was instantly acknowledged on first appearance to
be the most stylish and witty writer of the age—and that by a trained
audience accustomed to clap strokes of wit on stage as a modern
audience claps brilliant tennis strokes, and to appreciate style far more
than we do. (See Congreve's *Old Bachelor*: 'From Formula to Art',

Maximilian E. Novak, *Essays in Criticism*, April 1970.) Nor is he unthinkingly orthodox. Yet there is a more sober note to *The Way of the World* than is characteristic of earlier comedies. In a sense, it is the culmination of what went before, but rather as Marvell's *Coy Mistress* is the apogee of its kind, by absorbing something of the other side—and such ripeness preludes rottenness. In 1700, it is the last really interesting dramatic comedy before Shaw. Sir Richard Blackmore, writing in 1716, is therefore out of date and injuring the cause of his own class when he calls for stage censorship. His artless '*Essay upon Wit*' is of interest, however, as a revelation of precisely the bourgeois life-style that Restoration comedy had tried to laugh out of countenance and that Georgian comedy was to try to laugh into civility. Wit, Sir Richard sees as evil:

> That Distinction that seems common to Persons of this Denomination [*wits*] is an inferior Degree of Wisdom and Discretion . . . Wit and Discretion are almost incapable of friendly agreement [cf. Sedley's '*Fop Discretion*' and '*dull enough to grow/most miserably wise*'].

Wits scoff at

> the industrious Merchant, and grave Persons of all Professions . . . and expose them as stupid creatures, not supportable in good Company; yet these in their turn believe they have as great a right, as indeed they have, to reproach the others for want of Industry, good Sense, and regular Oeconomy, much more valuable Talents than those, which any mere Wit can boast of.

Worse, they live loose lives and 'expose the sacred mysteries of Christianity, and make its Votaries the Common Topic of their Raillery,' and are not struck down for their impiety:

> The Stage is become Impregnable, where loose Poets, supported by Numbers, Power and Interest, in Defiance of all Rules of Decency and Virtue, still provide new Snares and Temptations to seduce the People, and corrupt their manners. Notwithstanding the earnest cries of this great City, that Importune these Writers to reform the Theatre, and no longer to infect her Youth, and draw their Inclinations from their Professions and Employments; notwithstanding the Sighs and Tears of many once flourishing, but now disconsolate Families, ruin'd by the dissolute Lives of the chief Branches, who lost their vertue by fre-quenting the Fatal Entertainments of the Theatre; notwithstanding the wise and sober part of the Kingdom earnestly sollicit them to spare the People, to stop the spreading Plague and stay the destroying Pen,

they persevere with intrepid Resolution and inexorable Cruelty, to
poison the Minds, and ruin the Morals of the Nation.

(Augustan Reprint Society, Series One, No. 1, *Essays on Wit*, Ann Arbor
1946)

By contrast, he gives high praise to the complacent low-pressure
muddle of the new bourgeois *Tatler* and *Spectator*. Some of Sir
Richard's mud might stick to Etherege, little, if any, to Congreve or
Farquhar.

With *The Comical Revenge*, in 1664, Etherege was generally
allowed to have invented the new form of comedy, a comedy probable
enough for the Town to recognise itself, and polished enough for the
reflection to please. His third and last play, *The Man of Mode* (1676)
is contemporaneous with Wycherley's harsh *Plain Dealer*, but is
itself a development, not a change, from his own two earlier works
that established the basic form of Restoration comedy. Whether this
play, or Wycherley's *Country Wife*, or Congreve's *Way of the World*
is *the* masterpiece of the kind will no doubt always be a matter of
opinion, according as poise, plot, or personality is preferred in comedy,
but no-one doubts that it is Etherege's masterpiece. What sort of
masterpiece is in dispute.

Perhaps the trouble is that it is purposeful and revealing without
being moral or didactic. Etherege gives the evidence but withholds
judgement; presents characters who are complex but superficial—
appropriately so, for in their well-insulated world depth would be
superfluous.

The play is subtitled *or, Sir Fopling Flutter*. Why? He is not the
central character; that is clearly Dorimant. Nor is he a focal-point of
satire, though he clearly is what Dorimant calls him 'a person indeed
of great acquired follies' ('lately arrive piping hot from Paris'), and as
such is just the kind of fool Congreve thought deserving of satire.
But he is relished, as an entertaining clown and showpiece. By making
him the man of mode is Etherege nudging us towards the idea that
'all is vanity' (in a more colloquial sense, of course, than the preacher's)?
Sir Fopling is all manner, all modishness, whereas Dorimant, Medley,
Bellinda and Harriet all appear to be people of good sense, wits. Only
'appear', since all are in fact constantly preparing and trying to preserve 'a face to meet the faces in the street'—and, it might seem, despite
the insolent elegance of their style, their 'bel air', paying a heavy
price? To this problem Etherege provides no explicit solution, for
this seems a genuinely experimental comedy, in the sense that like a
natural scientist the author takes no side.

Of course, to take no side, to preserve a smiling abstention from praise or blame in matters of promise-breaking, infidelity, humiliation, double-crossing and loose living, at this period particularly, was in fact to take the un-Puritan side. Indeed, Etherege, like Sedley, must have been the more infuriating in giving no sign that such abstention might be called in question. Evidently, if all is vanity it cannot be. Why get upset about trifles—and in a toy world what is not a trifle? This seems to be *one* of the play's comic points. Finally, we feel it doesn't matter whether Dorimant has fallen in love with Harriet for keeps, whether he finds (like Young Bellair) that 'without church security, there's no taking up there', or whether he will get round Bellinda again. In this world, these are indeed vain frivolous trifles. But it is not quite such a toy world.

At one point in the twelfth-century *chantefable, Aucassin et Nicolette*, the aristocratic hero is searching the forest for Nicolette when suddenly he is confronted by a huge hairy horrible churl, dirty, ugly and uncouth, who says:

> Mais por quoi plorez vos et faites si grant duce? Certes, se j'estoie aussi riches on con vos estes, toz li monz ne me feroit mi plorer.
> [Why do you weep and show such sorrow? Why if I were as rich a man as you are nothing in the world would make me weep.]

Aucassin answers in a pretty metaphor that he has lost a white greyhound, the most beautiful in the world, gets a scathing answer from the literal-minded brute ('que vos plorates por un chien puant') and is then regaled with a tale of real trouble: hunger, poverty, and the threat of imprisonment for want of twenty sous. More, the churl is shown to possess a primitive sensibility:

> Une lasse mere avoie, si n'avait plus vaillant que une coutisele, si li a on sachiee de dessoz le dos, si gist a pur l'estrain, si m'en poise assez plus que de moi.
> [I have a poor mother who had nothing but an old mattress that they've pulled from under her, so that she lies on bare straw; I suffer more for her than for myself.]

It is as if some scribe had deliberately dropped a great blot in the margin of his beautifully illuminated manuscript. Money cures the churl's troubles, as it cannot cure those of a refined sensibility, and he appears no more in the tale. Why was he ever allowed in, and without wiping his boots? It doesn't alter our view of Aucassin and Nicolette in relation to each other and to their obstructive parents, but it does fleetingly juxtapose to theirs another world with a very different set of internal relationships—and this is apt to provoke second-order reflections thereafter.

In *The Man of Mode* there is a tactful equivalent. Mistress Loveit is Etherege's churl, so to speak, though she is well integrated into the whole work. Indeed, the main plot consists in nothing else but Dorimant's attempts to cast off Loveit 'honourably,' in order to secure a new mistress (or two) while still demonstrating his power (for 'reputation's' sake) by making her humiliate herself for him in public. What Dorimant and all the other main characters share with Sir Fopling is a fashionable surface; either they have no tender feelings, like him, or they successfully subdue them to a manner; unlike Puritans, they are not fanatics; unlike businessmen, they know life is not real and earnest; men are not to be oxen under the yoke. Loveit is different; in this world a sort of churl with undisguisably strong feelings.

Amongst several minor motifs, mostly contributing a sense of play and sparkle, a serious leitmotif is discernible; the recurrent concern with freedom (from love, marriage and, by implication, feeling). And this, together with other elements in *The Man of Mode* suggests a theme: apparently that emotion endangers freedom—but more subtly, it comes to seem, that though this is so there is only a choice of fire and fire since emotion is inescapable (even Dorimant, though subduing affection, is surely not free from emotion).

In such a world dissembling becomes a practical morality, and Loveit's inability to hide her love under a Manner—desperately though she tries—makes her uncomfortable or uncivil company for others,* a blot on the book, and an enemy to herself. Everyone else dissembles for the sake of power or reputation. Even Young Bellair may be suspected of some dissembling, if only in the way of self-deception, since when it comes to the crunch he does not react at all as a stage true-lover ought:

> MEDLEY Now's your time Bellair. Never had lover such an oppor-
> tunity of giving a generous proof of his passion.
> YOUNG BELLAIR As how, I pray?
> MEDLEY Why, hang an estate, marry Emilia out of hand, and provoke

---

* DORIMANT: You know a worthy principle of hers?
  MEDLEY: Not to be so much as civil to a man who speaks to her in the presence
  of him she professes to love.   (III. iii)

A very fanaticism of faithfulness!

E

> your father to do what he threatens. 'Tis but despising a coach,
> humbling yourself to a pair of galoshes, being out of countenance
> when you meet your friends, pointed at and pilloried wherever you
> go by all the amorous fops that know you, and your fame will be
> immortal.
>
> YOUNG BELLAIR   I could find it in my heart to resolve not to marry
> at all.
>
> DORIMANT   Fie, fie! That would spoil a good jest and disappoint the
> well-natured town of an occasion of laughing at you.
>
> (I. i)

The presentation is realistic, the persiflage amusing—and judgement is suspended. Is the town, young Bellair, or romantic love being
mocked? Etherege provides no standard by which to decide, but style
alone indicates that *something* is being smoothly ridiculed. Taken in the
context of the play as a whole, which includes a good deal of pure play-
wit, perhaps what mainly comes over is a diffuse sense of the absurdity
of taking love sufficiently seriously either to sacrifice for it or to pillory
the victim. This seems to support the idea that Loveit—and therefore passion—is the main target, since even Harriet, a favoured
character, joins in the fun of kicking her when she's down. Certainly
her undissembled love is enslaving and exposes her to general insult.
But who is to say that Harriet is here to be regarded as faultless? No
other major character fits neatly into any stereotype of the new moral
scale, going from Good Natured Wit (who helps himself without
harming others), through the Malicious Wit (helping himself and
harming others) and Good Natured Fop (neither helping himself nor
harming others), down to Malicious Fop (harming himself and failing
to harm others). Dorimant, like both Medley and Bellinda, is sometimes
good natured, sometimes malicious. In the first act he treats his servants
well, in the second he treats Loveit badly (and, later, worse)—a
point underlined by Bellinda:

> BELLINDA   H'as given me the proof which I desired of his love; but
> 'tis a proof of his ill nature too. I wish I had not seen him use her so.
> I sigh to think that Dorimant may be
> One day as faithless and unkind to me.
>
> (II. ii)

In fact, Loveit functions as a contrast, as passion punctuating the
persiflage that *passes for* cool reason. Sometimes the contrast *is* un-
favourable: she is possessive in trying to keep Dorimant when he has
tired of her, and she is self-destructive in being unable to overcome a
passion she knows can only hurt her. Sometimes, however, it must
seem favourable (short of reversal of almost impregnable standards).

Unlike Dorimant, Bellinda, and even Harriet, she commits no un-justifiable deceit, and her love passes the ultimate tests of genuineness: she would have been happy for Dorimant to marry to mend his fortune, remaining herself simply his loved mistress (v. ii), and would have gladly suffered public humiliation for it:

> Mrs. Loveit Public satisfaction for the wrong I have done you? This is some new device to make me ridiculous.
>
> ....
>
> Dorimant You will not satisfy my love?
> Mrs. Loveit I would die to satisfy that; but I will not, to save you from a thousand racks, do a shameless thing to please your vanity.
>
> (v. i)

Furthermore, in her verbal duel with Dorimant earlier in the same scene her points strike home simply because she is right and is known to be both by him and by the audience. Perhaps most telling is this rejoinder:

> Mrs. Loveit You take a pride of late in using of me ill, that the town may know the power you have over me, which now (as un-reasonably as yourself) expects that I, do me all the injuries you can, must love you still.

Now this indicates that a capacity for bantering stylishness in affairs of the heart is not evidence of all-round rationality—though it may well be circumstantial evidence of a lack of roundedness of personality, due to the period fear of emotion. To be governed by a need for power is no more rational (and therefore free) than to be governed by a need for undivided affection. Indeed, Dorimant's jealousy, however small the proportion of earnest to pretence, is positively *more* irrational than Loveit's. Indeed, hers is not irrational at all, save in so far as it distresses, without materially helping her—like grief. Her position is very different from that of the women in *The Country Wife.* They are all (poorly) married and therefore must keep their (purely sexual) affairs secret; and when Horner takes another woman he does not jettison the others; so their finally re-nouncing jealousy and agreeing to share him is entirely sensible. Loveit, however, will lose love and lover when Dorimant embarks on a fresh woman; she has good reason to be jealous. His, on the other hand, is a dog-in-the-manger jealousy—or, even less substantially, a dislike of losing the *reputation* of a man of power.

Both are free from some conventions, but not from others. He shows wit, she sincerity. His sexual life is richer in quantity, hers, one must assume on the basis of common experience, in quality. Neither of them is whitewashed, nor is either blackhearted.

Though the relative lack of plot and action does tend to direct attention to character and theme, *The Man of Mode* is not a moralistic comedy. On the contrary, it is comedy lying on the border of divertisement. That the action is carried forward almost entirely by a series of conversations and verbal confrontations also directs attention to tone; and the tone is mainly one of light detachment, if not of cynical frivolity. The way things are, it suggests, is not perfect; indeed it's absurd—but amusing to contemplate and listen-in on. The latest editor of the play, W. B. Carnochan (London 1967) takes it much more soberly, and calls in the formidable aid of Underwood's *Etherege and the Seventeenth-Century Comedy of Manners* (Yale 1957), when he argues that:

> The repeated images of love and sexual pursuit as religious experience, as gaming, as a business venture, lend weight to the puns and proverbs and colloquial rhythms of the dialogue. When Harriet asks Dorimant if he can 'keep a Lent for a mistress' and Dorimant answers 'In expectation of a happy Easter', the sexual joke mirrors ironic themes of the fall, of grace, of redemption, that are at the heart of the play.
>
> (xx)

It is not possible to prove a negative, but surely this is plain wrong: the result of an insensitivity to tone (nor does anything in Etherege's life give psychological support for such symbolic sobriety). Perhaps the passage should be quoted at length:

> DORIMANT You were talking of play, madam. Pray, what may be your stint?
>
> HARRIET A little harmless discourse in public walks or at most an appointment in a box, barefaced, at the playhouse. You are for masks and private meetings, where women engage for all they are worth, I hear.
>
> DORIMANT I have been used to deep play, but I can make one at small game when I like my gamester well.
>
> HARRIET And be so unconcerned you'll ha' no pleasure in't.
>
> DORIMANT Where there is a considerable sum to be won, the hope of drawing people in makes every trifle considerable.
>
> HARRIET The sordidness of men's natures, I know, makes 'em willing to flatter and comply with the rich, though they are sure never to be the better for 'em.
>
> DORIMANT 'Tis in their power to do us good, and we despair not but at some time they may be willing.

Now gambling is not one of the concerns of this play, and there is no reason to suppose that this passage of badinage is giving weight to anything connected with it or mirroring any theme about it. It is mainly playwit, a cleverly oblique way of talking about sex and seduction. The slight element of tendency-wit arises simply from mild debunking of love as a serious, romantic thing by the witty use of such a different register. When the dialogue goes on, surely, the same thing happens with religion. Themes of the fall, of grace, of redemption may be read *into* the text but cannot properly be read from it. The mere fact that the same topic is continued associates the religious imagery with that of gambling—but not ironically, not seriously, not blasphemously; no point is being made. Or, the implicit point is that no point is being made. Unlike bourgeois Puritans Etherege's characters do not take love, gambling or religion seriously enough to care whether the images are appropriate to the subject or congruous with each other. The *tonal* point is the unifying frivolity of treating weighty matters so lightly:

> HARRIET To men who have fared in this town like you, 'twould be a great mortification to live on hope. Could you keep a Lent for a mistress?
>
> DORIMANT In expectation of a happy Easter; and though time be very precious, think forty days well lost to gain your favour.
>
> (III. iii)

What matters is more the style than the content of this imagery. Here, as in Sedley's poem, the poise is the purpose. But Etherege's polished reflection of his world, a *beau monde*, makes no overt propaganda for it—unless it be propaganda to substitute pleasures and pains for virtues and vices, and to imply by tone that both are trifles to be relished, like the eponymous Sir Fopling, by the connoisseur of human absurdity. Certainly it may seem a preferable world to Sir Richard Blackmore's, but it is not shown as a good one—may seem preferable perhaps *because* it is not shown as a good one. In short, this is releasing comedy of a rather cynical kind, for though there are local discriminations the whole encourages laughter neither with, nor at, but *about*.

Steele, writing of *The Country Wife*, presumed that play likewise to be a reflection of life, since it exemplified no sentimental sexual morality, and he excused both *Wycherley* and later dramatists like himself on grounds of realism:

> ... a Poet had at that time discovered his want of knowing the manners of the Court he lived in, by a virtuous character in his fine gentleman,

as he would show his ignorance by drawing a vicious one to please the
present audience.

(Tatler, April 16, 1709)

The flaw in this species of reasoning is well brought out by R.
Edgley, in an excellent article:

> We must agree with Knights that, e.g. *The Country Wife* has no
> serious criticism of sexual morality as such, and in a certain sense with
> Knights and Wain that it has no direct criticism of morality at all.
> But it does not follow that it contains no social criticism . . . for the
> direct topic of criticism in *The Country Wife* is folly. . . . Folly is not
> itself a moral defect, for fools may be goodhearted and well-intentioned;
> and immoral people may be clever or intelligent. In Restoration comedy
> . . . the exposure of folly is mainly the work of immoral characters, who
> accomplish it by trick, fraud, deceit and dishonesty. The triumph of
> these characters is a triumph not of dishonesty but of wit and intelli-
> gence over stupidity.
>
> That is why these characters are sometimes associated with honest
> and upright men. In *The Country Wife* e.g., Horner's chief friend is
> Frank Harcourt, a kind of English honnête homme. To Wain this is a
> muddle . . . [but it] disappears if the triumphs of Horner and Harcourt
> are not looked at from a moral point of view, but are seen for what
> they are, triumphs of wit and sense over folly and stupidity. These
> are the common factors responsible for both successes: in each case a
> fool out of his folly, gives his woman to a man of wit.

('The Object of Literary Criticism', Essays in Criticism, July 1964)

The play, in fact, is perfectly coherent if regarded as a more radical
exploration than Etherege's of a rational 'morality' related to a
Hobbesian scale of pains and pleasures instead of the traditional
morality of vices and virtues related to theological principles. As in
nearly all Restoration comedies before the exemplary period, there is a
spin-off of anti-puritanism, if only because it is taken for granted that
chasing women in town is as proper a pursuit for the gallant as hunting
foxes in the country. Doing neither is by implication ungentlemanly.
Like Sir Fopling, Wycherley's fools are men of 'great acquired
follies'. Their mishaps are the result of defects of character and therefore justly the subject of scornful laughter, not sympathy. To this
extent Wycherley is a moralist where Etherege is not, but the morality
is aimed at folly not, in the religious way, at sex. Jealousy, however, is
the chief dramatic means of exploration, and a critique of marriage
becomes a recurrent concern, second only to that of folly.

That the consequences of folly are demonstrated in a sexual context
certainly means that libertinism looms large in the play. Even Har-

court, whose wit is to be 'legitimately' employed in 'bubbling' Sparkish of the chaste Alithea for the purpose of love in marriage, is carefully put forward as no prig but a Rochesterian libertine, upholding 'right reason':

> HARCOURT No, mistresses are like books. If you pore upon them too much, they doze you, and make you unfit for company; but if used discreetly, you are the fitter for conversation by 'em.
>
> (I. i)

Nor need we choose between Harcourt and Horner. The wit of the one obtains the reward of quality; of quantity the wit of the other. Furthermore, the comic emphasis of the action—Sparkish foolishly mistaking Harcourt's purport and forcing Alithea on him, Pinchwife delivering his own, disguised, wife to Horner, Sir Jasper abetting his wife in her quest for 'china'—properly highlights the Bad Examples, who can be shown as thoroughly absurd. (Addison and the sentimental dramatists misguidedly work the other way, setting up Good Examples with lovable little quirks and failings; in consequence they fall into an uncomic didacticism.) However, critics ever since Collier have been obsessed with the question whether Restoration dramatists were really satirising libertinism or were only pretending to. Kenneth Muir, for instance, writes as follows:

> Most modern critics believe that Dryden and the other dramatists were self-deluded or disingenuous about their motives and that they did not really expect the audience to condemn the libertinism of their gallants. Here . . . it is important to distinguish between Etherege and Wycherley, and between Congreve and Farquhar.
>
> (*The Comedy of Errors*, 1970, p. 17)

But Wycherley gives no condemnation of Horner, while Etherege at least shows shortcomings in Dorimant's particular mode of libertinism; further, the passage in Dryden that Muir quotes makes no mention of libertinism, only of folly:

> The business of the poet is to make you laugh: when he writes humour, he makes folly ridiculous; when wit he moves you, if not always to laughter, yet to a pleasure that is more noble. And if he works a cure on folly, and the small imperfections in mankind, by exposing them to public view, that cure is not performed by an immediate operation. For it works first on the ill nature of the audience; they are moved to laugh by the representation of deformity; and the shame of that laughter teaches us to amend what is ridiculous in our manners.
>
> (Preface to *An Evening's Walk*, 1671)

A statement that admirably describes the method of *The Country Wife*, provided we recognise that the laughter is *at* Sparkish, Pinchwife and Sir Jasper Fidget (and to a lesser extent the ladies of honour) and *with* Harcourt and Horner (in effect again *at* the dupes). As for Margery Pinchwife, we laugh *at* her natural simplicity, which is a handicap, but *with* her simple naturalness, which is a radical critique of the arranged marriage; we laugh *about* her acquired artfulness, which is a direct result of Pinchwife's determination to keep her simple and ignorant.

The chief device of the play, appropriately enough for the exposure of folly, is paradox—both structural, in the brilliant plotting that gives insistence to the *coups de théâtre* already mentioned, and textural, in speeches like this of Harcourt:

> Most men are the contraries to that they would seem. Your bully, you see, is a coward with a long sword; the little humbly-fawning physician, with his ebony cane, is he that destroys men.
>
> (I. i)

or Horner's thematic statement:

> No, a foolish rival and a jealous husband *assist* their rival's designs; for they are sure to make their women hate them, which is the first step to their love for another man.
>
> (III. ii)

Similarly, the supposed eunuch gets most women, the jealous husbands are easiest cuckolded, prudish ladies the most lecherous, and open aversion a sure sign of secret desire.

Everyone, it is assumed plays a role; in such a world, those who play according to right reason are clearly less absurd than those who play conventionally or foolishly. That traditional *morality* might well reverse this value-judgement is what makes this play radical and experimental as a *social* critique. It suggests that there are values other than the traditional moral ones in life.

Horner plays his role with full clarity of mind, and therefore is at the top of the comic scale (the magnitude of his sacrifice of masculine reputation and of his achievement in satisfying the appetites of four hungry women might well raise him to the status of Hero, in this saintless parallel-pantheon):

> HORNER Dear Doctor, let vain rogues be contented only to be thought abler men than they are, generally 'tis all the pleasure they have; but mine lies another way ...

HORNER Shy husbands and keepers, like old rooks, are not to be
cheated but by a new unpractised trick.

(I. i)

Sparkish comes at the bottom of the scale, as a man so thoroughly
affected that his mask has grown on to his face; his artificiality is such
that Alithea's maid is hardly paradoxical in calling him 'a natural'.
Running him close comes Sir Jasper, whose jealousy is as absurd in
the circumstances as Sparkish's lack of it, for he wants the reputation
of a husband without having to act the part in bed or out of it. His
bourgeois mistress is money:

> SIR JASPER Well, well—that your ladyship is as virtuous as any she
> I know, and him all the town knows—he! he! he! therefore now
> you like him, get you gone to your business together, go, go to your
> business, I say, pleasure, whilst I go to my pleasure, business.

(II. i)

A conceit significantly echoed by Pinchwife in the next Act, and
clearly placed in the scale of comic justice by Lady Fidget:

> LADY FIDGET Who for his business from his wife will run,
> Takes the best care to have her business done.

(II. i)

Lady Fidget and the other ladies of 'honour' come somewhere in the
middle, below Horner, below Margery Pinchwife (natural in her
desires, but so entirely unaffected that she cannot at first satisfy them
and give her husband his just deserts), but above the neglectful husbands. These ladies are satirised for wishing to preserve the appearance
of honour without the reality, but this acts even more as a satire on
the conventions. Anyway, when they finally blow the gaff, in a
women's get-together reminiscent of Dunbar's *Tua Mariit Wemen and
the Wedo*, they recover status, since their care for 'reputation' is
almost as rewarding as Horner's sacrifice of it:

> LADY FIDGET Our reputation! Lord why should you not think that
> we women make use of our reputation, as you men of yours, only
> to deceive the world with less suspicion? Our virtue is like the
> statesman's religion, the quaker's word, the gamester's oath, and the
> great man's honour; but to cheat those that trust us.

(v. iv)

All very well, provided those we cheat thoroughly deserve to be
cheated. In this play they do, and the final moral emerges naturally

enough from the interacting motifs of folly, jealousy, marriage and reputation:

> ALITHEA ... Women and fortune are truest still to those that trust 'em.
> LUCY And any wild thing grows but the more fierce and hungry for being kept up, and more dangerous to the keeper.
> ALITHEA There's doctrine for all husbands, Mr. Harcourt.

Wycherley hasn't quite the insolent ease of Etherege, or his imperturbable detachment; his is not so much a comedy of style and realistic surface, as one of matter; both his dialogue and action are pointed, and his characters tend to represent viewpoints. The general effect is less cynically releasing than Etherege's, and is more innovatory in that its social criticism has a positive aspect. What it lacks is human breadth; there is no *un*deservedly suffering Loveit to test the case or cast a complicating shadow.

Congreve, at first sight, combines the best of both authors, being as stylish as Etherege and as pointed as Wycherley, as realistic as the one and more reflective than either. He carries further than Etherege the concern of the Comedy of Manners with behavioural psychology (in contrast with the Comedy of Humour's concern with ethics) while also extending the range of Wycherley's social criticism. That being so, why did *The Way of the World*, his best play, fail?

True, his stylishness is less mimetic than Etherege's and therefore less of a comic weapon. In no imaginable society would so many say so much so well. Dryden surely exaggerated when he declared Congreve to be better than Shakespeare, but it is true that like Shakespeare he does often give his characters big set speeches that are unmimetic in their verbal excellence (yet often highly expressive of character or a characteristic human trait, or both). Take for instance, Mirabell's soliloquy:

> Think of you! To think of a whirlwind, tho' 'twere in a whirlwind, were a case of more steady Contemplation; a very Tranquility of Mind and Mansion. A fellow that lives in a Windmill has not a more whimsical dwelling than the Heart of a Man that is lodg'd in a Woman. There is no Point of the Compass to which they cannot turn, and by which they are not turn'd; and by one as well as another; for Motion not Method is their Occupation. To know this and yet continue to be in love, is to be made wise from the dictates of Reason, and yet persevere to play the Fool by the Force of Instinct.
>
> (II. vi)

Or, in very different vein, Lady Wishfort's 'boudoir Billingsgate':

> LADY WISHFORT Frippery! superannuated Frippery! I'll frippery
> the Villain; I'll reduce him to Frippery and Rags: a Tatter-
> demallion—I hope to see him hung with Tatters, like a Long-Lane
> Pent-house, or a Gibbet Thief . . . A slander-mouth'd Railer; I
> warrant the spendthrift Prodigal's in Debt as much as the Million
> Lottery, or the whole Court upon a birthday. I'll spoil his Credit
> with his Taylor. Yes, he shall have my Niece with her Fortune, he
> shall.
>
> FOIBLE He! I hope to see him lodge in Ludgate first, and angle into
> Blackfriars for Brass Farthings, with an old Mitten.
>
> LADY WISHFORT Ay dear Foible; thank thee for that, dear Foible.
> He has put me out of all Patience. I shall never recompose my
> Feature, to receive Sir Rowland with any Economy of Face. This
> Wretch has fretted me, that I am absolutely decay'd. Look Foible.
>
> FOIBLE Your Ladyship has frowned a little too rashly, indeed Madam.
> There are some Cracks discernible in the white Varnish.
>
> LADY WISHFORT Let me see the Glass—Cracks, say's thou?
> Why I am arrantly flay'd—I look like an old peel'd Wall. Thou
> must repair me, Foible, before Sir Rowland comes; or I shall never
> keep up to my Picture.
>
> FOIBLE I warrant you, Madam; a little Art once made your Picture
> like you; and now a little of the same Art must make you like your
> Picture. Your Picture must sit for you Madam.
>
> (III. v)

Perhaps Foible's last speech points to one reason for the play's failure
with the average theatregoer. It is brilliantly put—and where any
other writer would have been well content with the first witty antithesis, Congreve caps it with a clever conceit. One wouldn't lose this
speech for the world, but in terms of characterisation it is undoubtedly
too brilliant for a servant. Congreve complained that 'hasty Judges'
could not distinguish 'betwixt the Character of a Witwoud and a
Truewit'. Were they so very misguided? Moreover, Congreve
followed Shakespeare in sometimes using his personages as mouthpieces, but in an age less prepared to let action and characterisation
lapse for the pleasure of listening to a verbal aria. So Mrs Marwood, at
the beginning of Act II, might seem designed as a true wit, so cogently
does she put the libertine answer to the Puritan case:

> True, 'tis an unhappy Circumstance of Life, that Love should ever
> die before us; and that the Man should so often outlive the Lover.
> But say what you will, 'tis better to be left, than never to have been
> lov'd. To pass our Youth in dull Indifference, to refuse the Sweets

of Life because they once must leave us, is as to wish to have been born old, because we one Day must be old. For my part, my Youth may wear and waste, but it shall never rust in my Possession. (II. i)

Shortly afterwards, for no apparent reason (save perhaps to prepare for her appearance as a self-destructive malicious wit) she weakly renounces it: 'What I have said has been to try you'. Add to this a Loveit-like depth of feeling in mistresses Marwood and Fainall—not however presented with Etherege's total detachment—and one has something that may make for a deeper sort of play (as with Shylock and Malvolio) but at cost of blurring the comic line. Also, there is more intrigue than action; the plot works through words, not deeds, so that *The Way of the World* reads better than it plays.

Nevertheless, so excellent are its words that the chief reason for its unenthusiastic reception must have lain with the audience. Already, in 1700, it contained more cits that wits—people of relatively crude sensibility to both language and character. A perceptive audience could hardly fail to appreciate such dialogues as the following, but an unperceptive audience could hardly fail not to:

> FAINALL Faith, I am not jealous. Besides, most who are engaged are Women and Relations; and for the Men they are of a Kind too contemptible to give Scandal.
>
> MIRABELL I am of another opinion. The greater the Coxcomb, always the more the Scandal; for a Woman who is not a Fool, can have but one Reason for associating with a Man who is one.
>
> FAINALL Are you jealous as often as you see Witwood entertain'd by Millamant?
>
> MIRABELL Of her Understanding I am, if not of her Person.
>
> FAINALL You do her wrong; for to give her her Due, she has Wit.
>
> MIRABELL She has Beauty enough to make any man think so; and Complaisance enough not to contradict him who shall tell her so.
>
> FAINALL For a passionate Lover, methinks you are a man somewhat too discerning in the Failings of your Mistress.
>
> MIRABELL And for a discerning Man, somewhat too passionate a Lover; for I like her with all her faults; nay, like her for her faults. Her Follies are so natural, or so artful, that they become her; and those Affectations which in another Woman wou'd be odious, serve but to make her more agreeable. I'll tell thee, Fainall, she once us'd me with that Insolence, that in Revenge I took her to pieces; sifted her, and separated her Failings; I study'd 'em by Rote. The Catalogue was so large that I was not without Hopes one Day or other, to hate her heartily: To which End I so used myself to think of 'em, that at length, contrary to my Design and Expectation,

they gave me every Hour less Disturbance: 'til in a few Days it became habitual to me to remember 'em without being displeas'd. They are now grown as familiar to me as my own Frailties; and in all Probability in a little Time longer I shall like 'em as well.

FAINALL Marry her, marry her; be half as well acquainted with her Charms, as you are with her Defects, and my Life on't, you are your own Man again.

(i. iii)

This is discriminating about jealousy, it is perceptive, humorous and psychologically subtle; and it contrives to suggest the sweetness behind Mirabell's intelligence, the bitterness behind Fainall's; and throughout it is esthetically pleasing, as a model of urbane prose. Yet these very qualities signal decadence. Should the intelligence lapse, the language would seem precious; let characters sympathise a little less humorously with faults, and comedy could pass into whimsy, and if fundamental goodness were to get out of hand (is Mirabell already perhaps a shade too inclined to the Knightley-like reproof?) a sententious prig would appear. Congreve, in fact, preserves a delicate balance in these respects, and indeed carries it into matters of characterisation. Sir Wilful, for instance, is both mocked for unmannerliness and admired for goodheartedness, gaining rather than losing plausibility as a person in the process. Similarly Mrs Fainall, though tinged with malice, unexpectedly but not implausibly, comes at last to help Mirabell, for old love's sake, towards marrying Millamant.

With Farquhar, the decline is under way. Gone is the fop, and with him the 'morality' of pains and pleasures, the contrasts of ritual silliness and right reason, of malice and good nature. Gone too is the contrast of town and country (at last, a Restoration play is set out of London). There is no explicit, and little implied anti-puritanism; indeed *The Beaux Stratagem*, his best play, is clearly affected by the aftermath of puritanism: seduction is *not* taken for granted, and in fact doesn't happen. This means that a far worse husband than Sir Jasper escapes his just deserts, and the action of the play seems half-hearted— like that of those old Hollywood comedies which always baulked on the brink. A characteristic furthered by a relatively feeble structure. Act I gets the intrigue going by means of an implausible if informatory conversation between the beaux, Aimwell and Archer, the development in Act II, is the result of accident not of effort, and in Acts III and IV it proceeds still much more by chance than purpose. As for Act V ...

. . . the last act is marred by a most incongruous and sinister lapse. Aimwell and Dorinda are just about to be married; they have actually got a chaplain in attendance, waiting to marry them, when Dorinda hesitates.

DORINDA Pray, my Lord, consider a little——

AIMWELL Consider! Do you doubt my Honour or my Love?

DORINDA Neither: I do believe you equally Just as Brave——And were your whole Sex drawn out for me to choose, I should not cast a look upon the Multitude if you were absent——But, my Lord, I'm a Woman; Colours, Concealments may hide a thousand faults in me;——therefore, know me better first; I hardly dare affirm I know myself in anything except my Love.

AIMWELL (*aside*) Such Goodness who could injure? I find myself unequal to the Task of Villain; she has gained my Soul, and made it honest like her own——I cannot, cannot hurt her . . . I am no Lord, but a poor needy Man, come with a mean, a scandalous design to prey upon your Fortune:——But the Beauties of your Mind and Person have so won me from myself, that, like a trusty Servant, I prefer the Interest of my Mistress to my own.

DORINDA Sure, I have had the Dream of some poor Mariner, a sleepy image of a welcome Port, and wake involved in Storms—— Pray, Sir, who are you?

AIMWELL Brother to the Man whose Title I usurped, but Stranger to his Honour or his Fortune.

DORINDA Matchless Honesty!——Once I was proud, Sir, of your Wealth and Title, but now am prouder that you want it: Now I can show my Love was justly levelled and had no aim but Love—— Doctor, come in.

'Such goodness who could injure?' It is not merely that we can hear the gallery applaud. It is that we are in a world where generous actions and honesty are not what they seem, since we know perfectly well that generosity will pay; its reward, indeed, follows so quickly that we suspect for a moment that Aimwell knew he was safe. But if that were so it would not matter so much; he would be all the more efficient as an adventurer. Unfortunately it is not so. He is having it both ways: the thrill of reckless virtue, and the solid reward of a pretty wife and her fortune. That is the sort of thing that must not happen in comedy . . . The assumption is that a man who courts a woman for her money is bad (this is a sentiment foreign to the dispassionate truthfulness of Restoration Comedy); that he can make himself good by ruining in hot blood the whole plan he has carried through in cold blood (which merely proves him a fool or a hypocrite as well as a knave): and that Dorinda, who can hesitate to marry because 'she does not know herself', is quite right to rush into the arms of the man as soon as she knows he has no money or position, simply because he has confessed his double-dealing. And to crown everything, news arrives just after she has done so, that Aimwell's brother has died and that he has succeeded to the title and fortune. Surely *she* cannot have known that she too was safe? It is too much to hope.

(Potts, *Comedy*, pp. 145/7)

Certainly there is still witty dialogue in *The Beaux Stratagem*, and to some degree a continuation of earlier adventurousness (especially in its critique of marriage, in which the emphasis is interestingly shifted, perhaps by Milton's influence, from constancy and jealousy to compatibility and law); but the witty analogies are usually not quite so good, or are not relevant to any theme, and the serious critique is often so couched as not to constitute a *comic* seriousness:

> DORINDA But how can you shake off the yoke? your Divisions don't come within the Reach of the Law for a Divorce.
>
> MRS. SULLEN Law! what Law can search into the remote Abyss of Nature? what Evidence can prove the unaccountable Disaffections of Wedlock? Can a Jury sum up the endless Aversions that are rooted in our Souls, or can a Bench give Judgement upon Antipathies?
>
> DORINDA They never pretended, Sister; they never meddle, but in case of Uncleanness.
>
> MRS. SULLEN Uncleanness! O sister! casual violation is a transient injury, and may possibly be repaired, but can radical Hatreds ever be reconciled? No, no, Sister, Nature is the first Lawgiver, and when she has set Tempers opposite, not all the golden Links of Wedlock nor iron Manacles of Law can keep 'em fast.
>
> (III. iii)

In short, *The Beaux Stratagem* (1707) marks the last point at which Augustan comic drama is of living interest. Comic poetry and comic narrative prose succeed it, but do not continue its particular kind of comedy.

B. II. DRYDEN, POPE

That Dryden and Pope as poets do share with the dramatists something which can be classed as 'Augustan' is perhaps best evidenced in their style. They share a preference for clarity and balance, for parallelism and antithesis, for liveliness derived from syntax rather than from connotation, for analogical rather than emotional metaphor: all characteristics consonant with opposition to disorder and enthusiasm, and support for rule and decorum. Where both poets chiefly differ from the dramatists is in the orthodoxy of the rule and decorum that they espouse. They are not only Tory but also conservative; nothing is exploratory in their comedy. It is true that Dryden is typical of his age in using a good deal of argument, where Pope, later, uses a greater proportion of insult and implication, but it is the argument of a propagandist: his, so to speak, is forensic comedy; and he is always representing the Crown.

MacFlecknoe, of course, is Dryden's most amusing poem. With ingenious straining it can be taken as a comic denunciation of dullness, a sort of trial run for Pope's *Dunciad*. In plain fact, it is an heroic* and brilliant example of a low kind, invective satire; a lampoon on poor Shadwell. *The Medall* comes at the other end of the satiric scale, a formidable forensic onslaught on the Whigs and their policy, but again is what it calls itself, 'A Satyre Against Sedition', not a comedy. That leaves *Absalom and Achitophel*—possibly not a satiric comedy, but at least a comic satire. Remarkably, it is also what it has often been claimed to be, an heroic poem. Mocking, but not *mock*-heroic like most of *MacFlecknoe*, it treats a subject of heroic status—not merely the safety of the state but the survival of civilisation—in an appropriate way. Almost as remarkable, as nearly paradoxical, is the fact that most of the comic effect derives directly from the imposed structural form, of biblical allegory (and indirectly therefore, we may assume, from *Paradise Lost*!).

Absalom and Achitophel is very much of its period both in its basic assumption and in its practical propagandist purpose. That some knowledge of English politics around 1680 is required for its comprehension, however, does not mean that it is only of historical interest. For it seems to be ultimately based on a philosophic question of permanent relevance: the central question of Hobbes's *Leviathan* (1651)—can chaos be avoided save by submission to an absolute Sovereign? Dryden's answer, too, seems to be that of Hobbes: it cannot. The most cursory selection of passages sufficiently indicates that the Anglican Dryden is as deeply indebted to Hobbes as the atheist Rochester, and indeed thinkers of every persuasion. Dryden, like Hobbes, looked back with horror at the Civil War, and appealed with some confidence, in what was to become the typically Augustan way, to men of good sense:

> The sober part of *Israel*, free from stain,
> Well knew the value of a peaceful raign:
> And, looking backward with a wise afright,
> Saw Seames of wounds, dishonest to the sight;

---

* The model was in fact Boileau's 'poème héroï-comique', *Le Lutrin*.

> In contemplation of those ugly Scars,
> They Curst the memory of Civil Wars.
> The moderate sort of Men, thus qualified,
> Inclined the Ballance to the better side.   (ll. 69-76)

That is, the side of Charles II, at that time trying to ensure the succession for his obdurately Catholic brother James. Hobbes had put the issue in a wider context:

> Hereby it is manifest, that during the time men live without a common Power to keep them all in awe, they are in that condition which is called Warre; and such a warre, as is of every man, against every man. For WARRE, consisteth not in Battell only, or in the act of fighting; but in a tract of time, wherein the Will to contend by Battell is sufficiently known . . . In such condition, there is no place for Industry; because the fruit thereof is uncertain: and consequently no Culture of the Earth; no Navigation, nor use of the commodities that may be imported by Sea; no commodious Building; no Knowledge of the face of the Earth; no account of Time; no Arts; no Letters; no Society; and which is worst of all, continuall feare, and danger of violent death; And the life of man, solitary, poore, nasty, brutish, and short.
> (Part 1, Chap. 13)

Dryden takes the point, and plumps firmly for monarchy:

> . . . Kingly power, thus ebbing out, might be
> Drawn to the dregs of a Democracy.   (ll. 226-7)

And for conservation:

> Yet, grant our Lords the People Kings can make,
> What Prudent men a settled Throne would shake?
> For whatsoe'r their sufferings were before,
> That Change they Covet makes them suffer more.
> All other Errors but disturb a State:
> But Innovation is the Blow of Fate.
> If ancient Fabricks nod, and threat to fall,
> To Patch the Flaws, and Buttress up the Wall,
> Thus far 'tis Duty; but here fix the Mark:
> For all beyond it is to touch our Ark
> To change Foundations, cast the Frame anew,
> Is work for Rebels who base Ends pursue:
> At once Divine and Humane Laws controul;
> And mend the parts by ruine of the Whole.
> The Tampering World is subject to this Curse,
> To Physick their Disease into a worse.   (ll. 795-810)

These last lines, together with the following, are reminiscent of
several passages in *Leviathan*:

> Where Sanhedrin and Priest inslav'd the Nation,
> And justifi'd their Spoils by Inspiration;
> For who so fit for Reign as *Aaron's* Race,
> If once Dominion they could found in Grace?
> These led the Pack; tho not of surest scent,
> Yet deepest mouth'd against the Government.
> A numerous Host of dreaming Saints succeed;
> Of the true old Enthusiastic breed:
> 'Gainst Form and Order they their Power employ;
> Nothing to Build and all things to Destroy.
>
> (ll. 523-31)

For when Christian men, take not their Christian Soveraign, for Gods
Prophet; they must either take their own Dreames, for the Prophecy
they mean to be governed by, and the tumour of their own hearts for
the Spirit of God; or they must suffer themselves to be led by some
strange Prince; or by some of their fellow subjects, that can bewitch
them, by slaunder of the government, into rebellion, without other
miracle to confirm their calling, then sometimes an extraordinary
successe, and Impunity; and by this means destroying all laws, both
divine and humane, reduce all Order, Government, and Society, to
the first Chaos of Violence, and Civil warre.
>
> (Part 3, Chap. 36)

Justice therefore, is a Rule of Reason . . . [*for*] the preservation of
mans life on earth . . . [*not*] the attaining of an eternal felicity after
death; to which they think the breach of Covenant may conduce;
and consequently be just and reasonable; (such are they that think it a
work of merit to kill, or depose, or rebell against, the Soveraigne
Power constituted over them by their own consent). But because there
is no naturall knowledge of mans estate after death; much lesse of the
reward that is then to be given to breach of Faith; but onely a beliefe
grounded upon other mens saying, that they know it supernaturally,
or that they know those, that knew them, that knew others, that knew
it supernaturally; Breach of Faith cannot be called a Precept of Reason
or Nature.
>
> (Part 1, Chap. 15)

So that though God Almighty can speak to a man, by Dreams, Visions,
Voice, and Inspiration; yet he obliges no man to beleeve he hath so
done to him that pretends it; who (being a man) may erre, and (which
is more) may lie.
>
> (Part 3, Chap. 32)

So far, then, *Absalom and Achitophel* appears to be a didactic poem in
verse of heroic gravity and pungency, based on a considered political

philosophy. And it is true that this basis is what, strictly speaking, renders it still relevant today. If the conflict for us is not between religious radicalism and pragmatic conservatism, neither—at any rate, at the level of metaphysical abstraction—is it between communism and capitalism as economic systems, but essentially between conformity and non-conformity, absolutism and democracy—and therefore analogous to that which preoccupied Hobbes and Dryden. However, insofar as the poem remains amusing it depends on the particular political issue that prompted it.

Most comedy on behalf of the Establishment—not very common anyway—does not bother to argue. Dryden has to, for this was a rare case where power was not in the hands of the Establishment, but so delicately balanced that a comic satire might influence events. So delicately balanced, though, that argument alone, however cogent, however satiric (as in *The Medall*) could not be reckoned sufficient; hence, the element of comedy.

Fraudulent though it was, the Popish Plot 'revealed' by Titus Oates and Dr Tonge (1678), to murder Charles II and put James, Duke of York on the throne to rule with the aid of a Jesuit junta, came as a godsend to the various groups then coming to be known as the Whig party. Charles was in fact francophil and Catholicising, and had negotiated dangerous secret treaties with France. Moreover, he was inflexibly determined that James should succeed to the throne. When Shaftesbury and his supporters passed a bill, in the wake of the Popish Plot, to exclude him, the King prorogued and afterwards dissolved Parliament. Shortly thereafter two further exclusionist Parliaments were dissolved, pro-Whig judges were dismissed, to be replaced by more obliging ones, and Shaftesbury was put on trial for treason (plotting to put the King's illegitimate son, the Duke of Monmouth, on the throne). *Absalom and Achitophel* was published during this trial, probably—as Kinsley argues in the Commentary to his *Dryden* (Oxford 1958, IV. 1877)—with the design of prejudicing the result. A design that failed, despite a biassed summing-up by the Lord Chief Justice, for a Puritan London jury acquitted him. After its publication, however, according to Maurice Ashley, the Tory Lord Mayor of London

> was prevailed upon to revive an ancient custom whereby he was entitled to nominate one of the City sheriffs merely by drinking to him at the annual feast. He raised his glass to a Tory freeman. Aghast at such daring tactics the Whigs were thrown into confusion and after four months two Tory sheriffs were installed in office. The fate of

Whiggish juries was settled and the Whig leaders in fright for their
lives turned from open opposition to conspiracy.

(*England in the Seventeenth Century*, London 1952, p. 149)

A Protestant plot, as fraudulent as the popish one, was fabricated,
and a Tory, Anglican, Monarchical era set in. Tory domination was
to last until the death of Queen Anne (1714); the rights and powers
of Church and King were not to be seriously questioned for a hundred
years.

Both the need for argument and the fact that the events were well
known precluded a poem of action. Consequently, its main fault as a
comedy is prolixity in the more didactic parts; its main comic virtues
lie in the mischievous nature of the allegory and in the set-piece
characterisations that purport to show the inner personality of the
chief villains, *Achitophel* (Shaftesbury), *Zimri* (Buckingham), and
Shimei (Bethel, Sheriff of London). Brief, and straight, comparison
between Charles II and David was not unknown (as Kinsley shows),
but Dryden's extension of it into a detailed comic allegory was a
brilliant stroke: in general, because it used against the Puritans what
had been so often used by them as irrefutable evidence, the Old
Testament; in particular, because it overcame a prime difficulty, that
of recommending a loose-living, extravagant monarch to 'The
moderate sort of Men,' who not only held the balance, but were likely
to be thrifty and puritanical into the bargain. The Old Testament
parallel puts them in an inescapable dilemma, and enables Dryden to
arouse sympathetic laughter for the peccadilloes of holy *David*, while
reserving laughter of righteous scorn for the 'unholy'.

In pious times, e'r Priestcraft did begin

(it *sounds* anti-Catholic—and then goes on to use dream-nostalgia)

> Before *Polygamy* was made a sin;
> When man, on many, multiply'd his kind,
> E'r one to one was, cursedly, confind:
> When Nature prompted, and no law deny'd
> Promiscuous use of Concubine and Bride;
> Then, *Israel's* Monarch, after Heaven's own heart,
> His vigorous warmth did, variously, impart
> To Wives and Slaves: And, wide as his command,
> Scatter'd his Maker's Image through the Land.

(ll. 1-10)

Apart from the splendid comic idea of selling lechery to the bourgeoisie
on the authority of the Bible, there are the subtle tonal touches: in

'pious', the reference to marriage (so often a commercial matter), 'Nature,' 'vigorous warmth' (so different from lust), and the religious joviality of scattering his Maker's image. On the other hand, feelings of anti-semitism can be invoked to support anti-puritanism, which itself bolsters the Hobbesian view of the absurdity of hoping to find the good life in a free state of nature:

> The *Jews*, a Headstrong, Moody, Murmuring race,
> As ever tried th'extent and stretch of grace;
> God's pamper'd people whom, debauch'd with ease,
> No King could govern, nor no God could please;
> (Gods they had tried, of every shape and size
> That God-smiths could produce, or Priests devise:)
> These *Adam*-wits, too fortunately free,
> Began to dream they wanted libertie;
> And when no rule, no president was found
> Of men, by Laws less circumscrib'd and bound,
> They led their wild desires to Woods and Caves,
> And thought that all but Savages were Slaves.

(ll. 45-56)

Of the character set-pieces that of Shaftesbury is the finest—a fine stroke of heroic (not comic) satire for it gives to that

> ... fiery Soul, which working out its way,
> Fretted the Pigmy Body to decay:
> And o'r inform'd the tenement of clay.

(ll. 156-8)

a satanic power that makes its defeat seem all the more vital. The characters of Buckingham (who had annoyed Dryden by guying his heroic tragedies, in *The Rehearsal*) and of Bethel are also extended pieces, but of a racy, varied comic kind: wit, irony, hyperbole and incongruity blending into the strength of the argument and the strength of the heroic couplet.

Shaftesbury-*Achitophel's* temptation of *Absolon* (sic)-Buckingham constitutes a masterly parody of courtly sycophancy but, since such language has no contentual interest, it goes on far too long. The intervening reply by Buckingham (ll. 303-72), lets him down lightly (as a favourite of his father) but, far from being comic *tour de force*, like the similar excusing of Charles, is implausibly used to expatiate upon the virtues of the King. It is never more than merely didactic, and at one point is outright ridiculous: where of that bigheaded, bigoted, blockhead, James, it is said *by his rival* that he

> Of every Royal Vertue stands possest;
> Still Dear to all the Bravest and the Best.
>
> (ll. 335-6)

In short, the work is carried through on the surge of an inspired, detailed comic idea, it is dominated, texturally, by several great comic peaks—and between them there is a fair scattering of telling epigrams and paradoxes—but it cannot be said that it sparkles throughout. For that quality one must turn to the master-maker, Pope.

Like Dryden, Pope was mainly a didactic poet; perhaps only one major work, *The Rape of the Lock*, is indisputably comic throughout, though *Epistle II* of the *Moral Essays* ('Of the Characters of Women') and the *Epistle to Dr. Arbuthnot* have claims to be considered as comic satires on the whole (*The Dunciad* is surely a savage-farcical satire). All these works, like Dryden's comic and didactic satire, are *thematically* psychologically restraining and sociologically conserving. Pope, however, though committed to the Tory party is rarely directly concerned with politics. All the bitterness of party strife in the first half of the eighteenth century should not obscure the fact that Locke's second *Treatise of Government* (1690), expounding the doctrine of a constitutional balance of powers, had overthrown Hobbes's doctrine of absolutism in the minds of the majority of men. Some still feared it; but Pope is less concerned with saving civilisation than with civilising the saved, the 'moderate sort of men' who had come through and could now devote themselves to making money in safety and comfort.

To the connoisseur, the reader with a specifically *literary* sensibility, there is a sense in which it hardly matters what Pope is writing about. Dryden's mastery of the narrow couplet form is such that he can always say whatever he wishes as clearly as need be; he cannot always delight (or even interest, often, if the subject is inherently uninteresting) Pope's mastery of an even narrower couplet form is so marvellous one feels he could delight while versifying a timetable. He is *tonally* psychologically releasing.

Pope perfected the verse his age demanded, a form admirably adapted to express with the utmost clarity man as the oxymoron he was taken to be:

> Sole judge of Truth, in endless Error hurl'd:
> The glory, jest, and riddle of the world!
>
> (*Essay on Man*, ii. 17-18)

Such verse is typically in regular closed couplets, in iambic pentameter, rhyming always on a word of emphasis and usually on a long-vowelled

or diphthongal monosyllable; and it emphasises the regularity by
much use of chiasmus, antithesis and parallelism. A very exacting
form; but Pope increases its difficulty, firstly by keeping to the word
order, idiom and rhythm of colloquial prose (normally without
breaking metre), and secondly, by various syntactical and musical
manipulations:

> until in Pope a couplet will often suggest a figure in Euclid, its vowels
> and consonants, its sense-oppositions and sense-attractions, fitted to-
> gether like arcs and lines.
>
> (G. Tillotson, *Augustan Studies*, London 1961, p. 14)

Sometimes he wrote a first draft in prose, to master the sense, but
always endeavoured in verse to be *more* concise than prose could be,
and to be more than sensible, to 'tear the heart' (*Imitations of Horace*,
Ep. I I, i, 345).

What Pope does in this chosen form is miraculous: were it not
there in actuality we should not have believed it possible. Yet so much
are we under the spell of romanticism and post-symbolist modernism
that much of Arnold's and Macaulay's blindness and deafness to
Pope's poetry still persists; and unfortunately much of Pope's merit
in comedy is inseparable from verbal quality: insofar as it is celebratory not so much in what is said but (as with Joyce) in how it is said:
in the demonstrations of human fertility, inventiveness, and exuberant
mastery of a medium. Dr Johnson, brought up in a tradition now
somewhat alien to our sensibility, was alive to these facts. To
Boswell he remarked that 'a thousand years may elapse before there
shall appear another man with a power of versification equal to
Pope', and, in *Lives of the Poets*, that *The Rape of the Lock* was 'the
most attractive of all ludicrous compositions'—lavish praise from a
critic not given to extravagance.

The *Essay on Criticism* alone (written at nineteen) would sufficiently
demonstrate Pope's power of versification and creative invention:

> In fearless youth we tempt the heights of Arts,
> While from the bounded level of our mind
> Short views we take, nor see the lengths behind;
> But more advanc'd, behold with strange surprise
> New distant scenes of endless science rise!
> So pleas'd at first the tow'ring Alps we try,
> Mount o'er the vales, and seem to tread the sky,
> Th'eternal snows appear already past,
> And the first clouds and mountains seem the last;

> But, those attain'd, we tremble to survey
> The growing labours of the lengthen'd way,
> Th'increasing prospect tires our wand'ring eyes,
> Hills peep o'er hills, and Alps on Alps arise!

(ll. 220-32)

The metaphor is of epic extension, yet every detail is relevant and the scene as a whole accurate both on the figurative and the literal plane, it gives the true facts together with appropriate feelings that could not have been conveyed otherwise, its puns are unstrained (*heights, bounded, advanced*, and so on), the verse is always regular yet always aptly varied (note the rhythmical labouring of l. 230, for instance, or the repetitions of the last line). When Pope says 'Tho oft the ear the open vowels tire' the words in which it is so clearly and naturally said are in fact open-vowelled (and appropriately a little too much so), 'And ten low words oft creep in one dull line' with equally dismal appropriateness, or

> A needless Alexandrine ends the song
> That, like a wounded snake, drags its slow length along.

The last line is an alexandrine, is needless (for the sense), and it does drag. As a poet who took care to vary parts of speech, singulars and plurals, and areas of reference, in his rhymes, Pope could properly disparage others:

> While they ring round the same unvary'd chimes,
> With sure returns of still expected rhymes;
> Wher'er you find 'the cooling western breeze,'
> In the next line, it 'whispers through the trees:'
> If crystal streams 'with pleasing murmurs creep,'
> The reader's threaten'd (not in vain) with 'sleep.'

These examples all come from ll. 344-57, and it is tempting to go on quoting from this didactic poem. But Pope extends his range according to need. Thus, in the great passage towards the end of *The Characters of Women* much of the concluding line 'Alive, ridiculous, and dead, forgot' comes from a line by line increase in grammatical concentration that yet never obscures the sense, just as in the Atticus passage of *The Epistle to Dr. Arbuthnot* expectation is built up through a perfectly lucid sentence of eighteen lines whose main clause comes at the end as a long-awaited climax, everything before it being a sequence of dependent clauses, all hung economically and ungrammatically from one unrepeated auxiliary, 'Should'. This grammatically fuses three operations: should exist, act so, be such—and, to begin with, also suggests the question 'Should such a man . . . [be allowed to] . . .?'. The venomous *Sporus* passage in the same poem packs infinite riches in a little room, displaying a mastery of the form unequalled in our literature and unapproached by any writer other than Pope himself. One example must suffice:

> His wit all see-saw, between *that* and *this*,
> Now high, now low, now master up, now miss,
> And he himself one vile Antithesis.

'See-saw', itself an inspired image, is colloquially illustrated by an antithesis, which is immediately amplified by two more, suggesting respectively mental and physical imbalance, the whole being capped by a line equally destructive of Hervey's verse, character and sexuality. This is satiric rather than comic. However, it displays the exuberance, the triumphant creativity, that perhaps justifies our calling this *Epistle* as a whole an example of celebratory comedy, despite intermittent moods of bitterness. The first one hundred and twenty-five lines—and many other passages—are just as inventive and very amusing:

> Shut, shut the door, good John! fatigu'd, I said,
> Tie up the knocker, say I'm sick, I'm dead.
> The Dog-star rages! nay 'tis past a doubt,
> All Bedlam, or Parnassus, is let out:
> Fire in each eye, and papers in each hand,
> They rave, recite, and madden round the land

> (ll. 1-6)

Incomparably characterising and colloquial, too, one would add, were it not for such vignettes as that of Sir Plume (*The Rape of the Lock*) or, say, this:

> . . . Ye Rev'rend Atheists—F. Scandal! name them! Who?
> P. Why that's the thing you bid me not to do.
> Who starved a Sister, who forswore a Debt,
> I never named; the Town's enquiring yet.
> The pois'ning Dame—F. You mean—P. I don't.—F. You do!
> P. See, now I keep the Secret, and not you!

> (*Epilogue to the Satires*, ll. 18-23)

Incredible to find these are still perfectly regular heroic couplets. Like Joyce, Pope could truly have said, 'I can do *anything* with the English language'

Whatever may or may not be allowed to other poems in the way of celebratory comedy through textural or contentual fertility, there can be no doubts about *The Rape of the Lock*, which even Housman thought possibly the most perfect long poem in the language. It has long been known as the most humorous of satires, the most witty of moralities; it has not perhaps been recognised as a marvellously celebratory comedy as well. It is celebratory in so far as it exemplifies all the rhetorical *joie de vivre* already noted and, in addition, immense structural skill—witness the mixture of address: dedication, assertion, question, narrative, the changes of tense and viewpoint (e.g. 1, 13 and 15) and of voice (e.g. I, 27 and I, 115), so that the narrow form never wearies. It is celebratory, too, in its amplification (the addition of the sylphs to this account of a real-life incident), in being not only mock-heroic, but also mock-romantic and mock-magical, in its parody, and in its changes of pace. In a word, it is full to overflowing (though nothing is out of proportion). And nothing else so level-headed is so lighthearted. However, it is celebratory comedy in a more specific sense, as two quotations may make clear:

> In *The Rape of the Lock* Pope plays with the traditional imagery of love-sick poets, and while his treatment hints at the absurdity of their conventions it is clear that he is enjoying the licence which this gives his imagination. He demonstrates the superficiality of Belinda's world of fashion and scandal, of petty vanities and trivial mean absurdities; but he does not deny its transitory beauty—the beauty of which the sylphs, the inspired addition to the later version, are in some sort the symbol. Satire is absent from some of the descriptive passages of the poem, for, as Pope pointed out, 'since inanimate and irrational beings are not objects of censure . . . these may be elevated as much as you please and no ridicule follows . . .' the reader enjoys the game by which the things of everyday become transformed into objects of an unfamiliar beauty.
>
> (Ian Jack, *Pope*, 1954, ll. 13-14)

> That familiar things are made new, every paragraph will prove. The subject of the poem is an event below the common incidents of common life; nothing real is introduced that is not seen so often as to be no longer regarded, yet the whole detail of a female day is here brought before us with so much art of decoration, that, though nothing is disguised, everything is striking, and we feel all the appetite of curiosity for that from which we have a thousand times turned fastidiously away.
>
> (Dr Johnson, 'Pope', *Lives of the Poets*, 1779-81)

The end of Canto I provides a suitable example. Diction sustains the general mock-heroic manner—the use of 'a vast force to raise a feather', as Pope put it—but in a muted tone here, so that it may blend not only with other comic devices but also with devices that are not themselves exactly comic but which contribute to the celebratory *joie de vivre* by those celebratory transformations of the ordinary that Johnson notes (the Brobdingnagian combs and pins being the most obvious instances):

> Unnumber'd treasures ope at once, and here
> The various off'rings of the world appear;
> From each she nicely culls with curious toil,
> And decks the Goddess with the glitt'ring spoil.
> This casket India's glowing gems unlocks,
> And all Arabia breathes from yonder box.
> The Tortoise here and Elephant unite,
> Transform'd to combs, the speckled and the white.
> Here files of pins extend their shining rows,
> Puffs, Powders, Patches, Bibles, Billet-doux.
> Now awful Beauty puts on all its arms;
> The fair each moment rises in her charms,
> Repairs her smiles, awakens ev'ry grace,
> And calls forth all the wonders of her face:
> Sees by degrees a purer blush arise,
> And keener lightnings quicken in her eyes.
> The busy Sylphs surround their darling care,
> These set the head, and those divide the hair,
> Some fold the sleeve, whilst others plait the gown;
> And Betty's prais'd for labours not her own.

An element of satire is present, of course. The mock-heroic perpetuates Pope's gentle chiding of the two Catholic families whose quarrel over a clipped curl provided the poem's *raison d'être*, Bibles are rather reprovingly placed amidst the clutter of vanity, and the 'purer' blush of rouge is clearly ironic. Yet no-one could call it biting or even moralistic. If not flattering satire, a contradiction in terms, it seems at least flirtatious satire—and as such it models the thrust and tension that supports the whole airy structure as it arcs from 'the Vision at the beginning' to 'the Transformation at the end'. For it is constructed on a principle of interwoven paradox: of alternately seeming to celebrate what it satirises and (as here) seeming to satirise what it celebrates.

As a whole then, the work is rather more of a celebratory comedy, in the sense of gaiety and uplift resulting from a triumphant parade of style, than it is the comic satire it purports to be, on 'the little un-guarded follies' of the female sex—though it is certainly that as well. Johnson indeed neglects the implications of his earlier perception and

goes on, like most succeeding critics, to emphasise not only the fact
of moral satire but its importance too:

> The freaks, and humours, and spleen and vanity of women, as they
> embroil familes in discord, and fill houses with disquiet, do more to
> obstruct the happiness of life in a year than the ambition of the clergy
> in many centuries. It has been well observed, that the misery of man
> proceeds not from any single crush of overwhelming evil, but from
> small vexation continually repeated.
>
> (*Pope*)

The point is well taken; no doubt *The Rape of the Lock* is a more
significant restraining comic satire than might at first appear; but that
distracts attention from a more important point: that its creative *élan*,
its plenitude of Mozartian invention, is celebratory, and therefore
psychologically releasing, in effect. That it never wearies, though the
subject is slight and the treatment voluminous, is due to the combination of infinite variety and ceaseless tension.

A number of different characteristics of the passage quoted have
been mentioned, but a great many more have been passed over: the
variety of rhyme (within the rule of long-vowelled, emphatic monosyllable), the subtle empathetic activity ('*This* casket . . . *yonder* box,'
'*These* set . . . *those* divide'), the active verbs and compact syntax, the
sly touches of humour, or the complex reference (e.g. to the birth of
Venus, in the arming of this *female* epic hero: 'The fair each moment
rises in her charms'). This richness is typical of the whole poem, which
ranges from the ethereal to the Freudian-surreal (in the Cave of
Spleen, for example, 'Men prove with child, as pow'rful fancy works/
And maids turn'd bottles cry aloud for corks'), from semantic play-
wit:

> The Peer now spreads the glitt'ring Forfex wide,
> T'enclose the Lock; now joins it, to divide
>
> (II. ll. 147-8)

to genuine, though humorous, elevation:

> What Time would spare, from Steel receives its date,
> And monuments, like men, submit to fate!
> Steel could the labour of the Gods destroy,
> And strike to dust th'imperial tow'rs of Troy;
> Steel could the works of mortal pride confound,
> And hew triumphal arches to the ground.
> What wonder then fair nymph! thy hairs should feel
> The conqu'ring force of unresisted steel?
>
> (II. ll. 171-8)

or lightning character-sketch—astonishingly not merely in strict metre but *depending* on the metrical emphases for its colloquial compactness:

> (Sir Plume of amber snuff-box justly vain,
> And the nice conduct of a clouded cane)
> With earnest eyes, and round unthinking face,
> He first the snuff-box opened, then the case,
> And thus broke out —'My Lord, why, what the devil?
> 'Zounds! damn the lock! 'fore Gad, you must be civil!
> 'Plague on't! 'tis past a jest—nay prithee, pox!
> 'Give her the hair'—he spoke, and rapp'd his box
>
> (III. ll. 123-30)

This last quality is perhaps seen in even greater concentration in *Epistle II* ('Of the Characters of Women') where a 'romantic-marriage' story, an all too recognisable character, and a socio-moral point are condensed into four lines of comic satire:

> Papillia, wedded to her am'rous spark,
> Sighs for the shades—'How charming is a Park!'
> A Park is purchas'd, but the fair he sees
> All bath'd in tears—'Oh odious, odious trees!'
>
> (ll. 36-40)

Like the *Epistle to Dr. Arbuthnot* or Dryden's *Absalom and Achitophel*, this work hovers between comic and bitter satire. If anything tips the balance, it is (as in Dryden) the presence of a brilliant comic leitmotif: the idea of using the thesis that 'Most Women have no Characters at all' to ridicule the moral or emotional characters of a variety of females. Johnson saw this *tour de force*, rather humourlessly, as a mere lapse from logic, whereas it is in fact a piece of comic cheek, that bridges the logical gap by assuming that the thesis means no *constant* characters. Fittingly then the poem is climaxed by the extended portrait of 'Atossa':

> By what are these to great Atossa's mind?
> Scarce once herself, by turns all womankind!
> ....
> Superiors? death! and Equals? what a curse!
> But an Inferior not dependent? worse.
> Offend her, and she knows not to forgive;
> Oblige her, and she'll hate you while you live
>
> (ll. 115-138)

This clever satire is purveyed in a dose of lethal concentration. The Duchess of Marlborough was willing to pay £1000 to have Pope suppress it!

B. III SWIFT, FIELDING, STERNE

While Pope was attacking the wife, his friend *Swift*, on behalf of the Tory party, was attacking the husband, in his *Conduct of the Allies* and his 'Satirical Elegy'. However, both these pieces, like most of Swift's work, are clearly non-comic. Indeed, it is arguable that nothing of Swift's satire—save the brilliant but dated *Tale of a Tub* and a few poems—has a sufficient degree of gaiety or geniality to qualify as comedy; but the voyages to Lilliput and Brobdingnag may be claimed as exceptions—not, however, on account of the specifically contemporary mockery of courtly ropedancers, political high-heelers and low-heelers, religious big-enders and little-enders, or of corruption in elections and legal actions. These things have their modern analogues, of course, but are still too much of their age to be mainly what keeps *Gulliver's Travels* alive today. The exposure of the evil of war and the untrustworthiness of autocrats are more directly relevant, but quite properly the subject of satire that is hardly comic—culminating indeed in the outright invective of the king of Brobdingnag:

> I am well disposed to hope you may have escaped many Vices of your Country. But, by what I have gathered from your own Relation, and the Answers I have with much pains wringed and extorted from you; I cannot but conclude the Bulk of your Natives to be the most pernicious Race of little odious Vermin that Nature ever suffered to crawl upon the Surface of the Earth.
>
> (Chap. VI)

These aspects of the two books may profitably be marked, learnt and inwardly digested; but the learning that comes along with a sense of lighthearted liberation is to be sought elsewhere: in their mimetic merits.

A comedy, then, rather of imaginative exuberance than amusing statement; yet not thereby celebratory. One's sense of 'lighthearted liberation' in being made free of vividly detailed new worlds is at least uneasy, for delighted surprise at the detail of worlds seen first through one, then the other end of a telescope is constantly combined with shaming recognitions. The mimetic element in the books, in fact, merges into timeless satire. Amused wonder at the way the ordinary becomes amazing in a toytown perspective or a titanic one, is soon undermined by the realisation that nothing but a zoom lens is needed to see man as a dangerous toy or a revolting monster. (Gulliver, indeed, playing the role of an insensitive Lilliputian before the king of Brobdingnag represents humanity diminished to vermin.)

In general, Lilliputian pleasure is alloyed with unwelcome *social* implications—the impression of an antheap when Gulliver visits the capital, walking with 'the utmost Circumspection, to avoid treading on any Stragglers', or the toy men's considered ignorant verdict on the watch, 'some unknown Animal, or the God that he worships'—while, on the other hand, it is mostly *personal* implications that disturb the striking recognitions and surprises of scale in the Brobdingnag volume:

> For they would strip themselves to the skin, and put on their Smocks in my Presence, while I was placed on their Toylet directly before their naked Bodies; which, I am sure, to me was very far from being a tempting Sight, or from giving me any other Motions than those of Horror and Disgust. Their Skins appeared so coarse and uneven, so variously coloured when I saw them near, with a Mole here and there as broad as a Trencher, and Hairs hanging from it thicker than Pack-threads; to say nothing further concerning the rest of their Persons.
>
> (Chap. V)

Nevertheless, the pleasures are real enough and leaven the satire with a comedy of mimetic fantasy, whose delight comes not so much from anything that could be strictly called celebratory as from a related creative exuberance that allows us to see reality freed from the prison of habitual perception. The changes in Gulliver's role, his inconsistencies of character, though a problem in assessing the satire (especially in Book IV) are a positive asset to this rare and precarious kind of comedy, since to unsettle our assumptions, to bring home to us the strangeness of the world and the uncertainty of human character, is precisely the needling point of its perspectival absurdities.

Like Swift, *Fielding* wrote political satire against the Whigs, who sustained their supremacy under Walpole by bribery and corruption. The effectiveness of the dramatic form he chose is evidenced by the Licensing Act of 1737, which drove him from the stage and thereby gave us the two novels that preserve his place in the comic tradition, *Jospeh Andrews* (1742) and *Tom Jones* (1749), both of which (like *Jonathan Wild* (1743), his unsubtle, ironic allegorical satire on Walpole) have a greater breadth of concern than earlier Augustan comedies, but are less coherent in theme and less controlled and concentrated in style.

Jonathan Wild was intended to help in unseating Walpole, but he fell (1742) before the novel appeared—and nothing changed:

> Bills for the repeal of the Septennial Act and for the exclusion of placemen were thrown out as readily by Walpole's successors as by Walpole himself. It brought the realisation that the great hopes raised by the Revolution of 1689 were unlikely to be fulfilled so long as England retained its constitution unreformed . . .There was a steady growth of the feeling that Parliament was debased and rotten, and did not represent the power of the nation.
>
> (J. H. Plumb, *England in the Eighteenth Century*, London 1950, p. 105)

At the same time it was felt that the country was no longer endangered by the fanatical divisions of the past:

> In England it was an age of aristocracy and liberty; of the rule of law and the absence of reform; of individual initiative and institutional decay; of Latitudinarianism above and Wesleyanism below . . . Such an age does not aspire to progress though it may in fact be progressing; it regards itself not as setting out but as having arrived. . . .
>
> It is true that the men who were least content were those who looked closest at the realities of English life—Hogarth, Fielding, Smollett and the philanthropists; they indeed exposed particular evils . . . But even their strictures kept within the limits of the classical and conservative philosophy of the time.
>
> (G. M. Trevelyan, *English Social History*, London 1946, pp. 339-40)

Fielding's comedies, then, are particular and unphilosophical. Ethical rather than political, they work their admonitory benevolence within the framework of accepted bourgeois values. But can this be true of the novels? *Shamela* is wholly, *Joseph Andrews* and *Tom Jones* are considerably, inspired by opposition to Samuel Richardson's *Pamela*—and what could be more bourgeois than that book? However, their differences are not fundamental. Though the one was of the lower bourgeoisie, the other of the higher, the one Whiggish, the other Toryish, the one Low Church, the other High Church, the differences were rather of stance than matter, of tone than substance. The revived puritan 'enthusiasm' that Richardson represented was perhaps as repellent as its predecessor, but it was not revolutionary or republican; it was irritatingly priggish, but not dangerous; and Fielding evidently received from it no compulsion to go beyond personal morality.

Of these three moral comedies, the least regarded, *Shamela*, is esthetically the most consistent and accomplished—within its limits.

It is the vast expansion of those limits in the later books—especially *Tom Jones*—which makes them greater though less perfect comedies.

> The weakness of Richardson as a moralist is that he appears to be unconscious of the implications of the situations he describes. There are elements of hypocrisy and coarse-grained vulgarity in his heroine . . . By some perverse obliquity of the writer the intended moral is reversed. Instead of showing virtue rewarded Richardson has written an apologia for a self-righteous equivalent of Roxana or Moll Flanders. And in describing how she defended her 'honour' Richardson dwells with a lingering relish on scenes that are supposed to be the prerogative in English literature of the more pornographic playwrights of the Restoration.
>
> (Frank Bradbrook, 'Samuel Richardson', *Pelican Guide to English Literature*, ed. Boris Ford, London 1957, Vol. 4, pp. 298-9

On these weaknesses Fielding has fastened with a deadly parodic accuracy of which the title may act as paradigm. As *Pamela* is boiled down, so these elements are blown up till *Shamela* reveals

> to the dullest apprehension the moral insufficiency and dangers, not merely of *Pamela*, with its passing vogue, but also of all literature which proceeds to a description and interpretation of real life from ethical or religious preconceptions.
>
> (B. W. Downs (ed.), *Mrs Shamela Andrews*, Cambridge 1930, p. xi)

Limitation of space forbids any demonstration of the the closeness of the phraseology with the original, or any discussion of the framing letters showing *Shamela* to be true original, *Pamela* a whitewashing sham; but brief quotation may indicate something of Fielding's comic effectiveness:

> . . . I would have you to know, Madam, I would not be Mistress to the greatest King, no nor Lord in the Universe. I value my Vartue more than I do any thing my master can give me; and so we talked a full Hour and a half about my Vartue; and I was afraid at first, she had heard something about the Bantling, but I find she hath not; tho' she is as jealous and suspicious as old Scratch . . . We had not been a Bed half an hour, when my Master came pit a pat into the Room in his Shirt as before, I pretended not to hear him, and Mrs *Jewkes* laid hold of One Arm, and he pulled down the Bed-cloaths and came into Bed on the other Side, and took my other Arm and laid it under him, and fell a kissing one of my Breasts as if he would have devoured it; I was then forced to awake, and began to struggle with him, Mrs *Jewkes* crying why don't you do it? I have one Arm secure, if you can't deal with the rest I am sorry for you. He was as rude as possible to me; but I remembered, Mamma, the Instructions you gave me to

avoid being ravished, and followed them, which soon brought him to Terms, and he promised me, on quitting my hold, that he would leave the Bed.

Oh Parson Williams, how little are all the Men in the World compared to thee ...

Mrs *Jewkes* hath been with me since, and she assures me she is convinced I shall shortly be Mistress of the Family, and she really behaves to me as if she already thought me so. I am resolved now to aim at it. I thought once of making a little Fortune by my Person. I now intend to make a great one by my Vartue. So asking Pardon for this long Scroll, I am,

Your dutiful Daughter,
SHAMELA.

(Letter *X*)

Of the two wider comedies, *Tom Jones* is more accomplished than *Jospeh Andrews* and even more of a 'comic epic in prose.' It may fairly, then, represent Fielding's strength: it illuminates his age, and is often still relevant to ours; it is a landmark in the history of the novel, a still very readable masterpiece; most recent critics imply that it has no weaknesses, and would presumably deny that it is a *minor* masterpiece. Their valuation is not briefly disprovable, but it may now be of some service to the general reader to cast doubt upon it—even to suggest that it might itself not entirely escape the odium of showing the 'moral insufficiency and dangers . . . of literature which proceeds to a description and interpretation of real life from ethical or religious preconceptions'. Though he tries to found his evaluations in behaviour, Fielding is certainly not as free from ethical and religious preconceptions as Rochester or Etherege, nor is he in any radical way an independent thinker. He accepts almost wholly the ethical, religious and political compromises arrived at by the dominant classes of his day; and from this acceptance spring weaknesses as well as strengths.

In Book XIV, vi, for instance, Mrs Miller raves on for a couple of pages about the loss of her daughter's honour in a way that would not have disgraced Pamela's father (who would rather have had her in rags, or dead, than dishonoured, even by a lover). As Oscar Wilde said of the death of Little Nell, only a man with a heart of stone could refrain from laughing at it. But say what you will about multiple ironies, it does not purport to be funny. This is straight sobstuff anticipating (as do certain passages in Sterne) the sentimental novels that were soon to take over from sentimental drama. In the next chapter, Tom preaches a rather heavy sermon to Nightingale on his unwillingness to let love overcome class, to risk sacrificing his inheritance in order to make Nancy an honest woman. Admirable sentiments, and even cautiously *avant-garde*—but Fielding sees no hint of a parallel with Tom's own insultingly 'honourable' behaviour to Sophia, his assumption that her fortune would be more valuable to her than life with a poor man. Similarly, Fielding shares—and expects his audience to share—Tom's anguish and despair at the idea that he has unwittingly commited incest (compare the relative *sang-froid* with which Moll Flanders, in the earlier Augustan period, finds she's been committing it for years). A really sophisticated comic author—given to 'multiple ironies'—would have detached himself and us from Tom's no doubt realistic reaction; or at any rate have noted the distinction, both moral and psychological, between a horror that might naturally be felt after incest with someone actually lived with and in the family, and the quite uninstinctive, conventionally ingrained reaction after a night with an entirely unknown woman. Instead, Fielding uses this rare ill-chance (a false alarm anyway) to point a moral about sexual imprudence! The point is that radical unconventionality was not even on Fielding's horizon, but was possible fifty years earlier. And so one could go on. To define the poor, in passing as 'those who had rather beg than work' (Bk I, III) is a conventional Tory quip, and quite inconsistent with the liberal attitude, for example, to Black George at the beginning of Book III, x.

However, the middle-way, which is clearly Fielding's positive, may well be worth a little muddle. The real trouble is that Fielding is ideologically not dissimilar to Richardson, though temperamentally his contrary; so he must humorously recommend a stance rather than satirically attack a position. Since the stance advocated is one of unpriggish, undogmatic benevolence, he must be moral without being priggish or dogmatic, but his ideology being what it is there are inevitably cracks to be papered over, and some things that will seem less self-evident to many readers than they do to the author. Can we so easily take it for granted, for instance, that 'The cause of King George is the cause of liberty and true religion. In other words it is the cause of common sense' (Bk VIII. IX)? Above all, what is Fielding up to with Allworthy? Maurice Johnson (*Fielding's Art of Fiction*. Philadelphia 1965) finds nothing puzzling in his presentation, Andrew Wright (*Henry Fielding: Mask and Feast*, London 1965) sees something of the puzzle but believing, like Maurice Johnson, that Fielding can do no wrong briskly dismisses it by supposing the name Allworthy to be ironic and Tom himself to be the touchstone of values—but then he is also capable of saying that the pace of the book decelerates, simply because the earlier pages cover a longer span of time than the later. In fact, one of the strengths of the novel is its increasing acceleration. The groundwork is thoroughly laid; we have to wait till one-third of the way through before even the discovery of Molly Seagrim; and then everything happens. The grounds for thinking Allworthy to be what his name implies are firstly, that Fielding says as much, in his own person, in Book III, VII, secondly that innumerable passages in the novel support this, and thirdly that the dedicatory letter to Lyttleton makes it plain that he means what he has said. Why then is it that Allworthy is shown to be badly mistaken in almost every major judgement and decision he makes? Part of the answer is that the plot requires him to be: Fielding is more prepared to sacrifice character than action. Another part is implied by what Wright says of Parson Adams in *Joseph Andrews*:

> . . . in eighteenth-century terms Adams's opaque simplicity was something to be not merely condoned but approved—and, by Fielding, celebrated . . . to see far, to be profound, to be clever—these are to go down the paths of trickery and deceit; vanity and hypocrisy have an easier time establishing themselves on such soil. The armour of a good man is, to a certain extent, his very inability to see.
>
> (Ibid. p. 156)

However, Wright's omitting to apply this insight to Allworthy is not inexcusable:

> It was now the middle of May, and the morning was remarkably serene, when Mr Allworthy walked forth on the terrace, where the dawn opened every minute that lovely prospect we have before described to his eye; and now having sent forth streams of light, which ascended the blue firmament before him, as harbingers preceding his pomp, in the full blaze of his majesty rose the sun, than which one object alone in this lower creation could be more glorious, and that Mr Allworthy himself presented—a human being replete with benevolence, meditating in what manner he might render himself most acceptable to his Creator, by doing most good to his creatures.
>
> (Bk I, IV)

In context, this is not *attackingly* ironic; here we have a humour-character without satire, one who is lovably absurd like Addison's Sir Roger de Coverley or Goldsmith's Good-Natur'd Man. Why, though, introduce your touchstone in this *mock*-heroic fashion? Well, in what other fashion could a reader approving an anti-Richardson stance stomach the canting conclusion of that paragraph? One of Fielding's dilemmas, stemming from his limited moral position and his suspicion of intellectual daring, is that he wants to seem more permissive than he really is, and daren't appear priggish. Another problem is that he is very good at plot and action, at visual and other physical effects—as one might expect from his success in the theatre —but is not good at rendering feeling (witness the Nancy-Nightingale section already mentioned). Hence, it is reasonable to suspect, much of the paraphernalia of alienation devices, including apparently inappropriate mock-heroic, stylistic reversals, and the famous prefaces or digressions on the art of novel-writing. They avoid emotional involvement.

True, they are often fascinating and illuminating in their own right, true also that they are not always censurable as flaws of unity or verisimilitude, or as ways of hiding his weaknesses—but *sometimes*, it must be said, the effect is dangerously and damagingly alienating, though some degree of alienation is proper enough in a didactic comedy.

To find ingenious reasons for justifying everything in *Tom Jones*, as Johnson and Wright are not alone in doing—even to the extent of arguing that the playgoing scene is meant to relate Tom to Hamlet (Johnson, pp. 95-106) or that the Man of the Hill's tale is *Oedipus Rex* in reverse (Wright, p. 88)—is to risk missing the real merits of the book, which tend to be obscured by the defensive, and too often self-conscious artistry—frequently that of the complacent conjuror who insists on showing how his tricks are done.

Oddly enough, it turns out that the main weakness of the book is what underlies the multiple ironies and mock-heroics that enable him to hedge his bets, namely the matter. Conversely, its main strength is what often overlies the theme—happily, for the theme won't stand too close an examination—namely, tone and texture. There *is* a good deal of festiveness: in the panoramic sweep, in the very variety of pot shots —at Quakers, courtiers, politicians, parsons, soldiers, doctors, servants, innkeepers, magistrates, critics, philosophers, landladies, lawyers, prudes, coquettes, at avarice, marriage, jealousy, superstition, to name but a few—in the many patches of farce (such as the playgoing scene, and the crossing of trails at Upton that marks the climax of a playwright's plot) and, let it be confessed in those authorial intrusions which are not objectionable on other grounds. The narrator's personality does come through, and it seems a great deal better integrated

than his system of ideas. What remains in the mind is a picture of a
bad world controlled and commented upon by a sane, humorous,
kindly man, intelligent within limits, prejudiced, timid and class-
ridden outside them (the unjustly treated, much-suffering Partridge,
for instance, doesn't do nearly as well in Allworthy's settlement as
the exposed villain Blifil—but Partridge isn't a gentleman). Tonally,
Tom Jones is a highly civilised book, an organised reflection of the
spirit of compromise—perhaps necessarily a little tainted with complacency—that made Fielding's age in many ways easier to live in
than those preceding and succeeding it. The scatter of satirical bird-
shot, much of it at sitting targets, enhances rather than diminishes the
generally humorous, celebratory, conserving, and integrative effect.
But only by turning as blind an eye as Fielding did to many difficulties
would it be possible to deny that the integration is based on some
exclusion—indeed is largely based on the way the plot, in which all
turns out well, comforts primal disquiets aroused by the realistic
reversals, and on the author's gratuitous implications that all is under
control. Nor should it be overlooked that the celebratory exuberance
is often at odds with the didacticism, the playful structure with the
serious theme, and that the shifts of tone and style are often the
reflection of a basic acceptance of a world comically alleged to be a
bad one. Yet when all is said, it is big enough for us to bear with its
weaknesses.

To the casual eye Fielding may seem at times almost as eccentric
and experimental as Sterne, but Wright is correct in contrasting them:

> When Sterne says that *Tristram Shandy* will be 'digressive and pro-
> gressive at the same time' he is declaring war on the kind of art of
> which Fielding was a master. Sterne felt that the tidy straight-
> forwardness of the usual narrative did violence to the facts of life, and
> so he tried what he felt was a more accurate method.
>
> (*Fielding*, p. 74)

Doubts arise when he goes on to say:

> In a way, therefore, *Tristram Shandy* is far nearer to being a transcript
> of actuality than is *Tom Jones*—and in a sense Sterne is more realistic
> than Fielding.
>
> (p. 74)

Perhaps, but *only* 'in a way' and 'in a sense'. Reality and actuality are
not single concepts, and much modern experimentalism—anticipated,
and sometimes influenced by Sterne—abandoning traditional forms
in order to combat a supposedly false idea of reality has in fact been
conveying an idea not necessarily truer but only newer. Virginia

Woolf, who started from the assumption that 'Life is not a series of gig-lamps symmetrically arranged', would certainly have taken Sterne to be more realistic than Fielding. She is akin to Sterne, too, in that her works, like his, do not feature people with jobs, or undertaking persistent action. Fielding's novel, being set more in the world and less in the mind is more realistic if we mean by reality, things, the physical world, and by extension, action within it. For such a novel, linear time is appropriate. Sterne's monsterpiece is different.

It is different both absolutely and comparatively; absolutely by expressing a contrasting view of reality, comparatively by carrying further Fielding's belief in warm-heartedness as the essence of the good—carrying it so far in fact as to take it right out of the social sphere. At this point the comparative and absolute differences become congruent, for the limitation of interest to personal relationships squares with the view that 'reality' is interior rather than exterior; and these differences mark Sterne's work as the furthest reach of Augustan comedy from its social, rational and political beginnings in the previous century.

Indeed, *Tristram Shandy* (1760-7) is only just Augustan rather than pre-Romantic, and only just comedy rather than divertisement: Augustan, because its brilliant superficiality keeps it out of the clutches of the unconscious and within hailing distance of reason, comedy because it is purposive in its anarchic opposition to the idea that men are naturally reasonable and that, in Pope's words, 'the science of Human Nature is, like all other sciences, reduced to *a few clear points*'.

In effect, Sterne is the first anti-novelist; so if Fielding is the first novelist, there is a sense in which he may be said to have 'declared war' on Fielding's kind of art; but the radical differences of form, and the relative difference of theme, spring from a more than literary difference (the comedy would be of very restricted interest if they did not). Take two small marriage jokes, both implicitly against Richardson's stance:

> Now this was the affair which Mrs Western was preparing to introduce to Sophia, by some prefatory discourse on the folly of love, and on the wisdom of legal prostitution for hire, when . . .
>
> (*Tom Jones*, Bk XVI, vii)

> 'Pray, my Dear,' quoth my mother, 'have you not forgot to wind up the clock——'Good G—!' cried my father, making an exclamation, but taking care to moderate his voice at the same time,——'Did ever

woman, since the creation of the world, interrupt a man with such a
silly question?' Pray, what was your father saying?——Nothing.

(*Tristram Shandy*, Vol. I, III)

Fielding's style here is, significantly, formalised, extended, ordered;
Sterne's, equally significantly, is informal, fragmentary, elliptical—
not in any way romantic, but certainly not expressive of a view of
reality as order. Again, Fielding's joke is a social and moral one,
Sterne's has no such extension beyond the characters. Finally, Fielding
is indirect only in being parenthetic, whereas Sterne is obscurely
allusive throughout. When he explains the joke, three short chapters
later, after saying '———Shut the door———' he brings in
with unobtrusive economy the basic operator of, and theoretical
justification for, his kind of comedy—a consequence of Locke's
doctrine that had lain latent, as it were, throughout the high Augustan
period:

> As a small specimen of this extreme exactness of his, to which he was in
> truth a slave,—he had made it a rule for many years of his life,—on
> the first Sunday night of every month throughout the whole year,—as
> certain as ever the Sunday-night came,—to wind up a large house-
> clock, which we had standing on the back-stairs head, with his own
> hands:—And being somewhere between fifty and sixty years of age
> at the time I have been speaking of,—he had likewise gradually brought
> some other little family concernments to the same period, in order, as
> he would often say to my uncle Toby, to get them all out of the way
> at one time, and be no more plagued and pestered with them the rest
> of the month.
>
> It was attended with but one misfortune, which, in a great measure
> fell upon myself, and the effects of which I fear I shall carry with me to
> my grave; namely, that from an unhappy association of ideas, which
> have no connection in nature, it so fell out at length, that my poor
> mother could never hear the said clock wound up,——but the
> thoughts of some other things unavoidably popped into her head—
> and *vice versa*:——Which strange combination of ideas, the sagacious
> Locke, who certainly understood the nature of these things better than
> most men, affirms to have produced more wry actions than all other
> sources of prejudice whatsoever.

(Vol. I, IV)

It is Sterne's achievement to convince the reader, at last, that if Locke
didn't affirm as much he should have.

The element of literary mischievousness is certainly present—
Sterne announces early on that he will not obey Horace's or any other
man's rules. But as he also announces in various places that his

comedy is purely medicinal—against the spleen or the affliction of gravity—it is clear that it purports to be more than a literary reaction. Presumably it was written for personal support against his own persistent sickness, and therefore for similar quirky individuals (and who, it implies, is not one?), but its anarchy has wider significance —which that more solid Augustan, Dr Johnson, saw and disapproved of. Like the less funny but equally unequalled *Sentimental Journey* it is personal psychological comedy, far removed from the social, political or moral comedies that preceded it, and what's more is unsatirical about behaviour that is clearly irrational and, at any rate in its self-absorption, anti-social.

The self-absorption, and the consequent conversational *non sequiturs* that provide much of the comedy, comes in Sterne's view from men's addiction to hobbyhorses:

> some with large stirrups, getting on in a more grave and sober pace; ——others on the contrary, tucked up to their very chins, with whips across their mouths, scouring and scampering it away like so many little parti-coloured devils astride a mortgage.
> (Vol. I, viii)

And it is precisely those most addicted who think of themselves as most rational. Rochester's attack on the illusions of dogmatic reason ('an *ignis fatuus* in the mind') seems to be coming in again to round off the Augustan age where it began. But there are two major differences, one of form, one of content. Rochester writes in the rule-governed heroic couplet—properly enough as he holds to a doctrine of *right* reason, and his work has some social reference. Sterne holds to a doctrine of mentality as mere association of ideas given a misleading semblance of coherence by hobbyhorsical obsessions, his work has no social reference (though it has social *significance*, of course), and his style—structural, temporal, and textural—is that of ungoverned anarchy; or at any rate governed only by the sense of an all-pervading humorous personality, taking us into his confidence, selling us his own sense of Rabelaisian delight in absurdity, the sense that an acknowledged reign of Chaos might not, after all—*pace* Pope—be the end of humane civilisation. Moreover, he doesn't want to shame the world out of hobbyhorsing around:

> God speed them——e'en let them ride on without opposition from me; for were their lordships unhorsed this very night——'tis ten to one but that many of them would be worse mounted by half before tomorrow morning.
> (Vol. I, viii)

All Tristram's disasters result from his father's hobbyhorsical attempts at rationality—attempts twisted and biased by crankiness, association, the irrationality of other people, and the obdurate nature of the world. Indeed they spring fundamentally from the marriage articles agreed with his wife (surely written with an ironic awareness of Mirabell's and Millamant's much-praised attempt to bring sense into sexual partnerships). Yet even Tristram seems to relish, rather than reprove, Mr Shandy. Sterne's comedy, in fact, is so celebratory that it finds cause for rejoicing when the best laid plans of men gang agley. Even the patches of sentimentality are written with such awareness, including an awareness of the reader's and the author's tendency to emotional self-indulgence, that they become bitter-sweet celebrations of sorrow itself. Whether this is the last refinement of humour or of sentimentality is a nice point, but certainly they constitute a remarkable stylistic high-wire act.

Only one approach is consistently possible for Sterne, that of friendship, and this is in fact his method of operation. He takes the reader by the arm, and into his confidence. His direct addresses ('Shut the door') are not cases of author-intrusion, for the author intrudes everywhere, like floodwater. Even dialogue melts into direct address:

> ——'My sister, mayhap,' quoth my uncle Toby, 'does not choose to let a man come so near her * * * *.' Make this dash,—'tis an Aposiopesis.——Take the dash away, and write Backside,——'tis Bawdy.—— Scratch Backside out, and put covered-way in, 'tis a Metaphor; and I dare say, as fortification ran so much in my uncle Toby's head, that if he had been left to have added one word to the sentence,——that word was it.
>
> (Vol. II, vi)

Sterne's is the letter-writer's gift; it is intimacy brought to a fine artlessness; and the methods of his comedy are in keeping with it.

The theory of the association of ideas gives no opportunity for exploring the depths. Ideas lie fairly near the surface, and combinations of them as 'the sagacious Locke' allegedly affirms produce wry actions —not Romantic ones (in keeping as he does to the observable surface, or only just below it—as in one or two other respects—Sterne keeps one foot in the Augustan world). The natural result of such a theoretic background, and disorderly outlook, is a humour of innuendo, unexpected omission, sudden changes of direction and level. It depends on by-passing logic and avoiding sober statement. Since 'association' depends on the suppression of links it demands a comedy not of bawdry but of innuendo, which also depends on suppression. Innuendo, like sensibility, is related to the senses while pretending to be related to a moral code; so humour of innuendo lives happily enough with the high-wire wryness of sensibility. And the appearance of inconsequence is the result of an ever watchful and controlling wit, the appearance of spontaneity carefully contrived. His is not the real language of men, not even their real language caught on the wing, as it were, before being trapped in the nets of syntax and intellectual order. It certainly reads very much like it; but Sterne's music, with all its sudden reversals of tone, changes of key, jets and sparkles of variation for ever interrupting the melody, is obedient to the baton of a composer-conductor.

One finds constantly that the exact but unexpected word is used, the word that will convey without crude explanation the essence of a character or situation, as shown by some outward, observable detail; or the same thing is done by a typifying characteristic written in a uniquely personal way:

> It was a consuming vexation to my father, that my mother never asked the meaning of a thing she did not understand.
> —That she is not a woman of science, my father would say—is her misfortune—but she might ask a question.—My mother never did.— In short, she went out of the world at last without knowing whether it turned round, or stood still.—My father had officiously told her above a thousand times which way it was,—but she always forgot.
> (Vol. VI, xxxix)

At one time, he will use a sort of syncopation:

> But this is nothing to my travels; so I twice——twice beg pardon for it.

The natural beat would come on 'pardon', but the repetition throws the stress on 'twice', which would otherwise have been unaccented; attention is shifted from the mere fact to the sensibility behind it. At another time, the right detail is given extra vividness by apt rhythm— as in the hobbyhorse example, where the effect of toy dapperness in the last lines depends not only on the details of parti-colouredness, whips, and tucking up but on the change in rhythm from andante to allegro.

Not only is the *apparent* randomness of style esthetically complementary to the *apparent* anarchy of structure, both reminding the reader of the haphazard growth from acquaintanceship to intimacy in life, but also it serves to keep one on the *qui vive*. The diction is always about to tell some too too intimate secret. Was Uncle Toby's modesty due to his wound in the groin? The narrator half-hinted that it might be in the first book, and half-promises from time to time thereafter to become definite about it. That eddying movement, a turning breaking expanding progression down the stream of consciousness is never so far from the main current that it might not be caught up in it eventually.

To be eccentric and associatively irrational without losing touch with centrality, to be subtle and stimulating without going too deep, that is Sterne's problem. (Going deep would bring him to a level below Reason, where his chief gifts, observation and deduction, innuendo and unexpectedness, sensibility and uncommon sense would be wasted.) The problem is solved by the constant creation of a unifying persona, and most of the methods mentioned already contribute to that creation. Two less obvious ones remain to be mentioned: the cunning scattering of colloquialisms ('asthma got by *scating against the wind* in Flanders', or 'happening at certain changes of the moon to be both fiddler and painter, *according as the fly stings*'), and a hypnotising concentration, obtained by a literary use of perspective. Just as the structure plays tricks with Time so the texture plays tricks with Space: every so often, the wider world is faded out, so that what is nearer— to the narrator—looms larger than what is commonly thought important, and may even come to symbolise the whole (a whole become, of course, very different from that, seen in gross, previously accepted). This use of perspective, though essentially spatial, has the secondary effect of slowing down time, and while the narrator lingers innocently paddling palms or feeling pulses the reader has time to start associations of his own—often encouraged by asterisks.

The technique of digression, then, it is obvious, is in keeping with both the texture and structure, the theme and the idiom, of this book. It reflects the style, the melody, and the habit of mind he is comically setting up and celebrating as characteristically human (in opposition to received opinion). But above all it gives great opportunity for humour and characterisation—to say nothing of its use for those risky acts of virtuoso sensibility. As Sterne points out, in a digression, while one of his digressions is in progress, he may be leaving aside the story of Aunt Dinah (a form of innuendo, since Aunt Dinah is somehow embarrassing to Uncle Toby—and is herself a Digression) but he is subtly touching-in the outline of Uncle Toby's character. Moreover, since digression is integral to the theme it can properly be used, in a book in which the thesis is *everywhere* exemplified, to give necessary information about the theoretic background on which so much of the theme and the comedy depends—thus stating and enacting at the same time. Hence the early digressions on animal spirits, the association of ideas, 'homunculus', and hobbyhorses. Again, the digression is a very natural way of taking us further into the private worlds of characters who might seem to be just about communicating in a common one. Indeed, since the hero of *Tristram Shandy* is not born till near the end of the book of his 'Life and Opinions' it is clear that it could not have been written without digressions. In fact, it *is* Digression writ large; for life, it says, is not a series of gig-lamps symmetrically arranged.

The earliest Augustan comic writers would have bitterly agreed, and they did their best, from their experience of chaos in the outer world, to make it otherwise. For Sterne, writing in an exterior world made safer and more 'symmetrical', in part by their efforts, it was man's inner world, or at most his interpersonal world, that mattered. So, following Fielding, he finally turned Augustan comedy inside out by being celebratory, releasing, and innovating on the subject of human unreason—a kind of unreason, however, itself expressive of an Age of Reason, and therefore not unreasonably appreciated by the more civilised and sensitive members of its closing years: the unreason of the stream of *consciousness*, of the association of *ideas*.

8

Regency *c*.1800-1830

A. *General* B. *Jane Austen, Peacock; Byron, Shelley*

A. GENERAL

No period seems to demonstrate more clearly than this the under-lying function of comedy as a mode of psychological warfare. Between 1760 or so and the period of the Napoleonic Wars an Age of Com-promise passed into an Age of Extremism—with a sudden change into top gear at the time of the French Revolution. And sure enough in the 'Regency' period the major comic writers, Jane Austen and Peacock on the one hand, Byron and the supposedly humourless Shelley on the other, are found to represent in mutual mockery the opposition of neo-Augustanism and Romanticism—an opposition closely connected with an underlying ideological conflict more bitter than anything since the Civil War. The transition period, between Augustan and Regency ages, lacks major comic writers, and the minor comedy of Goldsmith and Sheridan is compromised by its Age and uncommitted to any ideological camp (Burns, combating elements in the very different climate of Scotland, is the exception that proves the rule). The temper of comedy in fact, matches that of Society.

True, reform had come to seem more desirable than stability as memories of the Civil War and its aftermath receded down the genera-tions, as corruption grew alongside commonsense and complacency. But in the transition period reform was expected and, in a mild sort, came about at the critical moment, just when dissatisfaction reached its height: when on top of heavy taxation, enclosures, and rising prices, the idea of relieving England by taxing America led to an expensive and unsuccessful war. In 1782 Parliament became more independent, and made much improvement, first under the Whig control of Rockingham, and then under Pitt the Younger (who later became intransigently reactionary). Corruption was reduced, the Cabinet system established, finances reconstituted, and a new empire was founded on the ruins of the old.

With the outbreak of the French Revolution—which affected the whole of the 'Regency' period—the movement of ideas accelerated but the reform movement came to a halt. The landowners' monopoly of power had not been broken, and a scared Tory government used it rigorously to defend the *status quo*, not merely against radicalism or revolutionism but against anything that might disturb the loaded balance of the constitution. Thomas Hardy, the Secretary of the London Corresponding Society, was tried for treason in 1794, having advocated 'representative government, the direct opposite of that which is established here.'

The Revolution crystallised Radical discontent, giving it a theory and an example of action. The reaction of the Tory party, in clamping down, aggravated the effects of the remorselessly proceeding Industrial Revolution. Romantic, rationalist, and dissenting Radicals joined in demanding a new order. In a land believed to be on the verge of violent revolution the Government felt that it could not afford to be mild. On the other hand, being without police and almost without an army, it was physically unable to be fully repressive. Spasmodic repression, therefore, was eked out with the propaganda of religious and ethical cant—anathema to the romantic poets—with argument, and with the ridicule of comedy. And the opposition answered with idealism (also not always free of cant), with argument, and with counter-comedy.

Committed though it may be, such comedy, springing from deeply opposed temperaments and principles transcends its own day more easily than comedy more narrowly based. The political satires of the preceding transitional period are now of interest only to the social historian, its moral comic verse, usually in couplet form, pales beside that of Pope; and the plays of Goldsmith and Sheridan, which do live, live more as farce, or divertisement than as comedy. Indeed, *She Stoops to Conquer* (1773) *is* farce, and *The Rivals* (1775) largely divertisement. *The Good-Natur'd Man* (1768) counts as comedy in that it uses laughter against sentimentally exaggerated virtue, and so does *The School for Scandal* (1783) since it mocks hypocrisy and scandal. All four, however, are second-order plays, more concerned with the world of literature than the world of their ostensible targets. Primarily concerned to rescue 'comic' drama from the sentimentalists, they live more for their pure amusement value than for anything else. No bad thing, of course, but a different thing from major comedy— and anyway the amusement-value is in fact somewhat undermined; for though they do revive something of Restoration comedy they also retain something of the sentimental comedy that succeeded it. In what was still, if increasingly unstably, an Age of Compromise they are compromised from the start.

Both Goldsmith and Sheridan are explicit about their intention of comically attacking sentimental comedy. Yet for all this, the first of their dramas—and the most anti-sentimental in purpose—betrays most strongly a sentimental implication. Certainly, the protagonist of *The Good-Natur'd Man*, Honeywood, seems to be a vehicle for comic satire upon unintelligent and ultimately calamitous benevolence. But there is never any doubt that he is precisely one of those delineated in Goldsmith's own essay on 'Sentimental Comedy', whose 'Faults and Foibles the Spectator is taught not only to pardon, but to applaud . . . in consideration of the goodness of their hearts.'

Sheridan has a harder edge. Sentimentality of a romantic kind in Lydia Languish, of a moral kind in Joseph Surface, are both amusingly exposed. No ambivalence here. But is it not a species of sentimentality to ask admiration for Charles Surface, just the type that has never lacked sympathy—nor ever deserved it ('God's life, don't talk about it: poor Stanley's wants are pressing, and if you don't make haste, we shall have someone call that has a better right to the money')? Again, could anything be less principled or more deserving of satire than Sir Oliver's generosity and forgiveness, simply because Charles has sentimentally spared his picture in the auction. Indeed, the introduction of Sir Oliver at all to make a test of the brothers' hearts is a piece of structural sentimentality. Restoration dramatists found no need for a moral arbiter and judge, but trusted to their own and the audience's intelligence to see that the characters were properly 'placed'.

The truth is that in Sheridan wit—mostly play-wit—is all-important. Not only was he liable to be sentimental while attacking sentiment, but he was also lacking in invention: even the much-laboured-over *School for Scandal* having some difficulty in keeping the action going. Goldsmith, on the other hand, a quicker and slacker writer, relies much more on situation, and consequently the characters are often 'humours'—but (Honeywood excepted) not of the Jonsonian kind; they are seen as funny but not as reprehensibly absurd. For instance, Hardcastle—like Honeywood and Croaker, like Marlowe —is a character one might hear of but would never meet:

> I love everything that is old: old friends, old times, old books, old wine; and I believe, Dorothy (*taking her hand*), you'll own I've been pretty fond of an old wife.

He is what he is not because Goldsmith has some comic point to make
but merely to raise a laugh by his oddity and subserve the situation to
come, when Marlowe takes him for an old-fashioned innkeeper.
Nevertheless, in the minor figures, Goldsmith often dispenses with
this 'idea' of a character; and even the major ones—perhaps in
proportion as they are *not* Jonsonian—do have some life. In part, no
doubt, because they are infused with feeling (as they are not armoured
in epigram the sentimentality doesn't have to go into the action as in
Sheridan*). In Sheridan, there is less feeling for idiosyncrasy and
idiom of character, but less need for it as there is more wit. Unlike
Honeywood and the others, Sheridan's characters start off as possible
beings. But as characters of wit, they remain fixed; that is, they do not
evolve or display unexpected facets, so as to become as rounded as the
requirements of the plot may allow; the nearest they come to it, or
rather, might seem to, is by way of speaking out of character occasionally, becoming mouthpieces for some felicity unlikely in them: witness
Fag's metaphor, nicely—and more plausibly—capped by his master:

> ABSOLUTE You blockhead, never say more than is necessary.
> FAG I beg pardon, sir—I beg pardon—but, with submission, a lie is
> nothing unless one supports it. Sir, whenever I draw on my invention
> for a good current lie, I always forge endorsements as well as the bill.
> ABSOLUTE Well take care you don't hurt your credit by offering too
> much security.

Sheridan's personages, in fact, are not humour-characters so much as
wit-characters. And where, comparatively rarely, there *is* amusement
from character, it is not of Goldsmith's sort. Where the latter shows
absurdity in *action*, the former shows it in *speech*. But not all the
glittering protection of an even surface of wit—'No, no; the merit of
these is the inveterate likeness—all stiff and awkward as the originals,'
'an old *gouty* chair,' 'and a damned disinheriting countenance'—nor
all the intelligence that can bring Lady Teazle by logical steps to
admit 'I must sin in my own defence, and part with my virtue to
secure my reputation', can keep sentiment from seeping in. Lady
Teazle does not part with her virtue (or lose her reputation)—any
more than Marlowe can bring himself to seduce the supposed chamber-
maid—and, what is worse, Sir Peter Teazle after all his ill-usage,

---

* In this they seem to reflect the general growth of sentimentality in the eighteenth
century. As Restoration, aristocratic wit declines, and *laissez-faire* attitudes
develop (thus hampering the practical expression of concern) so sentimentality
increases.

and quite unasked, goes loudly making money over to her, while she listens, and reforms, behind the screen. And Charles, like Honeywood, is rewarded rather for virtue of soul than deed—just as in sentimental comedy.

Burns too can be sentimental, even maudlin at times, but he doesn't let this sugar-water get into the whisky. His best comic poems, like those of Byron and Shelley are pure comedy, satirical or celebratory. This poetry also seems akin to theirs in its opposition to the Establishment, and to formality, in its support for freedom and nature. The kinship, however, is a distant one: Burns is opposed to the *Scottish* Establishment, in particular to the narrow restrictiveness of the Kirk (thus being in some ways more akin to seventeenth-century anti-Puritan writers). Best representing the two main aspects of his comic genius, perhaps, are *Holy Willie's Prayer*, an anti-clerical satire, and *Love and Liberty* (*The Jolly Beggars*), a comic celebration of freedom.

Holy Willie was of course a real contemporary, but the basic comic method of the poem makes him also a type: by concentrating attention on what was characteristic of the kind and congenital to the doctrine. Fundamentally the method is that of parody, both textural* and structural.† The modern reader *need* not know the original material mocked, or even the contexts from which various Biblical phrases are wrenched and distorted (though clearly his appreciation will be heightened if he does), since the linguistic shifts, the incongruous juxtapositions of diction and content, or divine matter and wordly, are sufficiently emphatic to produce comic irony anyway. Moreover, they are themselves a formal model of the implied theme: the distortion of character in Holy Willie himself, and the twistedness of the doctrine of predestination that he professed:

> O Thou that in the heavens does dwell!
>   Wha, as it pleases best thysel,
> Sends ane to heaven and ten to h-ll,
>   A' for thy glory!

* The poem is written in the 'language of the saints'—that improbable amalgam of biblical English and colloquial Scots which was characteristic of the Covenanter and the Presbyterian evangelical . . . [but] 'Burn's antitheses are not merely verbal; they are a matter of *ideas,* and their merciless irony strips bare the perverse barbarity of Willie's distorted Calvinism' (Crawford, p. 58). (J. Kinsley, *Burns,* Oxford 1968, p. 1048)

† The *Prayer* follows the traditional scheme of invocation (ll. 1-6); praise (ll. 7-30); confession and penitence (ll. 37-60); intercession (ll. 61-2) and petition (ll. 63-102). (*Ibid.* pp. 1048-9.)

> And no for ony gude or ill
> They've done before thee—

What keeps the poem within the bounds of *comic* satire is mainly the device of putting it in the first person. Holy Willie is thus not ostensibly attacked at all; rather he exposes himself—and there is a zestful voyeuristic delight in watching him do so at the very time he thinks he is covering up, from his own, our, and indeed God's critical scrutiny.

If *Holy Willie's Prayer* is comedy because its methods mitigate an otherwise bitter mood, *Love and Liberty* is so because rhythm, rhetoric and music transform what might be supposed a bitter reality into a mood of celebration: of drink, nature, and freedom. As Kinsley points out there is a tradition of popular beggar-songs and ballad-opera with similar implications. Burns's originality lies in treatment rather than theme: this poem is a fusion of pastoral tone and anti-pastoral realism:

> The cantata celebrates an old myth: the belief in the content and 'truest happiness' of the vagabond life . . . But for all that, and despite the reflection of current revolutionary ideas in the songs, there is nothing mythical or idealized about Burns's beggars . . . It is this pressure of reality—the reality of Poosie Nansie's—behind the poetical form that drives even Matthew Arnold to recognise . . . not only 'hideousness and squalor' but 'a breadth, truth and power which make the famous scene in Auerbach's cellar, of Goethe's *Faust*, seem artificial and tame beside it . . .'
>
> (Kinsley, *Burns*, p. 1150)

All these points—and the general quality of the work—are well exemplified by the opening recitative and the closing song. The first stanza begins with an economical evocation of bitter weather, in staccato rhythms and emphatic monosyllabic rhymes, moves indoors with jauntier rhythms and feminine rhymes, and concludes with gusto: 'Wi' quaffing and laughing . . . Wi' jumping and thumping . . .'. A mood that continues to accumulate jollity throughout the second stanza, by similar means: well-chosen detail well arranged, appropriate diction, rhythm, and increasingly lively rhyme ('order' 'Sodger', 'smack still' 'crack still'):

> First, niest the fire, in auld red rags,
> Ane sat; weel brac'd wi' mealy bags,
>   And knapsack a' in order;
> His doxy lay within his arm;

> Wi' USQUEBAUGH an' blankets warm,
> She blinket on her Sodger:
> An' ay he gies the tozie drab
> The tither skelpan kiss
> While she held up her greedy gab,
> Just like an aumous dish:
>   Ilk smack still, did crack still,
>   Just like a cadger's whip;
>   Then staggering and swaggering,
>   He roar'd this ditty up—
>
> tozie drab, *warm and tipsy slut*; skelpan, *smacking*; aumous, *alms*

The chorus of the concluding song reminds one of Burns's affinities with the romantic radicals:

> A fig for those by law protected!
> LIBERTY's a glorious feast!
> Courts for cowards were erected,
> Churches built to please the PRIEST.

But the last stanza of the song recalls the fact that, if this too is comedy as a mode of psychological warfare, it is in a more local war. The attack on courts and churches is subservient to an overriding concern with those who 'cant about DECORUM,/Who have character to lose'. This Scots comedy (like that in England specifically provoked by sentimentality) is narrower than that of the 'Regency', insofar as it seems to be specifically provoked by the unco' guid— who fought back not with counter-comedy but, as in England a century earlier, with the sermon. Burns's comedy, however, does have a universalising deep-structure, for it comes to seem the voice of an ageless and unregenerate paganism asserting its rights against the equally ageless tendency of the Super-ego to deny them entirely.

However, 'Regency' comedy, in one way or another, is undoubtedly wider in scope than comedy of the transition period, whether English or Scottish; further, there is much more of it; and it gains in importance by being part of the great debate* on the French Revolution.

Most of that debate, of course, was conducted in deadly earnest†, for the issues themselves were grave during the whole of the war period:

> Defeat in Europe [1793], disaster in the West Indies, bad harvests, and loss of markets—it was no wonder that discontent was rife at

---

* Well documented in Alfred Cobban, *The Debate on the French Revolution*, London 1950.

† Though the *Anti-Jacobin* did produce a number of amusing anti-romantic and anti-reformist parodies and burlesques.

home. The mob broke Pitt's windows, revolutionary clubs multiplied,
and Pitt began a policy of repression.

(J. H. Plumb, *England in the Eighteenth Century*, London 1950, p. 198)

The Tory Party [*between* 1790 *and* 1815] had become identified with
total opposition to movements of popular radicalism and political
reform. It remained the party of the Church of England, of public
order and administrative efficiency, of continuity and traditionalism in
methods of government. It clung to a hierarchical and aristocratic
notion of society . . . The Whigs shared in most of this outlook.

(David Thomson, *England in the Nineteeth Century*, London 1950, p. 23)

The Radical Party became really effective only when the pressures
relaxed after 1815. It is significant that all the major comedy—with
the exception of some of Jane Austen, who was not *directly* concerned
with the wider implications of the romantic stance—was written in
the period between Waterloo and the Reform Bill: a bill that marked
the end of the era of repression; but ushered in neither a new and
better Augustan age, as Jane Austen and Peacock would have wished,
nor the cantfree republic desired by Byron and Shelley, but rather that
reign of economists and calculators gloomily prophesied by the
romantic-reactionary, Burke, and the Augustan-radical, Peacock, alike.

Despite the Coercion Act, the Corn Law struggle, the reform
movement and Peterloo, this post-war period was a time in which
committed comedy was both appropriate and possible. Possible owing
to the relaxation mentioned and the redirection of energies formerly
channelled against an external enemy, appropriate because of the very
extremism and earnestness of the 'philosophies' bequeathed to the
Left and the Right: by revolutionaries, violent or (like Godwin) non-
violent on the one hand, and by the anti-jacobins (especially Burke)
on the other.

Burke's romantic temperament, moreover, added a certain quirky
element to the basic Tory inheritance of Augustan common sense,
which not only made it more open to comic attack but also tended to
complicate the alignment of the literary opponents:

You see, Sir, that in this enlightened age I am bold enough to confess,
that we are generally men of untaught feelings; that instead of casting
away all our old prejudices, we cherish them to a very considerable
degree, and, to take more shame to ourselves, we cherish them because
they are prejudices; and the longer they have lasted, and the more
generally they have prevailed, the more we cherish them. We are
afraid to put men to live and trade each on his own private stock of
reason; because we suspect that the stock of each man is small, and

that the individuals would do better to avail themselves of the general bank and capital of nations and of ages.

(Reflections on the Revolution in France (1790), Cobban, p. 247)

This element of cherished barnacled prejudice is what provides Peacock with cause for *radical* comedy, although he is temperamentally restraining and conserving. *Nightmare Abbey*, however, shows where his basic affinities lie. Like *Northanger Abbey* (and the less comic *Sense and Sensibility*) it turns romantic literature against the romantic life-style. Quite as firmly as Jane Austen, Peacock is opposed, like any good Augustan, to 'enthusiasm', sharing her belief that it was both self-indulgent and socially undesirable. But it is no accident that Shelley, the chief target of Peacock's book, admired it and remained firm friends with the author. For whereas Jane Austen unthinkingly accepts conventional orthodoxy, social, moral, and religious—her acute criticisms being entirely from within the system —Peacock is philosophically sceptical: broadly and amusedly critical of all current parties and notions. He might therefore seem to be a bridge between the comedy of conservation and the comedy of innovation—but is in reality a pier, attached to the Right Bank.

B. 1. JANE AUSTEN AND THOMAS LOVE PEACOCK

In respect of presenting or embodying opinion, there are two very distinct classes of comic fictions: one in which the characters are abstractions or embodied classifications, and the implied or embodied opinions the main matter of the work; another, in which the characters are individuals, and the events and the action those of actual life—the opinions, however prominent they may be made, being merely incidental.

(T. L. Peacock, 'French Comic Romances', *The London Review*, Oct. 1836)

If Peacock himself is clearly of the first class, like Voltaire, Jane Austen, just as obviously, is of the second—which is not to say that the one is entirely restricted to abstraction and the other to characterisation. Nevertheless it is unsurprising to find Peacock's sunny quality shining as warmly and illuminatingly in his essays as in his novels. The following passage, for instance, from The *Four Ages of Poetry* (which provoked Shelley's wholly serious *Defence*) displays the same range of mind, the same standards*, and the same comic device of

---

* It is interesting to note that he thinks of the 18th century as radical and sceptical, looking back to Hume, Gibbon, Rousseau, and Voltaire, whereas Jane Austen's intellectual ancestors were such pious and restraining moralists as Johnson, Cowper, Gisborne, Richardson and Crabbe (*v.* F. Bradbrook, *Jane Austen and her Predecessors*, Cambridge, 1966).

reductio ad absurdum—by condensed argument, perverted aphorism, and syllepsis—as are found so often in the novels:

> The contemporaries of Gray and Cowper were deep and elaborate thinkers. The subtle scepticism of Hume, the solemn irony of Gibbon, the daring paradoxes of Rousseau, and the biting ridicule of Voltaire, directed the energies of four extraordinary minds to shake every portion of the reign of authority. Enquiry was roused, the activity of intellect was excited, and poetry came in for its share of the general result . . . The success which attended these experiments, and the pleasure which resulted from them had the usual effect of all new enthusiasms, that of turning the heads of a few unfortunate persons, the patriarchs of the age of brass, who, mistaking the prominent novelty for the all-important totality, seem to have ratiocinated in the following manner: 'Poetical genius is the finest of all things, and we feel that we have more of it than anyone ever had. The way to bring it to perfection is to cultivate poetical impressions exclusively. Poetical impressions can be received only among natural scenes: for all that is artificial is anti-poetical. Society is artificial, therefore we will live out of society. The mountains are natural, therefore we will live in the mountains. There we shall be shining models of purity and virtue, passing the whole day in the innocent occupation of going up and down hill, receiving poetical impressions, and communicating them in immortal verse to admiring generations.' To some such perversion of intellect we owe that egregious confraternity of rhymesters, known by the name of the Lake Poets . . .

This is removed only by its comic mode from the notoriously unfair (and unfunny) onslaughts on Romantic poets in *Blackwood's* and the *Quarterly*, and is no more objective historical criticism than those were objective review-criticism. Both are different strategies in a common war against the new spirit that, internally and externally, was leading to so much disturbance.

It is with this *genre*, of the controversial comic essay, in mind that the texture of Peacock's novels should be savoured (their structure and cardboard characterisation seem to derive from his interest in opera) if justice is to be done to them For they are totally unnovelistic. The plots are sketchy and absurd, the personages merely mouthpieces, and all share the same style.

Thus, though they have in common an anti-romantic temperament, Peacock and Jane Austen are in all other ways as different as— Shelley and Byron.

Technically speaking, Jane Austen's comedy is quite alien to the essay form; she carries the traditional novel to a new peak precisely by integrating her comments and evaluations with a realistic action more successfully than her predecessors. If her kind of novel is assumed to be central, and used as a standard, then as a comic *novelist* she automatically outranks Peacock. As *comic* novelists the issue between them is by no means clear—perhaps indeed it is non-existent. For those able to take the demonstration of absurdity neat, unmixed with vagaries of character and plausibilities of plot, Peacock is much funnier. Naturally, for these matters are jettisoned in order that the ridiculousness of current assumptions and ideas may stand out the more graphically. Moreover, Peacock presents no moral impediments to laughter, for he is extremely tolerant, suffering fools with obvious gladness. It is views, not people, he shows as absurd, and rather because they are false than because they are immoral or indecorous. In Jane Austen's work the emphasis falls on particularities of behaviour not generalities of belief, on characters rather than ideas. Certainly these express wider implications, but the laughter is more personal than intellectual in origin. These distinctions, within a common cause, could well be displayed by a comparison of *Nightmare Abbey* (1818) and *Northanger Abbey* (1813) alone. But it is probably more profitable to take them along with each writer's other comedies.

Northanger Abbey is in fact the best introduction to Jane Austen's comedy, though it is not her best comedy And it is tempting to say that it is the nearest to Peacock, in its clear concern with romantic absurdity, in its inclination towards caricature, and in the broadness of the humour; and therefore that it does not fully exemplify her most typical gifts But this is true only by comparison with her other comedies, *Pride and Prejudice* (1813), *Emma* (1816), and (dubiously) *Sense and Sensibility* (1811) Compared with Peacock's, the heart of her mock-romance is found to lie not in its ostensible theme but, as always, in the social manners and morals of its characters.

The literary irony is mainly homespun burlesque, fun without wit; and, more importantly, without any intellectual basis save the unrealism of gothic romances. The comedy of character, however, is admirable, if somewhat less delicately incisive than that of the later works.* In some respects this relative crudity is an advantage The Thorpes are so abominable, General Tilney so blatant a money-hypocrite that there need be no uneasiness in appreciation; whereas in the other novels doubts about the standards invoked—mere 'propriety'?—sometimes prove inhibiting Similarly, the predominance of caricature

---

* The generally accepted chronology is followed here—that based on dates assigned to completed versions approximating to those published—though rewriting and revision make it difficult to say what period a work really represents.

characters here eliminates the sense of spinsterish spite that at times threatens the comic poise of other works. (In fact, were it not for the presence of minor characters, like Mr Collins or Mrs Elton, who verge on caricature, the preponderance of malicious smile and catty didacticism might well have tilted the other comedies into the mode of serious moral satire, like *Mansfield Park*.

Perhaps the vitality of Catherine, the anti-heroine, is a little underrated as a quality of value, but if so this discrepancy between the comic creation given and the moral judgement implied is rather less than in the case of Lydia of *Pride and Prejudice*, and much less than in that of Marianne of *Sense and Sensibility*, where it is fatally damaging. In general, *Northanger Abbey* is characterised by an apparently more tolerant tone than the other novels—a very desirable thing if conserving and restraining comedies are to work on others than the already converted: witness the high proportion of *humorous* comedy of character, like the following:

> 'You are fond of history!—and so are Mr Allen and my father; and I have two brothers who do not dislike it. So many instances within my circle of friends is remarkable! At this rate, I shall not pity the writers of history any longer. If people like to read their books, it is all very well, but to be at so much trouble in filling great volumes, which, as I used to think, nobody would willingly ever look into, to be labouring only for the torment of little boys and girls, always struck me as a hard fate; and though I know it is all very right and necessary, I have often wondered at the person's courage that could sit down on purpose to do it.'
>
> 'That little boys and girls should be tormented,' said Henry Tilney, 'is what no one at all acquainted with human nature in a civilised state can deny; but I must observe, that they might well be offended at being supposed to have no higher aim ...'
>
> (I. xiv)

On the other hand a number of typically barbed comments allow the reader the happiness—in this work usually unexceptionable—of a virtuous malice. *Northanger Abbey* is neither Jane Austen's best novel nor her best comedy, but as comedy it is much better than it is normally rated in her opus, for some things that might count as flaws in a realistic moral novel are virtues in a comic one.

Sense and Sensibility exemplifies within itself Jane Austen's general development from the predominantly comic to the predominantly didactic. And as Lerner says:

> By not remaining a comedy *Sense and Sensibility* fails in its professed aim: it does not succeed in winning us to the side of sense. The two

faults are one. Jane Austen set herself the task of making fun of
Marianne and engaging sympathy for Elinor: if sympathy for Marianne
becomes too violent, if Marianne more than Elinor seems to embody
the book's positives, then we shall not be led to the intended conclusion.
And this is what happens.

(L. Lerner, *The Truthtellers*, London 1967, p. 161)

Even in the early part of the work one comes across stylistic shifts,
within a single paragraph, from the sardonic geniality of comic distance
to the edgy censure of starchy moralism. Part of this comic insecurity
comes of telling the tale largely from Elinor's viewpoint, and this
minimises the chances of comedy against her. Later events do convict
Marianne of imprudence, and therefore of a sort of absurdity, but it is
difficult not to feel—and to feel that subconsciously the author
sometimes couldn't help feeling—that hers is the sort of risk one has
to take for vital life. Her absurdities of outlook and expression in the
early chapters are rightly chastised by laughter. But does the later
'absurdity' of passion quite deserve the preaching it provokes?

More even than in the other novels one feels that most of the values,
and therefore, since Jane Austen's comedy is not celebratory, most of
the comedy, depends on the acceptance of social patterns. Unlike
Shelley, she does not transcend her age, but rather, like Pope, represents it. In many ways this is a strength: it accounts for the assurance
and lucidity of her style (neither causes, nor results, nor judgements of
human behaviour pose doubts or problems); and of course a pattern
can be distorted, while remaining recognisable, for 'placing' comic
effect. However, such dependence also imposes limitations damaging
to moral comedy—damaging because they make it in part merely of
its age, not for 'all time'. Where there is neither philosophical questioning nor deep introspection, clearly manners and morals will sometimes be confused. Sunday travelling and dishonesty may be taken
for comparable evils, while judgements on pride and on elopement
with a lover will follow those of period convention rather than
reason.

A related result of being thus *subdued* to contemporary *mores* is
frequently a very narrow gap between what is supported and what is
opposed. Again, this is sometimes a strength, as it promotes subtleties
of discrimination within a type (the quality and degree of a characteristic being constantly brought out by the contrast of similar characters
or situations); but it sometimes also proves a weakness, by reflecting
the confusions and inconsistencies of custom—inevitable, since in any
society, 'morality' is bound to be a mixture of pragmatism, principle,

and prejudice. Lerner notes this narrow gap in connection with her clergymen:

> What is wrong with Mr Collins as a clergyman? His selfishness, his lack of imagination, would be faults in anyone: what is more specific is that he regards religion as a social institution, not as a personal experience. But so does Henry Tilney, in *Northanger Abbey*—so, even, does Edmund Bertram.
>
> (*The Truthtellers*, p. 24)

The same is true about marriage. Marriage for money alone is reprobated, and shown to lead to unhappiness. However, marriage for love alone is similarly reprobated and shown to lead to unhappiness. What is left? Only love *and* money; and all the heroines are lucky enough to achieve the double, thus getting the best of two moralities, of the heart and the head. But this solution hardly satisfies the Kantian touchstone of universality. Moreover, it is not always possible for the novelist to get the best of both worlds without some unintentional sacrifice. In *Sense and Sensibility*, for instance, the good sense of Elinor and Edward in deciding that 'they were neither of them quite enough in love to think that three hundred and fifty pounds a year would supply them with the comforts of life'—when in addition they have a rent-free rectory and a capital of two thousand pounds—effectively demolishes what little credence in their love Jane Austen has managed to build up, despite her lack of sexual empathy. After all, money then would be worth about twenty times its present value!

Similarly with pride and snobbery. A certain amount of either is approved, too much is reproved; and the line is drawn with dogmatic certainty—but not with the aid of any principle, philosophical or psychological. D'Arcy, 'with family, fortune, everything in his favour, should think highly of himself'; it is allowed that he 'has a *right* to be proud'—and to speak of 'the inferiority of your connections,' correctly enough in terms of current social beliefs, but without any authorial attempt to step outside those beliefs—as Shelley, Byron, and even Peacock did. It is only *excessive* pride that brings D'Arcy within the ambit of comic censure. Snobbery is strongly condemned by both Elinor and Marianne (and the narrator) in *Sense and Sensibility* but there is no hint of irony when Mrs Jennings, despite her vulgarity, is admitted to visit 'no one to whom an introduction could at all discompose the feelings of her young companions'—'excepting a few old city friends'.

This narrowness is clearly a result of submergence in a society limited in more than one sense. Only the strengths it gives rise to are normally commented on; in fact Janes Austen's work derives from it confusion as well as clarity. But Angus Wilson has honestly faced the drawbacks of

> the almost universal acceptance by modern writers on Jane Austen of her preferred range of artistic concern, as expressed in her letter to her niece Fanny of 'three or four families in a country village'. For some novelists, no doubt, this limitation would be a valuable discipline; for her, I believe, the constriction, however inescapable, was a deforming one; it distorted the balance between the two views of life whose conflict made her art. If only they would admit this, modern critics would feel less compelled to tie themselves in knots in order to give a moral unity to the continuous contradiction that exists not only between her different novels but also within each of them.
>
> ('The Neighbourhood of Tombuctoo: Conflicts in Jane Austen's Novels', Southam, p. 182)

The moral placing, of course, is done with a remarkable combination of clarity and subtlety, it is mediated with precise and varied irony, with sharp intelligence; yet, even when it is not merely conventionally correct but humanly right (as in the case of Emma's little gibe at the gabbling Miss Bates, which brings down such condemnation), it often seems trivial, or anyway, the product of an overprotected and unrepresentative little world which hid from itself not only the real problems of the world beyond but also the deeper of its own inner human problems. Restoration writers are commonly accused of triviality, but they do come to grips with sexual problems, betrayal, fortune-hunting, at a deeper level. Jane Austen's is a softer, cushioned society, and for this reason hers is probably a slighter kind of comedy than theirs—certainly than Jonson's. Frank Churchill, in *Emma*, is severely condemned for having perpetrated an almost harmless deception: that of keeping secret his engagement to Jane Fairfax in order not to lose his inheritance. Jonson would have given not only much more comic approval to his gaiety and charm but also to the rogue-intelligence that enabled him to manage others so much more successfully than Emma (who thinks she's managing him). Jonson, of course, does tend to favour much more deeply-dyed rogues than Frank Churchill—and this makes his comedy more universal, for ultimately the qualities shown by such rogues are not only more likable than those of the Establishment dupes but more fitted for survival. Like the qualities of the tragic hero they may be a threat, but they are basic qualities mankind cannot afford to lose. By comparison with Jane Austen, Fielding *is* coarse, as she thought him, but it is arguable that like Chaucer he had a robust strength that gives his comedy deeper foundations. So, in context, Emma's tact in not telling her father of her engagement 'till Mrs Weston were safe and well' (from giving birth), so that 'No additional agitation should be thrown at this period among those she loved' seems no more than we should have expected in this pampered world. Stand back, though, and it is difficult not to feel that Mr Woodhouse, who *is* laughed at, is only relatively more valetudinarian than the others, who are *not*. In a Himalayan world, Jane Austen's often seems to be a morality, however refined, of the foothills. Clearly her comedy aims at being integrative as well as conserving, at reconciling head and heart, pride and prejudice, but in so far as it succeeds it does so only by fastidious exclusion.

Such animadversions are necessary to correct the critical balance— though in fact its one-sidedness is not so misleading as might have been expected, for the defects are much less damaging in comedies of Peacock's second type 'in which the characters are individuals, and the events and the action those of actual life' than they would be in those of the first type, where 'the implied or embodied opinions [are] the main matter of the work'.

Pride and Prejudice and *Emma* remain major comedies, no matter what the limitations, because their heroines are fully realised characters, and the heroines are keystones of the constructions. Which is the better of the two? Most modern critics favour *Emma*; and there is no doubt that it is bigger and more complex, and moreover the only novel not marred by too obvious contrivances for the sake of plot (the convenient and unprepared-for marriage of Lucy and Robert Ferrars in *Sense and Sensibility* being only the most glaring example). There is good reason for Lerner's conclusion:

> *Emma* is a full and rich and human book, all the responses it arouses dig deep into warmth and anger, grief and fear. But in no situation does any of these emotions take charge. The author's eye is fixed so steadily on the contrast between what is and what is believed, that however powerfully we are moved by one or the other half, we remain aware of the whole as a balanced situation. The harm and grief are never violent enough to run away with our attention. The richer the human material, the harder it will be for the author to maintain the judicious, amused balance of comedy: to be amusing is always easier when one is merely amusing. Perhaps *Emma* is as profound as pure comedy can be.
>
> (*The Truthtellers*, p. 102)

However, if one questions the word 'profound'—on the grounds given above—then the last sentences indicate reasons for preferring *Pride and Prejudice*. The reasons are precisely those given by Q. D. Leavis for *not* doing so—but then she is seeing Jane Austen, not unreasonably, with more emphasis on the moral, than the comic novelist (as indeed did the author herself: 'The work is rather too light, and bright, and sparkling; it wants shade'):

> . . . in *Emma* and *Persuasion*, we see her foregoing the immediate effect of witty rejoinder and humorous character to analyse motive and build up total effects; in this new manner the human heart is investigated in a new way, every impulse noted and considered with respect, instead of inspiring the easy comments of the earlier automatic and rather unfeeling sprightliness.
>
> ('Jane Austen', *A Selection from Scrutiny*, Cambridge 1968, Vol. 2, p. 59)

It is perfectly true that in both novels Jane Austen almost always manages to be serious without being solemn, as she did not in *Sense and Sensibility*. But there are certainly many more occasions in *Emma* when it seems she is on the verge of forgetting that though comedy, in contradistinction from farce and divertisement, is in some sense serious it must also be amusing—and, in short, if status as comedy is in question, Angus Wilson's heretical preference for *Pride and Prejudice* has much to commend it:

> In any case Lizzie is so real and D'arcy so unreal that we cannot take the compromise seriously. *Emma* is the tale I cannot swallow despite all its great artistry, its reverberating intricate ironies. For what has Miss Woodhouse learned? That she cannot make up daydreams of grandeur to sugar the pill of Highbury's pettiness . . . Mr Knightley, so much admired by modern critics, seems to me pompous, condescending and a bore. His manliness consists in the looming spectre of a Victorian paterfamilias . . . What has he learned but to treat her as 'the little woman', 'my Emma', who has made him think better of spoiled children. It is a sad sort of father-daughter marriage that has been achieved—Rochester and Jane Eyre without the passion . . . Emma hates Hartfield where nevertheless all her affections lie, all her limited young life has been spent. She knows that it is a neighbourhood of voluntary spies, not, as Miss Bates, whose battle is lost, asserts, 'such a happiness when good people get together—and they always do' Only regulated hatred—regulated now by the lessons Mr Knightley and Jane Austen have taught her—can reconcile Emma to Hartfield, where her affections and roots lie. It is a sad ending, a depressing compromise.
>
> ('The Neighbourhood of Tombuctoo', *Critical Essay*, ed. Southam, pp. 198-9)

As W. A. Craik points out (*Jane Austen, the Six Novels*, London 1968) both novels ridicule romanticism by the ironic use of romantic literary conventions and clichés; and thus they somewhat mitigate Jane Austen's tendency to social solipsism. And both novels centre on flawed heroines, so that ironies of texture and structure are perfectly appropriate. Both, too, show great mastery of dialogue: apt, accurate, and self-revealing; in both, actions and characters interact naturally and consequentially, and in both, there is a spectrum of characters, from lifelike to almost pure caricature, that permits degrees of qualities and characteristics to be dramatically established. In all these respects, both are a great advance on the earlier comedies. *Pride and Prejudice* does have one advantage, other than the less unsatisfactory com-promise noted by Angus Wilson: namely, that *all* the characters are deficient in some way; there is no one like Knightley to encourage the author's priggishness. In this respect, too, the greater proportion of action to characterisation is also beneficial, as is the more witty style that goes along with it. On the other hand, *Emma* manages larger groups of characters in a more complex plot with greater facility, and thus offers greater possibilities for structural ironies and for the esthetic pleasure of variety-in-unity. But then it is Jane Austen's longest novel and has fewer active characters—and therefore for comic purposes might seem to stand in the greater need of that 'sprightly' style that is the perquisite of *Pride and Prejudice*. Ultimately, it comes down to a matter of taste: what proportions of entertainment and seriousness one prefers in a comedy.

Neither work can be said to be mithridatic, like Jonson's con-serving comedy, or celebratory like Shakespeare's, or releasing and innovatory like some Restoration comedy; but both works do con-tribute to the evolution of social sensibility within an accepted culture, both finely carry on the Augustan comic tradition of civilising the bourgeoisie while accepting its basic values—and by doing so they also set themselves, though less directly than Peacock's works, in opposition to the new, radical romanticism of the day.

Paradoxically, it is also true to say of Peacock that he partly supports, if not the radical romanticism of his day, at least the radical romantics. Indeed, he is better approached not through Jane Austen but rather by way of the phenomenal Robert Bage—like Peacock a self-educated, but brilliant and learned member of the trading class, and like Peacock avant-garde but not revolutionary. He was accused, by contemporary standards quite righly, of being anti-social, anti-moral, and anti-religious; he was opposed to divisions of class and divisions of sex. Long before Mary Wollstonecraft, Bage championed the cause of sex equality, and created some very un-Austenish heroines (like *Hermsprong*'s Miss Fluart: 'A kiss! Lord bless me, I thought your lordship had wanted to undress me!'), and he sardonically slaughtered any number of other sacred cows of the period. Like Peacock, he differed from the romantic radicals by keeping cool and being ironic and logical rather than heated, idealistic and metaphysical. And he shares with Peacock a refusal to believe in any grand cure for all the separate failings of man and society. For both, the remedy at its most positive is piecemeal progress by liberal common sense, at its most negative by Voltairian withdrawal: theories are all very well, but 'il faut cultiver notre jardin.' This 'wisely sceptical Epicureanism' (Ian Jack, *English Literature* 1815-1832, Oxford 1963, p. 223), while comically useful by introducing a cool draught of cynicism into an atmosphere of romantic hot air, can also bring radicalism to the brink of conservatism, or over it. Teleologically, therefore, as well as tonally, Bage and Peacock are against the romantics though sharing many of their views (and, in Peacock's case, friendships).

Bage's one major novel, *Hermsprong* (1796), however, is interesting less for its likeness than its unlikeness to Peacock's works. The same clear sardonic Augustan style, it is true, ironically insinuates heresies:

> . . . [my begetting] was a clandestine act, for which my valiant father had no warrant, and for which I am to be punished with all the disabilities the prudence of our laws can provide . . .
>
> (Chap. 1)

There is the same comic use of syllepsis:

> My mother was a blooming girl, brought up in a cottage, and knew nothing but innocence and spinning, till my valiant father undertook to be her preceptor. My maternal ancestors had, I suppose, few records, but many traditions; one of which is that my mother defended the citadel of her honour all the preceding summer, and had surrendered at the close of it, subdued by a too tender heart and a flowered cotton gown. On the twentieth day of her lying-in, she died of kindness and caudle.
>
> (Chap. 1)

And there is the same anti-clericalism:

> I did not at this time know the turpitude of the crime I was going to commit; I did not know it was murder, and of all murders the most flagitious. I might kill another man, and repent; but I could not repent of killing myself; nor could God ever forgive me for rushing into his sacred presence without a passport.
>
> (Chap. 1)

This last example corresponds to Peacock not only in its social tendency but in its method of logical wit:

> 'I am really astonished,' said the Reverend Doctor Gaster, gracefully picking off the supernal fragments of an egg he had just cracked, and clearing away a space at the top for the reception of a small piece of butter—'I am really astonished, gentlemen, at the very heterodox opinions I have heard you deliver: since nothing can be more obvious than that all animals were created solely and exclusively for the use of man.'
>
> 'Even the tiger that devours him?' said Mr Escot.
>
> 'Certainly,' said Doctor Gaster.
>
> 'How do you prove it?' said Mr Escot.
>
> 'It requires no proof,' said Doctor Gaster: 'it is a point of doctrine. It is written, therefore it is so.'
>
> 'Nothing can be more logical,' said Mr Jenkinson.
>
> 'It has been said,' continued he, 'that the ox was expressly made to be eaten by man: it may be said, by a parity of reasoning, that man was expressly made to be eaten by the tiger: but as wild oxen exist where there are no men, and men where there are no tigers, it would seem that in these instances they do not properly answer the ends of their creation.'
>
> 'It is a mystery,' said Dr Gaster.
>
> *(Headlong Hall,* 1816, Chap 2)

Here, Dr Gaster's complacent absurdity is mocked, but so are the views of Mr Escot, the deteriorationist, and Mr Jenkinson, the status-quo-ite (and Mr Foster, the Shelleyan perfectibilian) elsewhere; and in no case is there any question of *blame*. We are not required to dislike Dr Gaster, for he is not a person but a point of view (and we are not surprised to find the reverend Dr Opimian in *Gryll Grange* serving as a focus for anti-clerical comedy simply by being the favoured mouthpiece for Peacock's own Epicurean paganism; if feelings were to come into the matter we should have to dislike and like him at the same time!) This fact is related to the great difference between these works and *Hermsprong.* Bage can't, won't or daren't rely on his essayistic gifts; he gives much more importance to story than Peacock does, and it is not always appropriate to comedy; he dislikes his villain and can't keep comic distance with him; worse still, he likes his hero, the impeccable Hermsprong, the natural man without religious or moral training who nevertheless can do no wrong. The book thus turns out to be simulating, and often witty and amusing but, on the whole, not a comic whole. Some comedy clearly thrives on character and story; comedy of ideas does not: Peacock gains by discarding.

Mills speaks of Peacock being

> intellectually detached almost to the point of enjoying sophistry and hypocrisy as a pure intellectual challenge, to be attacked for itself rather than for its social effects: his concern seems to be reason and intellectual clarity rather than honesty and justice.
>
> (Howard Mills, *Peacock, his Circle and his Age*, Cambridge 1969, p. 131)

Tonally speaking there is a good deal of truth in this. It is the result of his being, like Shelley, not concerned with flesh and blood. One reward, however, is 'ridicule without abuse, and satire free from bitterness' (A. Martin Freeman, *Thomas Love Peacock*, London 1911, p. 209). Another reward, oddly, is that it leads to both wider and more specific social *reference*, if not 'concern'. So, for instance, his personages are based on real people, romantic and reactionary, but only on those aspects of them that are representative of a body of opinion—the same thing, in Peacock's view, as a psychological type, since he seems to have taken all obsessive and general ideas to be really rationalisations: that is why his characters never change their views as a result of argument. They thus have a specific and a general reference. Anti-clericalism may again be used to illustrate this point. Jane Austen satirises particular clergymen, much more for their personal than their clerical inadequacies, and not at all in reference to any general social philosophy. Peacock's much greater range of mind, and lack of emotional concern about particular characters, enables him to link the Middle Ages with specific matters of contemporary politics, particular historical personages with general ideas:

> ... for the sake of pious discipline, and what was in those days called social order, namely the preservation of the privileges of the few who happened to have any, at the expense of the swinish multitude who happened to have none, except that of working and being shot at for the benefit of their betters, which is obviously not the meaning of social order in our more enlightened times: let us therefore be grateful to Providence, and sing *Te Deum laudamus* in chorus with the Holy Alliance.
>
> (*Maid Marion*, 1822, Chap. 9)

> ... that most legitimate and most Christian king, Richard the First of England, the arch-crusader and anti-jacobin by excellence—the very type, flower, cream, pink, symbol, and mirror of all the Holy Alliances that have ever existed on earth ...
>
> (Ibid.)

Not that Peacock is at his best when most concerned with contemporary matters. The present-day reader, for instance, is likely to be more engaged by those witticisms that, starting from the author's current antipathies, straightway generalise them—as, say, in the case of bishops: '. . . the meek who had inherited the earth' (ibid) or '. . . Druidism was still struggling with Christianity. The lamb had driven the wolf from the rich pastures of the valleys to the high places of the wilderness . . .' (*The Misfortunes of Elphin*, 1829, Chap. 6). Or, to change the subject, while remaining in the same novel—a procedure that could as easily be reversed, owing to Peacock's essayistic concern with *topics*, and, therefore, relative independence of novelistic context—there is Seithyn's timeless defence of leaving ill alone. The speech seems in fact to derive from speeches of Canning 'in Parliament in 1817, to his electors in 1820 and again in the House in 1822' (Freeman, p. 286), but it might equally have derived from Burke; and it must have made most impact in its own day, as it does in ours, as the expression of archetypal conservatism. The speech does not so much refer the reader to Canning as use Canning as a concrete universal. Here, as elsewhere in Peacock, literary detective-work is of little critical importance—and if successful might even be a hindrance.

> 'It is well,' said Elphin, 'that some parts are sound: it were better that all were so.'
> 'So I have heard some people say before,' said Seithyn; 'perverse people, blind to venerable antiquity: that very unamiable sort of people who are in the habit of indulging their reason. But I say, the parts that are rotten give elasticity to those that are sound: they give them elasticity, elasticity, elasticity. If it were all sound, it would break by its own obstinate stiffness: the soundness is checked by the rottenness, and the stiffness is balanced by the elasticity. There is nothing so dangerous as innovation. See the waves in the equinoctial storms, dashing and clashing, roaring and pouring, spattering and battering, rattling and battling against it. I would not be so presumptuous as to say I could build anything that would stand against them half-an-hour; and here this immortal old work, which God forbid the finger of modern mason should bring into jeopardy, this immortal work has stood for centuries, and will stand for centuries more, if we let it alone. It is well: it works well: let well alone. Cupbearer, fill. It was half rotten when I was born, and that is conclusive reason why it should be three parts rotten when I die.'
>
> (*The Misfortunes of Elphin*, Chap. 2)

Seithyn happens to be a rather less unrounded character than most of Peacock's. That quality, however, is not used to add animus to amusement. On the contrary, though Seithyn's neglect leads to the ruin of his country and the drowning of most of its population, he is presented as a Falstaffian rogue who goes on to prosper in another country and comes to a good end. In short, like much of Peacock's work, this seems to be comedy of a kind as nearly impossible as Pope's humorous satire in *The Rape of the Lock*, namely, celebratory satire. Seeing men—save a small 'Grecian' élite—as ingenious rationalisers of ineradicable irrational attitudes, especially destructiveness and possessiveness—he seems to have resigned himself to enjoying the absurd spectacle. Yet this is not quite the case; it does not take account of the element of cynicism, increasing in the later books. More profitably, Peacock's comedy can be seen as the creation of a style from a despair, the celebratory element being part of a generally mithridatic comedy, designed to enable the reader to grin and bear the human condition while 'the common daylight of commonsense' makes its snail-like progress—with the help of such marginalia on the page of history as his work provides.

This abstention from blame, as one would not blame a cat for catching birds—and might possibly appreciate its gruesome skill—is seen most clearly in the anti-romantic comedy. To know all is to forgive all, and Peacock knew romanticism intimately; Shelley's friendship was the greatest influence in his life, he was fond of old ballads, well-versed in picturesque theory, and shared the romantics' love of rural walks and wild scenery. Peacock admired Shelley, Shelley Byron, and Byron Peacock: a symbolically closed circle, from which he escapes into comedy only by reinforcing the preponderantly Augustan element in his character with an effort of will. This closeness gives shade, and therefore a sense of depth, to the light surface of his essentially plane comedy. 'The War-Song of Dinas Vawr,' from *The Misfortunes of Elphin*, may act as a paradigm case—a song, as Peacock truly says:

> put upon record as being the quintessence of all the war-songs that ever were written, and the sum and substance of all the appetencies, tendencies, and consequences of military glory:

THE WAR-SONG OF DINAS VAWR

> The mountain sheep are sweeter,
> But the valley sheep are fatter;
> We therefore deemed it meeter
> To carry off the latter.
> We made an expedition;
> We met a host, and quelled it,

We forced a strong position
and killed the men who held it.

On Dyfed's richest valley,
Where herds of kine were browsing,
We made a mighty sally,
To furnish our carousing.
Fierce warriors rushed to meet us;
We met them, and o'erthrew them:
They struggled hard to beat us;
But we conquered them, and slew them.

As we drove our prize at leisure,
The king marched forth to catch us:
His rage surpassed all measure,
But his people could not match us.
He fled to his hall-pillars;
And, ere our force we led off,
Some sacked his house and cellars,
While others cut his head off.

We there, in strife bewild'ring,
Spilt blood enough to swim in:
We orphaned many children,
And widowed many women.
The eagles and the ravens
We glutted with our foemen;
The heroes and the cravens,
the spearmen and the bowmen.

We brought away from battle,
And much their land bemoaned them,
Two thousand head of cattle,
And the head of him who owned them:
Ednyfed, king of Dyfed,
His head was borne before us;
His wine and beasts supplied our feasts,
And his overthrow, our chorus.

A great comic song because it appreciates what it is against. The tone
is self-congratulatory, and therefore at sardonic odds with the content,
while the form (particularly in the matter of flippant feminine
rhyming) emphasises the shallow callousness of the heroic theme. Yet
these satiric counterweights are not so heavy as to cancel entirely the
joviality and exultation of conquest and victory, which thus flesh out
the civilised surface.

Douglas Hewitt interestingly refines this point:

> We do not so much investigate the ideas in such books as imagine what it would be like to hold them. We may be said to entertain them, and the festive metaphor is appropriate because they are frequently not the ones with which we spend every day. Our vicarious enjoyment, indeed, is often the enjoyment of entertaining somewhat outrageous ideas or a succession of incompatible ones. In this promiscuity such novels correspond to that argumentative and dialectical process by which we are often said to 'make up our minds'.
>
> ('Entertaining Ideas: A Critique of Peacock's *Crotchet Castle*,' *Essays in Criticism*, April 1970, p. 201)

Very often the ideas that Peacock entertains are indeed specific and local, but the majority of them have not gone dead, since he seems to have had a knack—associated with his philosophic gift—of picking out problems that were going to last; so that even when he is not universalising there is at least an impression of astonishing modernity. In the age of Malthus he naturally deals with overpopulation, but there is also popular education ('The reading public has increased its capacity of swallow in a proportion far exceeding that of its digestion'), pollution, evolution (or *de*volution, from the better-natured, healthier orang-utan), industrialism versus agriculturalism, heredity versus environment—carried on into the realm of crime and punishement:

> I no more blame or praise a man for what is called vice or virtue, than I tax a tuft of hemlock with malevolence, or discover great philanthropy in a field of potatoes, seeing that the men and the plants are equally incapacitated, by their original internal organisation, and the combinations and modifications of external circumstances, from being anything but what they are. *Quod victus fateare necesse est.*
>
> 'Yet you destroy the hemlock,' said Squire Headlong, 'and cultivate the potato: that is my way at least.'
>
> (*Headlong Hall*, 1816, Chap. 14)

Women's Lib., too, gets a a very fair airing, though there is more than a little irony in his portrait of Stella (which renders understandable Scythrop's equal attraction, despite his principles, to the frivolous Marionetta—a rare novelistic touch):

> Stella, in her conversations with Scythrop, displayed a highly cultivated and energetic mind, full of impassioned schemes of liberty, and impatience of masculine usurpation. She had a lively sense of all the oppressions that are done under the sun; and the vivid pictures which her imagination presented to her of the numberless scenes of injustice and misery which are being enacted at every moment in every part of

the inhabited world, gave an habitual seriousness to her physiognomy, that made it seem as if a smile had never once hovered on her lips. She was intimately conversant with the German language and literature; and Scythrop listened with delight to her repetitions of her favourite passages from Schiller and Goethe, and to her encomiums on the sublime Spartacus Weishaupt, the immortal founder of the sect of the Illuminati.

(*Nightmare Abbey*, 1818, Chap 10)

This knack of picking out problems of the age that also show signs of being problems for all time comes from the habit of seeking particular examples of the more general categories which were of primary interest. Like Mr Crotchet, he set

The sentimental against the rational, the intuitive against the inductive, the ornamental against the useful, the intense against the tranquil, the romantic against the classical.

(*Crotchet Castle*, 1831, Chap. 2)

Though, in the last analysis, he came down on the side of the latter in all these pairs, he did not, like Mr Crotchet, hope to see such 'great and interesting controversies . . . satisfactorily settled' before he died. In Chapter 6, Mr MacQuedy's paper on one aspect of one problem from one pair, never gets beyond the first sentence, and Dr Folliott sums up for Peacock by observing that 'you can scarcely find two to agree on a scheme, and no two of those can agree on the details'.

The drawback, of course, to essayistic comedy in novel form is that novels are longer than essays, and therefore—especially when you go from novel to novel and necessarily repeat some things (since the number of great and interesting controversies is limited)—such comedy is found to need what might well seem generically incongruous, a plot. The problem then arises of finding the right balance between form and content, structure and texture; a problem Peacock solves perfectly only once, in *Nightmare Abbey*.

In *Headlong Hall*, plot is almost non-existent, and despite Mr Escot's marriage, it rather breaks off than ends. Essentially it consists of a number of mouthpieces delivering themselves of set speeches, witty, stimulating and formal. Fortunately it is a very short novel, despite the range of topics it concerns itself with; and the fact that the characters all speak like books is part of the satiric point. *Melincourt* has too much plot: there is a split between plot and ideas (Sir Oran Haut-Ton being used for irreconcilable purposes: to mock Monboddo's ideas on evolution, and, accepting Monboddo's view of primitive ape-man as a Noble Savage, to satirise modern man and his political system): further, absurd though the plot is, it is treated far too cavalierly; it bulks too large to be forgotten by the reader, and it is therefore irritating to find it forgotten by the characters most concerned: for instance, when Forester seeking for the abducted and endangered Anthelia takes a great deal of time off to philosophise with Fax on overpopulation and political economy. Again, Peacock seems to be far too much under the spell of Shelley, of whom Forester is an idealised and impossible portrait—yet treated wholly seriously (as indeed is the unlovable, priggish Anthelia). They are Peacock's Bertram and Fanny. It follows that the topics are also treated more seriously than in the other books, and at tediously greater length. That the characters speak like books is not now a comic point. It may well be right that no change of system will materially effect the world's problems so long as there is increasing overpopulation, as Peacock seems to believe, and thus there is clearly a case for treating this and related matters earnestly and at length. But it makes for didacticism more than comedy—though, to be fair, *Melincourt* is not without a good deal of light relief. *Maid Marion* and *The Misfortunes of Elphin* suffer from an attempt to mix oil and water: old romance, to which Peacock is attracted despite himself, and speculative comedy. *Crotchet Castle* and *Gryll Grange* are far more witty, much less didactic, than *Melincourt* but tend to suffer a similar hiatus between problems and irrelevant plot. Moreover, there is every now and then a sense that the greater proportion of humour in these novels is a sign that despair has passed into *je m'en foutisme*. Peacock's remark to Trelawny, 'Don't talk to me about anything that has happened for the last two thousand years,' now seems significant not so much of a large perspective as of ultimate retirement from the field. Earnest debaters are dismissed with greater celerity, and though discussion may 'find favour' it is merely because, as Dr Opimian puts it, 'I have found it very absorbent of claret'. Only in *Nightmare Abbey* are plot, character, concern and cynicism blended to best advantage.

The comic satire in this novel is more unified than in any other, being almost entirely directed against various forms of self-induced romantic melancholy and Germanic mystification and metaphysics. Furthermore, he seems to be at just the right distance from Shelley and is able at once to satirise Scythrop while using him, not as a mouthpiece, but an example of 'lived romanticism' (Mills, p. 164). In Scythrop, Peacock has taken to a logical conclusion the view that fervently held general systems are (if not poses) rationalisations of underlying emotional states. Scythrop utters few systematic ideas, and when he does we are shown the personal motives behind them. How this characteristic is turned to comic account can be seen nowhere better than in the hilarious Chapter 13, which is also the climax of the plot (where Scythrop's intrigue is discovered not only by his father but also by Marionetta and Stella). It is externalised by having Scythrop, in romantic manner, misuse science and literature to explain away difficulties due to private passions, and is later internalised in Scythrop's retreat into the dignity of suicidal mystery. In this novel, too, the art of formal conversation, mixing wit with wisdom, folly with sympathy, is brought to a brilliant peak.

B. ii. BYRON, SHELLEY

For Restoration playwrights men became absurd by pretending to wit they hadn't got, for Peacock, in the Regency, by pretending to feelings they hadn't, and by not admitting to the real feelings they had. Amongst those he satirised—or at any rate used as a basis for satire—was Byron. And the later Byron himself adopted a similar view. There are, however, radical differences: on the whole—despite some self-criticism in *Don Juan*—Byron projects this perception about his own romantic self on to established society, so that his is a comic satire on varieties of social hypocrisy; and further, for all his radicalism, Peacock's stance and tone is more acceptable to the general public than Byron's—and therefore Byron has to use a very different comic method. Though he admired Pope above all other poets, and despised most of the romantics, his comedy is essentially *romantic* satire. Like Shelley, and unlike Jane Austen and Peacock (who rightly choose prose as their medium), he starts from feelings rather than conventions or ideas, and appropriately avails himself of the greater range of rhetorical devices normally permitted by verse. But it is a different range from that of Pope; there is a sense in which the romantic satirist needs verse more than the Augustan satirist does.

Pope, defending the norm in the name of Nature-as-Reason, had his readers with him in a straight fight against backsliders, and could afford to hammer home his points straight away in telling couplets. His problem was merely one of economy: to get maximum impact in minimum time. He could afford, usually, to write didactic rather than comic satire. Byron needed to disarm an antagonistic public before he could attack its assumptions. His problem was one of sales-manship; so he needed a larger scope than the couplet could give, and a wider range of tone (including a much larger admixture of frivolity, to jolly his readers along till it was time to slip in a punch). The typical casual, conversational style, appealing to the fellow-feeling of unpretentious men, is therefore an essential tool; for his values are the unconventional ones, and while he may be irreverent he must not be alarmingly serious.

This style, and the ottava rima stanza, is common to *Beppo* (1818), and the more specifically social poems, *The Vision of Judgement* (1822), and *Don Juan* (1819-24), the works of his greatest maturity. The final couplet of this stanza is admirably suited to a surprise ending which underlines incongruity—one of Byron's main comic methods for mocking absurd disparities between seeming and being in society. The ridiculous rhyme on a serious subject serves the same purpose. Even the despotism of this very demanding rhyme-scheme and the contrasting liberties of the diction are appropriate to the theme of freedom. The strained rhymes, too, often emphasise an irreverence implicit in the matter.

Beppo and *The Vision of Judgement* are at opposite ends of the comic spectrum. There is one passage of sustained social satire in the former (stanzas XLVII-XLIX, beginning 'England, with all thy faults I love thee still'), and there is a good deal of generalised satire of sexual morality in this land of 'cloudy climate' and 'chilly women', in contrast with the warmer Italian, but this is sweetened by comic irreverence to the moral and sentimental, and this in turn by a great deal of pure humour: sometimes from ingenious rhyme alone, sometimes from neat typology:

> He was a lover of the good old school
> Who still become more constant as they cool. (XXIV)

Some comes from clever punning:

> Crush'd was Napoleon by the northern Thor,
>   Who knocked his army down with icy hammer,
> Stopp'd by the *Elements*, like a Whaler, or
>   A blund'ring novice in his new French grammar. (LXI)

And some from characterisation:

> 'Tis true, your budding Miss is very charming,
>   But shy and awkward at first coming out,
> So much alarm'd that she is quite alarming,
>   All Giggle, Blush, half Pertness and half Pout;
> And glancing at *Mamma* for fear there's harm in
>   What you, she, it or they may be about.

> The Nursery still lisps out in all they utter—
>   Besides, they always smell of bread and butter.
>   (xxxix)

It is arguable, indeed, that *Beppo* is divertisement rather than comedy
as defined. And were it not for the necessary element of play-wit
mentioned, it would be arguable that *The Vision of Judgement* was
invective satire, for it is essentially a bitter attack on what 'this old,
blind, mad, helpless, weak, poor worm' George III stood for ('He
ever warr'd with freedom and the free') and on the turncoat Southey
who had unwisely hymned him in bad verse:

> He had written praises of a regicide;
>   He had written praises of all kings whatever;
> He had written for republics far and wide,
>   And then against them bitterer than ever:
> For pantisocracy he once had cried
>   Aloud, a scheme less moral than 'twas clever;
> Then grew a hearty anti-Jacobin—
>   Had turn'd his coat—and would have turn'd his skin.
>   (xcvii)

But the heavenly setting, of course, provides a natural source for a
saving irreverence and play-wit.

Of *Don Juan*, Byron's greatest work, and the only really long poem
in English that is never dull, it might be said that the first six cantos
are largely humoristic like *Beppo*, the remaining ten satiric like *The
Vision of Judgement*. But even in the early cantos the ridiculous rhyme,
for instance, now lightly carries weighty implications, the mockery of
woman merges into pity:

> . . . for man to man so oft unjust,
>   Is always so to women; one sole bond
> Awaits them; treachery is all their trust;
>   Taught to conceal, their bursting hearts despond
> Over their idol, till some wealthier lust
>   Buys them in marriage—and what rests beyond?
> A thankless husband, next a faithless lover,
> Then dressing, nursing, praying, and all's over.
>   (2, cc)

Moreover, even in these early cantos the irony is often a result of the
mingled bitterness of one who feels and the laughter of one who
thinks; while the later cantos pass from the fierce attacks on war and
despotism in cantos eight and nine to the infinitely varied effects of the
succeeding cantos on England, where Juan is advised to 'Be hypocritical, be cautious' (11, lxxxvi). *Don Juan* is far too long to be

analysed here (and fortunately there is no shortage of analyses). Its essence, however, the flexibility that can cover so many aspects of falsity, capture so many moods, and victims, with its net of rhyme, reason and ridicule, may be found encapsulated in the brilliant *ubi sunt* passage in Canto 11 (LXXVI-LXXXV). Unique in English literature, it mingles comically but not incompatibly love, literature and politics, pity, anger and laughter. The style runs a gamut to deal with matter from 'The world' to 'an old Opera hat'. What unifies it is what unifies the whole created universe of *Don Juan*: that earnest belief in the freedoms of body, mind, and morality which is the better side of the romantic reaction to emotional conflicts set up by the spirit of the age. This is the side Peacock sympathised with. No doubt it shows the difference between a basically Augustan temperament and a basically romantic one that in Byron's case cynicism never got out of hand. Perhaps his middle period had sometimes betrayed a mixture of soft sentiment and hard cynicism, but in *Don Juan* the attitude is realistic, he

> ... would not be a tortoise in his screen
> 　Of stubborn shell, which waves and weather wear not.
> 'Tis better on the whole to have felt and seen
> 　That which humanity may bear, or bear not:
> 'Twill teach discernment to the sensitive　.
> 　And not to pour their ocean in a sieve.

(14, XLIX)

This comedy is not only innovatory in its radicalism, integrative in its blending, and releasing in its freedom from cant (in an age addicted to it*), but also celebratory in its sustained creative élan, its ceaseless invention, and formal virtuosity.

Jane Austen mocks the Gothic novel, Peacock uses it to mock an attitude, *Don Juan*, in the last cantos, uses it mainly as a setting (but in part, more purposefully, to make a contrast with civilised insipidity), and Shelley turns it into a mechanism for wild fantastic humour.

---

* 'As to Don Juan, confess, confess—you dog and be candid—it may be profligate but is it not life, is it not *the thing*? Could any man have written it who has not lived in the world?—and fooled in a post-chaise?—in a hackney-coach?—in a gondola?—against a wall?—in a court-carriage?—in a vis-à-vis?—on a table?—and under it? I have written about a 100 stanzas of a 3rd Canto, but it is damned modest—The outcry has frightened me. I have such projects for the Don, but the Cant is so much stronger than the—, nowadays, that the benefit of experience in a man who had well weighed the worth of both monosyllables must be lost to despairing posterity.' (P. Quennell (ed.), *Byron, A Self-Portrait*, London 1950, II, p. 491.)

His comedy, in fact, like his serious work is tinged with hysteria. Not that there is much comedy in Shelley, most of his radicalism is expressed in deadly earnestness, most of his satires are invective. There are touches of wit and humour in various passages of prose and verse, but in the end only two pieces could claim to be complete comedies. *Oedipus Tyrannus, or Swellfoot the Tyrant* (1820) starts with the brilliant comic conception of using the King's gout to link him with Sophocles's Oedipus, thereafter in mock-tragedy attacking his divorce proceedings against Queen Charlotte. The execution, however, does not live up to the conception. It is too specific in its now tedious reference to *merely* contemporary details, and the fantasy is often too bitter to be comic—sometimes, indeed, verging on hysteria and, therefore, melodrama. We are left with one great comic poem, *Peter Bell the Third* (1819).

This is not without flaws: there is very little story, considering its length, and both chronology and development are occasionally obscure (as might be gathered from the rather odd order of the seven parts: Death, The Devil, Hell, Sin, Grace, Damnation, Double-Damnation). These flaws, however, are quite outweighed by the amplification and subtlety of mood and the highly original use of the fantasy element in Gothic romances for psychologistic ridicule: witness Part III— Hell—which perceptively shows that in an unjust society *all* classes are corrupted and basically unhappy, and ends with a stanza surely deriving from Dante and the last pages of *Vathek* but original and subtle in form:

> All are damned—They breathe an air
> Thick, infected, joy-dispelling;
> Each pursues what seems most fair,
> Mining like moles through mind, and there
> Scoop palace-caverns vast, where Care
> In thronèd state is ever dwelling.

Peter Bell the Third is essentially a gayer *Masque of Anarchy* (1819) whose inner purpose is to satirise contemporary conditions and attitudes, social, sexual and metaphysical. It is comedy, as the *Masque* is not, because of its indirection: the use of a symbolic Wordsworth as a vehicle. Mostly, of course, it deals with the later, turncoat Wordsworth, when

> His eyes turned up, his mouth turned down;
> His accent caught a nasal twang;
> He oiled his hair; there might be heard
> The grace of God in every word.

(I, ii)

This is the Wordsworth who is made symptomatic of his society:

> For he now raved enormous folly,
>   Of baptisms, Sunday schools and graves.
> 'Twould make George Colman melancholy
> To have heard him, like a male Molly
>   Chanting those stupid staves.
>
> Yet the Reviews, who heaped abuse
>   On Peter while he wrote for freedom,
> So soon as in his song they spy
> The folly which soothes tyranny,
>   Praise him, for those who feed 'em.
>
> He was a man too great to scan;
>   A planet lost in truth's keen rays;
> His virtue, awful and prodigious;
> He was the most sublime, religious
>   Pure-minded poet of these days.
>
> (VI, xxxii-xxxiv)

The ambiguity of the last stanza—are the first two lines ironic inherently or only by contagion from context?—indicates the chief reason for the poem's comic success: it is more inwardly and intimately appreciative of the best in Wordsworth than anything else on him. Therefore the adverse criticism is given full credence, and the social criticism carries through on its coattails. If such a genius could be so smitten, why should not the world and the people in it all grow 'dull as Peter's self'?

Shelley is wonderfully sensitive to the particularly Wordsworthian strength:

> Yet his was individual mind,
>   And new-created all he saw
> In a new manner, and refined
> Those new creations, and combined
>   Them by a master-spirit's law.
>
> Thus—although unimaginative—
>   An apprehension clear, intense,
> Of his mind's work, had made alive
> The things it wrought on; I believe
>   Wakening a sort of thought in sense.
>
> (IV, ix-x)

And the precise sort of sort is unforgettably evoked in Part V:

But Peter's verse was clear, and came
　　Announcing from the frozen hearth
Of a cold age, that none might tame
The soul of that diviner flame
　　It augured to the earth:—

Like gentle rain on the dry plains,
　　Making that green which late was grey,
Or like the sudden moon that stains
Some gloomy chamber's window-panes
　　With a broad light like day.

For language was in Peter's hand
　　Like clay, while he was yet a potter:
And he made songs for all the land
Sweet both to feel and understand,
　　As pipkins late to mountain cotter.

(xiii-xv)

No better or more appreciative criticism of Wordsworth has ever been written. Yet, 'although unimaginative' prepares the way for the later humorous fantasy of Peter's dread disease, as do certain other witty but just reservations about even the uncorrupted Wordsworth: the egotism:

He had a mind which was somehow
　　At once circumference and centre
Of all that he might feel or know;
Nothing went ever out, although
　　Something did ever enter.

He had as much imagination
　　As a pint-pot;—he never could
Fancy another situation,
From which to dart his contemplation.
　　Than that wherein he stood.

(IV, vii-viii)

the inhibitions:

But from the first 'twas Peter's drift
　　To be a kind of moral eunuch:
He touched the hem of Nature's shift,—
Felt faint,—and never dared uplift
　　The closest all-concealing tunic.

(IV, xi)

Clearly a man liable to damnation and double-damnation, a man who could have been a reformer but chose to 'die' into conformity:

And the Third is he who has
O'er the grave been forced to pass
To the other side, which is—
Go and try else—just like this.

(Prologue)

This rather Dantean assumption enables Shelley to take a god's-eye view of his subject, and so the poem turns out—taken in the round—to be a remarkably charitable comedy, a comedy characterised by a sort of metaphysical sensitiveness, a sense of pity for the fatal flaw in human nature, for the paradoxical fact that the pursuit of one's own happiness and interest produces personal as well as general damnation. It is kept comic by the cheek of turning Wordsworth's own idea of reincarnation against him, by the hyperbole this leitmotif permits, by the deft use of snide details—the oiled hair, the gravelled drive and so forth—by the shafts of wit, and above all by the versification: 'un-Shelleyan', folk-ballad metre, sharp and often feminine rhyming, plain diction and homely imagery, all of which create a tension between potentially high-faluting theme and apparently low-faluting form, so that each is constantly putting the other in comic perspectives varying according to their relative weighting. It is more tolerant than Byron's or Jane Austen's opposed kinds of comedy, less dispassionate than Peacock's. It contributes not so much to social reform, to civilising the bourgeoisie, or the pursuit of philosophic ungullibility, as to the evolution of metaphysical sensibility.

The opposition of neo-Augustanism and Romanticism in mutual mockery, then, is not so straightforward a confrontation of parties as might at first appear. Yet neither is it illusory; our representative pairs come out right in the end. If Jane Austen and Byron remain the more rooted in their age, they purvey very different views and feelings about it. If Peacock and Shelley, rather, take off from their times, they do so in different ways and arrive at different ends. Reversing the common case, Regency comedy masks fundamental differences beneath superficial similarities.

9

Brave-New-World *c.*1870-1970

A. *General* B. *Butler, Shaw; Waugh, Heller; Joyce, Stoppard*

A. GENERAL

Quite apart from the sheer bulk of amusing writing extant in the modern period (most of it, however, clearly classifiable as farce or divertisement), post-regency comedy presents several new problems. For one thing, there are great differences, between the earlier and later comedies of this period, yet all, as the products of men in a new sort of society—an industrial one—share *something* not found previously. For another thing, at least some American comedy must be taken into account; even if we restricted ourselves to the novel only (obviously the dominant form in this period) at least two or three works would qualify as outstanding. Moreover, it is often impossible —and certainly unprofitable—to place certain writers in national pigeonholes. James wrote most of his work in England, though often about Americans, and finally became naturalised; much the same applies to Eliot; the reverse to Auden and Isherwood. This sort of interchangeability, indeed, is less surprising than it might at first appear. Differences of language and culture, though many, are not so deep as they are often made out to be; and as Nabokov has said:

> Nothing is more exhilarating than philistine vulgarity. But in regard to philistine vulgarity there is no intrinsic difference between Palearctic manners and Nearctic manners.
>
> ('On a Book Entitled *Lolita*', *Lolita*, London 1959, p. 305)

Again, despite many differences, both civilisations—a word increasinly queried by comic writers on both sides of the Atlantic—now have more in common with each other than either has with its eighteenth-century past. Power, population and wealth during the nineteenth century passed from country to town, but the relative stability of rural life and traditional values was not felt to be adequately replaced, in a rapidly changing industrial society, by the various social philosophies associated with the change. We might, then, expect

English comedy in both countries to be increasingly disillusioned and mithridatic during the last hundred years—and this is indeed the case for a good deal of it, though not for all, and usually not so directly as this implies. Much more puzzling and problematic is the dearth of such comedy—in fact, almost of *any* complete comedies—between about 1830 and about 1870.

A partial explanation of this dearth was advanced towards the end of chapter 4: the mid-Victorian writer was himself committed to many values inseparable from abuses he disliked and was therefore incapable of a unified comic vision, and Darwin seemed to show that Nature itself supported the utilitarian philosophy of ruthless competition—which indeed, both in England and America, did seem to be making the country as a whole richer and richer, fitter and fitter to survive. We may add to this Mumford's point:

> Try as they would, the most optimistic minds of the nineteenth century were all obsessed by the utilitarian ideology: Bellamy no less than Marx, Engels no less than Spencer, could conceive of a better future only in terms of the widening triumphs of industrialism . . . beyond that their notions of a developing human life were nebulous.
>
> (Lewis Mumford, *The Condition of Man*, London 1944, p. 329)

In an inhumane and psychologically disintegrative society, though, what was needed was a centrally 'human' and integrative vision—something all these factors conspired against. Coherent, full-scale comedy, then, had to wait upon disillusion at least with utilitarianism and industrialism (and later, in the twentieth century, also with the remedies for their ills). In the meantime, the expression of comic genius seems to have been hampered by the fact that the Victorians for forty years or so behaved and believed in a utilitarian way but felt in a post-romantic one. (Thus, both Dickens and Thackeray invariably blur satiric comedy with sentimentality.) Further reasons for a trough in the comedic graph—namely a combination of basic optimism and basic religious earnestness—are implicit in Trevelyan's assessment:

> if any real unity is to be ascribed to the Victorian era in England, it must be found in two governing conditions: first, there was no great war and no fear of catastrophe from without; and secondly, the whole period was marked by interest in religious questions and was deeply influenced by seriousness of thought and self-discipline of character, an outcome of the Puritan ethos . . . 'Self help' was a favourite motto. . . .
>
> (G. M. Trevelyan, *English Social History*, London 1944, p. 509)

This religious earnestness, showing itself in the 'respectability' that oppressed Tom Sawyer and Huck Finn as much as their English contemporaries, must also help to account for the high proportion of good farce, divertisement and nonsense in both countries during this interim period. These provide escape or regressive retreat, temporary but refreshing, from a conformity that is accepted, or half-accepted, though obscurely felt to be oppressive. Writer and reader go back to childhood, through the looking-glass, into wonderland, or off to the land of the Jumblies. The other common result of conformist pressures, of course, is likely to be thwarted rage; and the period is in fact also rich in lampoon and invective.

Some of this work, inevitably, borders on comedy (though comedy of a restricted scope); some of it might be mistaken for comedy. Hood's brilliant punning poems, for instance, share with much other work of the period a horrid fascination with physical disaster and decay as a source of laughter. Surely, from the writer of the 'Song of the Shirt', this must be mithridatic comedy, inuring people to the inevitable gruesomeness of a non-welfare state? But no, the pathetic tale of Ben Battle and faithless Nellie Gray does not use laughter to show up war or women, it uses *them* merely as sources of laughter. It is all play-wit, not tendency-wit. Similarly, at the other end of the century, Wilde's best play, *The Importance of Being Earnest*, is surely not a 'monument in comedy', as W. W. Robson maintains (*Modern English Literature*, Oxford 1970, p. 44), on the grounds that it undermines the Victorian concept of earnestness. For one thing, the action demonstrates only the importance of having the name Earnest. True, a pun is intended, but nothing much is made of it, ironically or otherwise. The frivolous dialogue *can* be seen as reformist mockery of Victorian seriousness, but we are not particularly encouraged to see it so; only to enjoy the frivolity. If there is mockery of anything, it is surely of the well-made romantic plays that dominated the theatre, disgusting Shaw, and infecting Wilde's own earlier plays. And even this seems rather doubtful. Are not they too rather a source of amusing absurdity than a subject of it?

The highpoint of Victorian repression was not reached until the 1870s—just about the time that a small circle of advanced thinkers were garnering the harvest of earlier sporadic forays against it; just about the time, too, that the interaction of growing population and growing industrialisation, each promoting the development of the other, was coming to be seen as a vicious spiral rather than a mark of Progress. This is when modern comedy begins, with Butler and

Shaw—but theirs is not so much a comedy *for* liberty or human values as one *against* hypocrisy, inconsistency, and inefficiency.

Increasingly thereafter, however, suspicion grows that the technology and *laissez-faire* philosophy of an overcrowded society were, more importantly, *dehumanising*—and shortly afterwards suspicion (among those able to value freedom more than protection) that the bureaucracy designed to control them was equally so. Unsurprisingly, then, as the dream of a brave new world, supposed first to be ushered in by the French Revolution, next by industrial free enterprise, and finally by single-party State control, comes to look ever more like a nightmare, the most striking comedy of Industrial Man seems to be founded in a fear of dehumanization.

Where most comedy of the past has been concerned with *civilising*, so to speak (still setting-up scaffolding), most of the more recent comedy that seems likely to last has been concerned with *humanising*. In a sense, English comedy has come almost full circle: being against the Establishment in the medieval period; by, for, and against the bourgeoisie in the renaissance-to-regency period; and against the Establishment, again in the modern period—this latter Establishment, too, giving rise to a sense of individual powerlessness before something vast, international, and inimical to the development of a fully human being. Mumford, along with many others who are far from comic writers, clearly reflects fears of barbarism and automatism similar to those so exuberantly fountained forth in the witty projections and paradoxical inventions of Huxley's satiric, ironically-titled *Brave New World* (1932):

> Man himself did not mirror the perfection of his instruments. Behind this empty technical fabric was an emptier ideology: one which multiplied quantities and forgot qualities: one which centred on the means of life and forgot its consummations.

> (Lewis Mumford, *The Condition of Man*, London 1944, p. 395)

Such views are now widely held and clearly articulated. They were less so in the first half of the present period; and are hardly discernible at all before about 1870. Though human-scale communities, and the accompanying 'sense of community', declined with the growth of industrial towns, it did not die out until the advent of the new housing estates and the development of ribbon development (based on car-ownership). And more relevant still is the fact of a genuine sharp increase in complexity and control: necessary to meet such calamities as World War I, the Slump and Depression, and World War II:

Until August 1914 a sensible, law-abiding Englishman could pass through life and hardly notice the existence of the state, beyond the post office and the policeman. He could live where he liked and as he liked. He had no official number or identity card. He could travel abroad or leave his country for ever without a passport or any sort of official permission. He could exchange his money for any other currency without restriction or limit. He could buy goods from any country in the world on the same terms as he bought goods at home.

(A. J. P. Taylor, *English History* 1914-1945, London 1970, p. 25)

To this change—especially unpalatable to writers, and others of the middle class—Larkin's 'Toads' expresses in brief a not-uncommon modern attitude, combining a longing for 'free' primitivism with a wry comic resignation, born of the knowledge of necessity—at any rate if one also wants civilised comfort and security in an overcrowded world:

> Why should I let the toad *work*
>> Squat on my life?
>
> ....
>
> Ah, were I courageous enough
>> To shout *Stuff your pension!*
> But I know, all too well, that's the stuff
>> That dreams are made on:
> For something sufficiently toad-like
>> Squats in me, too . . .
>
>> (Philip Larkin, *The Less Deceived*, Hull 1955, p. 30)

Already in 1872, Butler had written of stopping the development of machines lest they enslaved man (but only under the pretext of satirising the idea). In 1900, however, Bergson's assertion that the spectacle of men acting like automata was the chief source of laughter, found instant favour. Today comedy connected in some way or other with the idea of an ant-heap society is rather the rule than the exception. For since *Erewhon* the pace of change has progressively increased; so has population and collectivism; and Conservative and Labour, Democratic and Republican, Fascist and Communist governments have all conspicuously failed to provide a society fit for people to become fully human in—facts naturally reflected in the development of comedy.

Vanity Fair (1848), the best of the few complete comic works of the interim period, to some extent asserts the value of human vitality, set against a deadening social structure. But this is merely a by-product of Thackeray's desire to satirise the upper social circles, and any such valuation of Becky Sharp comes out in the novel as unconscious implication, not ostensible purport. Furthermore Becky did not *have* to be in that circle, whereas the modern protagonist is trapped in an unsought web. Anyway, Thackeray's real subject is human nature and individual morality, and his standards (like his setting) are backward-looking rather than forward-looking. Meredith's *The Egoist* (1879) consciously set forth the values of vitality and authenticity against those of egotism, sentimental ruthlessness, and hypocrisy, and thus marks a stage in the evolution of modern sensibility. But, again, the morality is wholly individual. There is truth, too, in Caudwell's suggestion that his style is significant of a fundamental weakness: '. . . the babble of a man unsure of himself and trying to distract attention from this' (Christopher Caudwell, *Romance and Realism*, ed. S. Hynes, Princeton, 1970, p. 82). Wilde puts it more wittily, in *The Decay of Lying*:

> Ah! Meredith! Who can define him? His style is chaos illumined by flashes of lightning. As a writer he has mastered everything except language: as a novelist he can do everything except tell a story: as an artist he is everything except articulate.
>
> (Oscar Wilde, Intentions, London 1891)

The most striking example of the divisive and inhibiting effect of the interim period is undoubtedly that of Dickens, who produced not a single complete comedy despite acute awareness of gross contemporary absurdities and an immense comic gift. *Pickwick* is farce; elsewhere there are many pockets of comedy, and a great gallery of comic characters; but only *Martin Chuzzlewit* (1844) bears any resemblance to a complete comic work. Indeed, the first few pages of Chapter IX might well be seen—though not without eyestrain—as an early symbolic representation of the unnatural intricacy and complexity of the new society (as the fog in *Bleak House* provides a central symbol of that book's main satiric concern, the law):

> You groped your way for an hour through lanes and byways, and courtyards, and passages; and you never once emerged upon anything that might reasonably be called a street. A kind of resigned distraction came over the stranger as he trod those devious mazes, and, giving himself up for lost, went in and out and round about and quietly turned back again when he came to a dead wall or was stopped by an iron railing, and felt that the means of escape might possibly present themselves in their own good time, but that to anticipate them was hopeless. Instances were known of people who, being asked to dine at Todgers's, had travelled round and round for a weary time, with its

very chimney-pots in view; and finding it, at last, impossible of attainment, had gone home again with a gentle melancholy on their spirits, tranquil and uncomplaining. Nobody had ever found Todgers's on a verbal direction, though given within a few minutes walk of it. Cautious emigrants from Scotland or the North of England had been known to reach it safely by impressing a charity-boy, town-bred, and bringing him along with them; or by clinging tenaciously to the postman; but these were rare exceptions, and only went to prove the rule that Todgers's was in a labyrinth, whereof the mystery was known but to a chosen few.

(Chap. IX)

However, the initial hypothesis would be overthrown by that 'tranquil and uncomplaining' if by nothing else. But there is also the extraordinary vitality, the sense rather of gladly *partaking* in this world than being overwhelmed by it. One is not so much amused, even, as elated. In fact, it represents that mixture of optimism and opposition, criticism and basic acceptance mentioned earlier amongst other possible reasons for the surprising shortage of complete comedies in this period. What the passage really symbolises (especially in context) is society's inconvenient yet fascinating complexity, its interesting cussedness and explorable ramification.

In any case, the proportion of melodrama connected with Jonas Chuzzlewit is large enough to rule out the book as a comedy. There is too the appalling sentimentality associated with Tom Pinch, of which the concluding paragraph of the work provides a more than sufficient sample:

And coming from a garden, Tom, bestrewn with flowers by children's hands, thy sister, little Ruth, as light of foot and heart as in old days, sits down beside thee. From the Present, and the Past, with which she is so tenderly entwined in all thy thoughts, thy strain soars onward to the Future. As it resounds within thee and without, the noble music, rolling round thee both, shuts out the grosser prospect of an earthly parting, and uplifts ye both to Heaven!

Moreover, the focus of the book—as with Thackeray and Meredith —is individualistic. Dickens's concern, like theirs, is with 'self':

Self; grasping, eager, narrow-ranging, over-reaching self; with its long train of suspicions, lusts, deceits, and all their growing consequences; was the root of the vile tree.

(Chap. III)

Yet oddly enough *Martin Chuzzlewit* does contain Dickens's most sustained piece of comedy, the largely self-contained American section, which shows in concentration the same greed, crookedness, and vulgarity revealed more dilutedly in the English scenes. But it is still only comedy of a New World not of a new age.

In America, that new comedy is symbolically bracketed by Twain's *Huckleberry Finn* (1884) and Heller's *Catch-22* (1961); in England by Butler's *Erewhon* (1872) and Stoppard's *Jumpers* (1972). Not that *Huckleberry Finn* is concerned with an industrial civilisation, any more than Butler is centrally concerned with machines. But, like Butler, Twain does make a radical break by unreservedly holding up to ironic mockery the accepted values of his age. During the course of the book, Huck Finn is to be re-educated *out of* Christian and civilised standards, and into a natural humanity. That slaves are treated as machines and thus dehumanised is as significant a part of this theme as the fact that the book opens with Huck's feeling 'all cramped up' by coming into money and the 'sivilization' going with it, and ends with his final rejection of the emerging society that was to become modern America, the paradigm of industrial civilisation:

> I reckon I got to light out for the Territory ahead of the rest, because Aunt Sally she's going to adopt me and sivilize me, and I can't stand it. I been there before.

The raft acts as an image of a better society: smaller, drifting rather than power-driven, non-racialist, free of such feuds as that of the Shepherdsons and Grangerfords; and it is on the raft that Huck is ironically shown as going to the dogs, losing the last vestiges of the morality of a civilised, Christian, property-owning new world:

> They went off and I got aboard the raft, feeling bad and low, because I knowed very well I had done wrong, and I see it warn't no use for me to try to learn to do right; a body that don't get *started* right when he's little, ain't got no show—when the pitch comes there ain't nothing to back him up and keep him to his work, and so he gets beat. Then I says to myself, hold on,—'spose you'd a done right and give Jim up; would you felt better than what you do now? No, says I, I'd feel bad— I'd feel just the same way I do now? Well then, says I, what's the use you learning to do right, when it's troublesome to do right and ain't no trouble to do wrong, and the wages is just the same? I was stuck. I couldn't answer that. So I reckoned I wouldn't bother no more about it, but after this always do whichever come handiest at the time.

(Chap. 16)

Heller is equally inspired in choosing another slave-world, the Air Force, as his symbol of contemporary society. His rendering is more

fantastic than Twain's but is still founded in reality; whereas Butler
and Stoppard more obviously write comedy of ideas. There does indeed
seem a slight tendency for British writers to be cooler, somewhat more
philosophical, keeping a greater comic distance—perhaps because
Americans, starting with ideals higher than ours but less deeply rooted
in society, always found the reality (usually more extreme anyway)
worse than they expected. Stoppard is rather a special case, since his
subject itself is philosophical. But it holds true of Nathanael West
and Samuel Beckett, both classifiable as nihilists; and of Vladimir
Nabokov and Evelyn Waugh, both cynics. *Lolita* (1955) is set in a
more fully realised, realistic world than any of Waugh's novels, and
cannot quite sustain its comic distance; at the end of the novel the
cynical poise falters and moralism creeps in (which does not prevent
its being rather better than the best of Waugh). In a different way—
a more formalistic way—it holds true also of, say, E. E. Cummings and
W. H. Auden. Both 'Next to of course God' (america i/love you land
of the pilgrims and so forth . . .) and 'Miss Gee, A Ballad' (Let me
tell you a little story/About Miss Edith Gee . . .) deal with dehumanisation, but Auden's tone is so consistently detached, in keeping with the
ballad pastiche, that the poetic experience itself becomes rather
inhumane. Cummings on the other hand is warmer, and a little
muddled, for the speaker, though generally regarded ironically,
occasionally seems to be a sincere mouthpiece for the author. Shaw,
too, keeps further from involvement and indignation than, say,
Elmer Rice, despite the alienation-effect of the expressionist technique
of *The Adding-Machine* (1923)—a bitter fantasy rather than a
comedy. But not too much should be made of this tendency.

More fruitful for appreciating particular works, is the realisation
that the brave-new-world comedy falls into three basic classes. For
there are three ways of reacting to what is felt—obscurely or clearly
—to be a complex, mechanised, bureaucratic system: the *optimistic*,
the *pessimistic*, and the *humanistic*. In the first case—that of Shaw
and Wells—the writer, like Marx and the other reformers noted by
Mumford—tacitly accepts something of the utilitarianism that has
produced the system and conceives of a better future 'in terms of the
widening triumphs of industrialism'. In the second case—that of
Twain, Beckett, Waugh, Eliot, and the West of *Miss Lonelyhearts*—
the persona (or the protagonist) washes his hands of the whole business,
lights out for some other territory: religion, death, some far-off land;
or becomes a recluse. In the third case—that of Auden, Orwell,
Huxley, and the author of the greatest of modern comedies, Joyce—

the writer tries to step outside the utilitarian and industrial framework of thought and assert other, more fundamental values. The first two classes produce a negatively 'human' comedy, in so far as they are against dehumanisation; the third produces a more positive 'human' comedy. The first group, so to speak, advocate perfecting, the second defecting, the third converting. The first are in some sense psychologically at home in the society they mock, the second would like to 'get the hell out it', the third gradually to transform its nature by insinuating more human values, or at the very least to ensure that these values should not be forgotten.

Obviously, the divisions will not be clear cut. A writer may well not be very optimistic about the prospect of transforming the values of the ant-heap from within, and so slide from conversion to defection. Or he may intellectually place himself in one group, like Wells, while being emotionally drawn to another. And, of course, writers may very properly differ in different works . . .

Wells, for instance, clearly thought of himself as a member of the first class. Until his later years, at any rate, he was optimistic about the shape of things to come; and that shape was the current shape projected into the future, but grown up: no longer a grubby, untidy little capitalist but a clean shining well-developed socialist. The two comedies for which he is remembered, *Kipps* (1905) and *The History of Mr. Polly* (1910) certainly endeavour to fulfil this role—sometimes rather desperately. In Chapter V I I, of *Mr. Polly*, for instance, he intrudes in his own person, with elephantine humour, to introduce 'a certain high-browed gentleman living at Highbury', and goes on to quote him at length:

> 'A rapidly complicating society,' he writes, 'which as a whole declines to contemplate its future or face the intricate problems of its organization, is in exactly the position of a man who takes no thought of dietary or regimen, who abstains from baths and exercise and gives his appetites free play. It accumulates useless and aimless lives, as a man accumulates fat and morbid products in his blood; it declines in its collective efficiency and vigour, and secretes discomfort and misery. Every phase of its evolution is accompanied by a maximum of avoidable distress and inconvenience and human waste . . .'

At the end of the intrusion he excuses himself by asserting:

> I feel this has to come in here as the broad aspect of this History.

In fact, it comes in rather as an intermittent aspect. The novel does not really bring out much sense of the deeper social causes of Mr

Polly's unhappiness; and if it survives today it does so in spite of
Wells's dutiful and vague gestures towards socialist solutions, not
because of them. In *Kipps* a socialist *guru* is hauled in by the hair.
But what does his final message turn out to be? 'Get the hell out
of it'!

> 'I wonder what I said,' said Masterman in parenthesis. 'Anyhow,
> you're doing the right and sane thing, and that's a rare spectacle. You're
> going to marry your equal, and you're going to take your own line,
> quite independently of what people up there or people down there
> think you ought or ought not to do. That's about the only course one
> can take nowadays, with everything getting more muddled and upside
> down every day. Make your own little world and your own house first
> of all; keep that right side up whatever you do, and marry your
> mate...'

(Chap. IX, 1)

This squares well enough, too, with the Huck Finn solution in
Mr. Polly:

> He could, for example, 'clear out'.
> It became a wonderful and alluring phrase to him—'Clear out!'

And clear out he does, from town to country, leaving his wife a
little capital in the form of insurance money and finding himself a
modest prosperity at the idyllic Potwell Inn—rather as Kipps finds
a second fortune at the same time as his socialism, after escaping first
from the restraints of the commercial system and next from those of
the snob-system.

The truth is that Wells's socialism is superficial, though he *is*
deeply concerned with the plight of people trapped in the webs of
commerce and convention—especially the former. How blighting to
a full life that could be is shown graphically in the opening chapters
of Kipps; and even more in the following fascinating document from a
survivor from the period:

> These were the requirements of employment at a Burnley cotton mill
> office before the turn of the century. The 'requirements', under the
> heading of 'Office Staff Practices' are listed thus:
>
> 1. Godliness, Cleanliness and Punctuality are the necessities of a
> good business.
>
> 2. This firm has reduced the hours of work, and the clerical staff
> will be present between the hours of 7 a.m. and 6 p.m. on week-days.
>
> 3. Daily prayers will be held each morning in the main office. The
> clerical staff will be present.
>
> 4. Clothing must be of a sober nature. The clerical staff will not
> disport themselves in raiment of bright colours, nor will they wear
> hose, unless in good repair.

5. Overshoes and topcoats may not be worn in the office, but neckscarves and headwear may be worn in inclement weather.

6. A stove is provided for the benefit of the clerical staff. Coal and wood must be kept in the locker. It is recommended that each member of the clerical staff bring four pounds of coal each day during the cold weather.

7. No member of clerical staff may leave the room without permission from Mr. Rogers. The calls of nature are permitted and clerical staff may use the garden below the second gate. This area must be kept in good order.

8. No talking is allowed during business hours.

9. The craving of tobacco, wines or spirits is a human weakness, and as such is forbidden to all members of the clerical staff.

10. Now that the hours of business have been drastically reduced, the partaking of food is allowed between 11.30 a.m. and noon, but work will not, on any account, cease.

11. Members of the clerical staff will provide their own pens. A new sharpener is available on application to Mr Rogers.

12. Mr Rogers will nominate a senior clerk to be responsible for the cleanliness of the Main Office and the Private Office and all boys and juniors will report to him 40 minutes before prayers, and will remain after closing hours for similar work. Brushes, brooms, scrubbers and soap are provided by the owners.

13. The new increased weekly wages are as hereunder detailed: Junior boys (to 11 years) 1s. 4d., boys (to 14 years) 2s. 1d., Juniors 4s. 8d., Junior Clerks 8s. 7d., Clerks 10s. 9d., Senior Clerks (after 15 years with owners) 21s.

The owners recognise the generosity of the new Labour Laws but will expect a great rise in output of work to compensate for these near Utopian conditions.

(*Nottingham Evening Post*, 28 August 1971)

Having experienced this sort of cramping existence Wells seems to have been very naturally sympathetic to the wish to escape at all costs. So despite periodic attempts to regard his characters in a scientific way, as biological specimens, despite good intentions of relating them to socialist doctrine, we find luck and private enterprise providing solutions and the characters humanising themselves by *dropping out* of the petty bourgeoisie. In so far as his comedies are integrative, they are so in an individualistic way, and depend on quirky, untypical characters. The tone and tenor is tolerant, not doctrinaire, and in short his comedies are nearer to the second class than the first.

Beckett, on the other hand, is completely unified and very definitely in the class he seems to be in: the comedy of withdrawal and despair, of hilarious pessimism. So much is this so, that it is questionable whether *Waiting for Godot*, his one indisputable masterpiece, should count as comedy or not. It exists at the common vanishing-point of tragedy, farce, and nihilistic comedy; but can in fact be profitably seen as minimal comedy,* of a philosophical sort. There are two acts, covering two days: the minimum required to suggest endless sequence. In one act, a tree, the only stage-prop, has leaves, in the other it is leafless—just enough to suggest endless repetition. Of the two pairs of characters, one suggests man's psychological division into extrovert and introvert, optimistic and pessimistic, the other, his class-division into boss and bossed. The names are Russian, French, Italian and English. So the localised action, motivated plot, and personalised characters of the normal play are abandoned for the grander concerns of metaphysical philosophy: Mankind Anywhere and Always.

Beckett is clearly not the sentimentalist (who knows the value of everything and the price of nothing), but neither is he quite the cynic (who knows the price of everything and the value of nothing); nor does he take the humanistic middle-way (knowing both the price and value of everything). In fact, he is a nihilist, for whom everything has no value and no price. Thus life is taken to be entirely pointless (though we cannot be *sure* even of this negative certainty) and all human activities, spiritual or physical, are merely ways of passing the time (which, as Estragon says, would have passed anyway). As *any*thing will pass the time, there is no point in positive effort:

VLADIMIR   Nothing you can do about it.
ESTRAGON   No use struggling.
VLADIMIR   One is what one is.
ESTRAGON   No use wriggling.
VLADIMIR   The essential doesn't change.
ESTRAGON   Nothing to be done.

(Act 1)

Thus absolved from responsibility, we can revel in the textural absurdities of *non sequitur* and non-listening, and even in the structural progression from fairly healthy inertia, through decay, towards the grave we are 'born astride' of. Despite the grim situation of the protagonists the play is hilariously funny. In this philosophical context, and dealing with types rather than persons, we can be amused

* A case made out more fully in Rodway, 'Minimal Comedy: *Waiting for Godot*', *The Truths of Fiction*, London 1970.

at truths of moral and logical absurdity in human behaviour that would normally arouse only pity or horror (that is why the work can profitably be regarded as a work of *comic* art):

> Pozzo Well to begin with he should pull on the rope, as hard as he likes so long as he doesn't strangle him. He usually responds to that. If not, he should give him a taste of his boot, in the face and privates as far as possible.
>
> Vladimir (*to Estragon*) You see, you've nothing to be afraid of. It's even an opportunity to revenge yourself.
>
> Estragon And if he defends himself?
>
> Vladimir I'll come flying to the rescue.
>
> Estragon Don't take your eyes off me.
>
> (*He goes towards Lucky*)
>
> Vladimir Make sure he's alive before you start. No point in exerting yourself if he's dead.
>
> Estragon (*bending over Lucky*) He's breathing.
>
> Vladimir Then let him have it.
>
> *With sudden fury Estragon starts kicking Lucky, hurling abuse at him as he does so. But he hurts his foot and moves away, limping and groaning. Lucky stirs.*
>
> Estragon On the brute!

If all our serious activities are really absurd rituals to pass the time as we decay, all our civilisation an elaborate Meccano-game, then nothing has point, and the only worthwhile value is stoicism. This is indeed the value purveyed by *Waiting for Godot*, and by Beckett's other works (which, however, probably pass beyond the bounds of comedy, funny though many of them are in places). An unusual mood in comedy, for 'stoicism' traditionally smacks of nobility, whether real, as with Boethius and Socrates, or religious—putting the clock fast—as with Seneca. Beckett's, however, is an *ig*noble stoicism.

His non-character in the short non-story 'The End' refers to '. . . the story I might have told, a story in the likeness of my life, I mean, without the courage to end or the strength to go on.' (*No's Knife*, London 1967, p. 67). This *is* the story Beckett tells, over and over, edging—from *Godot* onwards—to a literary 'death', as his impersonages edge to a literal one: sans action, sans character, sans plot, sans words, sans everything. He shows stoicism not in exhortatory word or exceptional deed, but during the daily creep of a backward evolution from human to animal to stock-and-stone. While waiting, his derelicts neither despair nor defy; they endure, as if anticipating the earth they are to become. Beckett's minimal comedy, then, the comedy of characters who have opted out in every possible way, is *mithridatic* It indicates a way of death-in-life for the aged, the imprisoned or the bedridden; shows the spirit of non-resistance needed to pass the time with fewer and fewer resources, to make do with less and less, make the best of bad businesses, be thankful for ever-smaller mercies. His works, as it were, are Get Worse cards for those in hospital, in the end bed; and they gradually get more gruesome and less funny after *Waiting for Godot*.

Beckett's nihilism is philosophical, Nathanael West's is not; and therefore his comedy is less logical and consistent. Moreover, it is less hilarious. Since he is not quite sure whether he is opting out or not, we sometimes feel for his stricken characters, rather than sharing the comic viewpoint of the gods, 'who kill us for their sport'. Beckett's consistency, however, is not necessarily wholly beneficial. It is arguable that he is logical but not reasonable, metaphysical rather than sensible, and therefore—starting from two fashionable, but fallacious assumptions—arrives eventually at a half-dead-end.

That the universe is absurd and thus at every point pointless, is the first assumption; the fallacy being that though *existence as a whole* may be absurd—and very disappointing to those brought up to believe otherwise—it by no means follows that the *whole of existence* is absurd. The second assumption is that the universe is absurd because it acts arbitrarily, and thus unjustly, towards mankind. Anthropomorphically speaking, this is allowable; victims of fire, flood, earthquake or disease, may well feel they live in a hostile world—but still it is not an *absurd* one, for even its most violent acts are not arbitrary; rather, they are the results of unalterable law. To be generally pessimistic on this account and complain of injustice is to confuse natural law with human law—the absurdity lying with the plaintiff, not the universe. For all their façade of modernism, Beckett's plays are medieval in their assumption that the end of life is the whole of life, that no purpose or reason beyond life entails none within it. But in fact, as we read or watch, we are apt to realise that we are not all the time ill, poor and filled with boredom, that along with the self-deception, the absurdity, the fundamental isolation and pointlessness of the human situation, goes the achievement, the gusto, the variety and (at any rate before we are too stricken) the worthwhileness of life. That is why we are able to find the gruesomeness funny.

West's nihilism, like that of the Absurdists, springs from the modern world; but in not springing so far from it, in sticking to the local and temporal, he gains more in plausibility than he loses in consistency. Like Beckett, he shows people at the end of their tether, but they are still fully alive and reacting. Ultimately his novels suggest an 'Absurd' universe of suffering, but proximately they deal with the here-and-now of the Depression. Like Joyce, he shows the absurdity of men's pretence to grandeur and nobility, the inability of people to be more than human, but he can't quite achieve Joyce's Homeric laughter. He is destructive of self-deception—which one could regard as a sort of game—but the laugh is on the civilisation that drives people to it, not on the characters:

> Why laugh at himself, however, when Shrike was waiting at the speakeasy to do a much better job? 'Miss Lonelyhearts, my friend, I advise you to give your readers stones. When they ask for bread don't give them crackers as does the Church, and don't, like the State, tell them to eat cake. Explain that man cannot live by bread alone and give them stones. Teach them to pray each morning: "Give us this day our daily stone".'
>
> He had given his readers many stones; so many, in fact, that he had only one left—the stone that had formed in his gut.
>
> (*Miss Lonelyhearts*, New York 1933, Chap. 2)

Miss Lonelyhearts's column is not only a symbol of that self-deception, but also a symbol of West's view of society (and life); and he is not finally affirmative of both, like Joyce. As the truly dreadful, ill-expressed letters roll in, 'all of them alike, stamped from the dough of suffering with a heart-shaped cookie knife', to be answered—and no better answer seems possible—with 'Life *is* worth while, for it is full of dreams . . . and faith that burns like a clear white flame on a grim dark altar', we come to feel that nothing can be done save to sugar pills for an incurable disease, life, and try hard to find the hypocrisy funny.

A Cool Million (1934) is more directly sociological, and might seem to come into our first category of optimistic socialist reform. Certainly it mocks the capitalist dream. Lemuel Pitkin seeks fortune through free enterprise. In the event, he loses his teeth, his eyes, a leg, his scalp, and is finally shot by a political assassin. However he has previously been the dupe of both Communist and Fascist organisations:

> 'But he did not live or die in vain. Through his martyrdom the National Revolutionary Party triumphed, and by that triumph this country was delivered from sophistication, Marxism and International Capitalism. . .'

We are left feeling wryly that the sickness is beyond any cure, social or personal:

> ... Ought I commit suicide?
> Sincerely yours,
> Desperate.

The implied, cynically mithridatic answer seems to be *Yes*.

If West, among other things, is exposing capitalism, in bitter, witty comedy, Orwell in *Animal Farm* (his only comedy) is exposing communism. His comedy is structural more than textural—though the famous afterthought, the pigs' revision of 'All animals are equal' to 'All animals are equal but some animals are more equal than others', is both a structural turning-point in the fable and also a brilliantly condensing witticism. More importantly, though, Orwell differs from West (and Beckett) by being in the third category. Implicit in *Animal Farm* (explicit in *Nineteen Eighty-Four*, which satirises clerical and fascist totalitarianism as well as communist) is the positive of empirical humanism. Societies, he implies, should not be based on an all-embracing theory, nor operate through an all-embracing system. Also implicit (though more obviously in *Nineteen Eighty-Four*) is the idea that society should provide units of a 'human' scale. For him, as for other modern comic writers, giantism is suspect.

His limpid style is admirably adapted to the kind that *Animal Farm* is cast in, the beast fable. Such fables were normally used to reduce moral problems to diagrammatic form, to clarify what was essential out of the multifarious detail of reality—till the veriest fool could see the point. Orwell is concerned to demonstrate, however, not a moral absurdity but an intellectual one. If moral feelings come into the book at all (for example, pity and indignation at Boxer's being sold to the knackers) they do so only slightly. The mere fact that the characters are animals, not human beings, diminishes such feelings —which Orwell was never good at conveying anyway; we do not expect animals to show loving-kindness and are not, therefore, morally outraged when they don't. The beast-fable uses animal characteristics to illustrate and objectify certain *aspects* of human nature: foxy cunning, doglike devotion, piggish greed, and so on; and the animals are humanised just sufficiently to indicate that their chief characteristic is to be found in man. Inevitably this suggests that any man who is dominated by one trait, like an animal, is sub-human: satirisably absurd.

History, of course, had already given Orwell the fabulous facts,

H

the Revolution having revolved one turn too many. The beast-fable technique gave him various other elements of his satiric comedy: detachment, so that the demonstration of paradox in the relationship of Marxist theory with communist practice should not be blurred by feeling; automatic comment on classes of people (such as the sheep who bleat in droves whatever the propagandists choose to put into their silly heads, or the fanatically faithful but uncritical and amoral dogs); a smallscale, fundamental, practical realm (the farmyard) where the difference between theory and practical results could be clearly shown; but above all it gave him a self-evident positive, that needed no preaching: a standard of full humanity—and by implication a social structure that would permit a richer life than that of 'Animal-ism'. The technique also provided a constant supply of relevant textural ironies, such as the turning point of the Revolution when 'Comrade Napoleon sprang forward with a cry of "Death to Human-ity!" and sank his teeth in Jones's leg,' or for that matter, the name Napoleon itself, with its reminder of a previous Revolution that went wrong.

Where Huxley satirised the brave new world of Wellsian science, and the utilitarian 'greatest happiness' principle (though constantly slipping into uncomic nostalgia for Victorian Christian hymns and sexual mores, to say nothing of occasional neurotic masochism—thereby ending with a conserving and restraining comedy), Orwell satirises the *political* brave new world, because in practice—since it is single-party—it departs from a human norm, and he thus ends with a didactic comedy that is integrative and life-enhancing in tendency, though its rather cynical surface suggests a mithridatic purport.

Auden also falls, and more obviously, into the third group, at any rate in his later period. Both earlier and later, much that is called 'comic' verse would be better styled 'light verse' ('divertisement' by our definitions). The little that would properly count as comedy in the earlier period is, of course, 'optimistic' directly or indirectly since it is based on the assumption that a *communistic* industrial, bureaucratic society will provide the good life currently in abeyance. Mostly the assumption is pretty far in the background, and the tone is uncertain: sometimes one feels that the irony is in fact self-protective, disguising doubts about the stance taken. These doubts became conscious and explicit as early as the *Letter to Lord Byron* (1937):

> Hail to the New World! Hail to those who'll love
> Its antiseptic objects, feel at home...

....
Preserve me from the Shape of Things to Be ...
(Section II)

More, neurosis—once symbol of economic and personal corruption,
curable only by communism—comes to be approved:

> I hate the modern trick, to tell the truth,
>   Of straightening out the kinks in the young mind,
> Our passion for the tender plant of youth,
>   Our hatred for all weeds of any kind.
> Slogans are bad: the best that I can find
> Is this: 'Let each child have that's in our care
> As much neurosis as the child can bear.'

(Section IV)

This change is confirmed by a confession in his latest collection of
shorter poems:

> A dishonest poem is one which expresses, no matter how well, feelings
> or beliefs which its author never felt or entertained. For example, I
> once expressed a desire for 'New styles of architecture': but I have
> never liked modern architecture. I prefer *old* styles, and one must be
> honest even about one's prejudices.

(*Collected Shorter Poems*, 1927-57, London 1966, Foreword)

For a short period the political zeal and censoriousness that militated
against comic geniality tended to be transferred to religion. But after
1950 or so, by which time his conversion had been digested, Auden
became relaxed and tolerant—on the same principles that brought
Kierkegaard to despair. If the world and its inhabitants are both
fallen and blessed, and therefore people are 'human' only if frail and
inconsistent; if the divine is necessarily unknowable; and if (since in
fallen ignorant man *any* course of action will be imperfect) nothing in
life on earth is of fundamental importance—then *angst* or, as in
Auden's case, a serene human comedy are equally possible. From
1950 onwards there is almost no specifically religious poetry, apart
from 'Horae Canonicae', but the 'absurd' human condition is celebrated.

His real comic period begins at this time. He is now *anti*-Utopian
(and pro-Arcadian), now *opposed* to the well-regulated society of
bureaucracy and management, and in favour of a more 'human'
golden mean:

> For Sun and Moon supply their conforming masks, but in this
> hour of civil twilight all must wear their own faces.
> And it is now that our two paths cross.

Both simultaneously recognize their anti-type: that I am an Arcadian, that he is a Utopian.

He notes, with contempt, my Aquarian belly: I note, with alarm, his scorpion's mouth.

He would like to see me cleaning latrines: I would like to see him removed to some other planet.

Neither speaks. What experience could we possibly share? Glancing at a lampshade in a store window, I observe it is too hideous for anyone in their senses to buy: He observes it is too expensive for a peasant to buy.

Passing a slum child with rickets, I look the other way: He looks the other way if he passes a chubby one.

I hope our senators will behave like saints, provided they don't reform me: He hopes they will behave like *baritoni cattivi*, and, when lights burn late in the Citadel,

I (who have never seen the inside of a police station) am shocked and think: 'Were the city as free as they say, after sundown all her bureaus would be huge black stones':

He (who has been beaten up several times) is not shocked at all but thinks: 'One fine night our boys will be working up there.'

You can see, then, why, between my Eden and his New Jerusalem, no treaty is negotiable.

('Vespers', 'Horae Canonicae', *The Shield of Achilles*, 1955)

In 'The Managers' (*Nones*, 1952) the organisers of our complex society are regarded with humorous contempt—not satiric contempt: the perspectival references to history and art and the esthetic game of the rhyme-scheme both combining to block indignation:

> . . . Could one of them
>   Be said to resemble
> The tragic Hero, the Platonic Saint,
>   Or would any painter
> Portray one rising triumphant from a lake
>   On a dolphin, naked,
> Protected by an umbrella of cherubs? Can
>   They so much as manage
> To behave like genuine Caesars when alone
>   Or drinking with cronies,
> To let their hair down and be frank about
>   The world? It is doubtful.
> The last word on how we may live or die
>   Rests today with such quiet
> Men, working too hard in rooms that are too big,
>   Reducing to figures
> What is the matter, what is to be done.

'The Fall of Rome' in the same volume is also perspectival, looking backwards, forwards, and sideways, to achieve a comedy not of laughter but quizzical resignation. Two rigid, complex societies are compared with each other:

> Caesar's double-bed is warm
> As an unimportant clerk
> Writes I DO NOT LIKE MY WORK
> On a pink official form,

and then—sideways—are contrasted with the great natural simplicity that will outlast them, and beside which they are found absurdly wanting:

> Altogether elsewhere, vast
> Herds of reindeer move across
> Miles and miles of golden moss,
> Silently and very fast.

Elsewhere, too, small signs are seen as significant of coming disaster, the crash of the whole elaborate edifice:

> A small grove massacred to the last ash,
> An oak with heart-rot, give away the show:
> This great society is going smash;
> They cannot fool us with how fast they go...
>
> ('Woods', *The Shield of Achilles*, 1955)

But Auden is not quite opting out; rather he is 'laying bets upon the human race/Retaining enough decency to last' ('Woods'); for there is always Nature to help it when civilisation has failed. Thus the celebratory comedy of the nature poems supports the 'human' comedy —the possibility of transformation, in the current crisis, if men will live more naturally, cease trying to be gods or Caesars, and settle for average, *moyen sensuel* humanity. The conception finds its finest expression in the long-lined, much-modulated poem 'In Praise of Limestone' (*Nones*, 1952), which is, as Replogle says 'mildly funny' but a 'comic masterpiece', the amusement coming largely from dictional 'incongruities . . . many of them subtle and delicate and unobtrusive' (Justin Replogle, *Auden's Poetry*, London 1969, p. 237). Here the limestone landscape, small-scale, moderate, easily turns into a symbol of the centrally human, neither greatly good nor vilely evil:

> What could be more like Mother or a fitter background
> For her son, the flirtatious male who lounges
> Against a rock in the sunlight, never doubting
> That for all his faults he is loved; whose works are but

> Extensions of his power to charm? From weathered outcrop
>   To hill-top temple, from appearing waters to
> Conspicuous fountains, from a wild to a formal vineyard,
>   Are ingenious but short steps that a child's wish
> To receive more attention than his brothers, whether
>   By pleasing or teasing, can easily take.
> Watch, then, the band of rivals as they climb up and down
>   Their steep stone gennels in twos and threes, sometimes
>   Arm in arm, but never, thank God, in step...

Saints and Caesars seek more 'immoderate soils', and are allowed to be right in doing so, for their landscapes are more in tune with the modern world, their idealistic abstraction comparable to our 'greatest comfort . . . music/Which can be made anywhere, is invisible,/And does not smell.' Nevertheless, the limestone land is not now a mere irrelevance, 'A backward/And dilapidated province . . . with a certain/ Seedy appeal . . . .':

>   . . . Not quite;
>   It has a worldly duty which in spite of itself
>   It does not neglect, but calls into question
>   All the Great Powers assume; it disturbs our rights.

And finally limestone man and his landscape are preferred; in the very last analysis this moderation is better than the overreaching of high endeavour:

>   . . . when I try to imagine a faultless love
>   Or the life to come, what I hear is the murmur
>   Of underground streams, what I see is a limestone landscape.

Space forbids any further examination, however brief, of other varieties of comedy within the brave-new-world spectrum. Perhaps mention should be made, however, of those not in it, or at best only on the ultra-violet or infra-red fringes. Synge's *Playboy of the Western World*, for example, may *signify* a reaction against Edwardian civilisation but its comic identity, its *meaning*, antedates civilisation. James and Conrad, not normally thought of as writers of comedy (though James, like Dickens, has a good deal of comic writing throughout his works), each wrote one indisputable comedy: *The Bostonians* and *The Secret Agent*. Both are masterpieces of sustained irony—and therefore, rather unusually, use the omniscient narrator technique—both aim for what James desiderated in the Preface to his first novel, 'the greater complexity, the superior truth', and both are conserving and restraining—and slightly biassed: James implying that because

some feminists were neurotics feminism was nonsense, Conrad rather
too easily reducing anarchist idealism to personal laziness and shiftless-
ness. They could, then, be related to our governing concept, since
feminism and anarchism represent two attempted contributions
towards the nineteenth-century vision of a brave new world. But these
movements provide only the subjects, not the real themes of the novels.
Conrad's main concern is with the question of morality: What is
'trustworthiness,'? 'idealism',? 'faithfulness,'? 'respectability'? James's
with matters of self-delusion and psychological domination. Similarly
Anthony Powell's as yet uncompleted *Music of Time*, though set
firmly within its society, derives its comedy, as the title suggests,
mainly from time not space, from closely observed people rather than
any general vision of the modern world, whether for or against. Not
all modern comedy, then, can be included in the three, fluid categories embraced by the term 'brave new world'; but when time has
finished its sifting it seems likely to be such comedy that is regarded as
characteristic of the industrial age. So it seems proper to conclude with
a somewhat closer look at one or two representative examples from
each category.

B. i. Butler, Shaw

Man's very soul is due to the machines; it is a machine-made thing;
he thinks as he thinks, and feels as he feels, through the work that
machines have wrought upon him, and their existence is quite as much
a *sine qua non* for him, as his for theirs. This fact precludes us from
proposing the complete annihilation of machinery, but surely it
indicates that we should destroy as many of them as we can possibly
dispense with, lest they should tyrannize over us even more completely.

True, from a low materialistic point of view, it would seem that those
thrive best who use machinery where its use is possible with profit;
but this is the art of the machines—they serve that they may rule.
They bear no malice towards man for destroying a whole race of them
provided he creates a better instead; on the contrary they reward him
liberally for having hastened their development . . . Though our
rebellion against their infant power will cause infinite suffering, what
will not things come to, if that rebellion is delayed?

They have preyed upon man's grovelling preference for his material
over his spiritual interests, and have betrayed him into supplying that
element of struggle and warfare without which no race can advance . . .
even now the machines will only serve on condition of being served,
and that too upon their own terms . . .

(Samuel Butler, *Erewhon*, London 1872, Chapter XXIV)

The argument against machines is developed at great length, and with formidable plausibility (though under the thinnest guise of satire); so too, is the argument for treating crime as illness (in this case by the devastating inversion and parody involved in an Erewhonian trial of illness as crime). Behind such arguments seems to lie the criterion of a 'human' norm. Surely their tendency is innovatory and humanising? It is; yet Butler turns out to be more akin to the first group than the third, insofar as he is thoroughly at home with his society's basic utilitarianism though bitterly against its superficial romanticism, especially as it showed itself in religion, culture, and hypocrisy. In short, his comedy purports to be innovatory but is fundamentally conserving; it is however psychologically releasing, though not integrative. Butler is against the machine society but for capitalism in its most ruthless form; he opposed Victorian religion and the puritanism and hypocrisy that went with it, but accepted the basic assumptions of his age, its *real* principles—as shown in action— as against its theoretical ones. His is comedy of ideas, but it is far from philosophical.

P. N. Furbank, in his excellent *Samuel Butler* (Cambridge, 1948), speaks of *The Way of All Flesh* (1884, published 1903) as belonging essentially to the literature of conversion: a remark that may be extended to include all the essential Butler. He doesn't painstakingly correct dogmatism, Darwinism, and science, but suddenly has a bright idea—behind which one senses an emotional rather than an intellectual impetus—and straightway turns the old idea inside out:

> Everything is like a purse—there may be money in it, and we can generally say by the feel of it whether there is or not. Sometimes, however, we must turn it inside out before we can be quite sure whether there is anything in it or not. When I have turned a proposition inside out, put it to stand on its head and shaken it, I have often been surprised to find how much came out of it.
>
> (*The Note-Books of Samuel Butler*, ed. H. F. Jones, London 1912, p. 224)

There were psychological complications too. Butler obviously had a need to revolt against authority (as we see not only from his attitude to his own stern clerical father but from his attitude to all father-figures). He also had a need for security (witness his attitude to money, for him the stated root of all *good*—as it was in practice for his less honest contemporaries). He is therefore the most conservative and bourgeois of rebels, next to Dr Johnson. And most of his rebellion seems to be the product of fear and thwarted rage, which resulted in destructiveness and possessiveness—somewhat incompatible qualities.

True, there is a sense of unity in Butler, as the same ideas crop up again and again in different contexts; but it is constantly offset by a sense of perversity, coming from evident desires to shock and rebel, combined with acquiescence in bourgeois behaviour, money worship, and timidity. All these points could be illustrated from the novels, but are more handily available, as isolated items, in the *Note-books*, which are the source of many of the best things in the novels:

> There are two great rules of life, the one general and the other particular. The first is that everyone can, in the end, get what he wants if he only tries. This is the general rule. The particular rule is that every individual is more or less an exception to the general rule.
>
> *(Note-books*, p. 11)

A typical Butlerian puzzle, Is this ironic? Or plainly true? If so, is *what* true? Or is he perversely shooting us and drowning us?

> Man is but a perambulating tool-box and workshop, or office, fashioned for itself by a piece of very clever slime, as a result of long experience; and truth is but its own most enlarged, general and enduring sense of the coming togetherness or con-venience of the various conventional arrangements which for some reason or other it has been led to sanction. Hence we speak of a man's body as his 'trunk'.
>
> (Ibid. p. 18)

A shocking and perverse definition of truth combined with a plausible and serious idea of a human body—an idea used in the anti-machinist brief in *Erewhon*. But what of the following? A point Butler makes over and over again, and not only in comic works, but impossible to take wholly seriously (and unprofitable if one did):

> All eating is a kind of proselytising—a kind of dogmatising—a maintaining that the eater's way of looking at things is better than the eatee's. We convert the food, or try to do so, to our own way of thinking, and, when it sticks to its own opinion and refuses to be converted, we say it disagrees with us. An animal that refuses to let another eat it has the courage of its convictions and, if it gets eaten, dies a martyr to them. So we can only proselytise fresh meat, the convictions of putrid meat being too strong for us.
>
> It is good for a man that he should not be thwarted—that he should have his own way as far, and with as little difficulty as possible. Cooking is good because it makes matters easier by unsettling the meat's mind and preparing it for new ideas. All food must first be prepared for us by animals or plants, or we cannot assimilate it; and so thoughts are made more easily assimilated that have been already digested by other minds. A man should avoid converse with things that have been stunted or starved, and should not eat such meat as has been overdriven

or underfed or afflicted with disease, nor should he touch fruit or vegetables that have not been well grown.

Sitting quiet after eating is akin to sitting still during divine service so as not to disturb the congregation. We are catechising and converting our proselytes, and there should be no row. As we get older we must digest more quietly still, our appetite is less, our gastric juices are no longer so eloquent, they have lost that cogent fluency which carried away all that came in contact with it. They have become sluggish and unconciliatory. This is what happens to any man when he suffers from an attack of indigestion.

(Ibid. p. 81)

An anticipation of psycho-somatic medicine? A muddle, in which metaphor is mistaken for argument? A leg-pull? Or an idea for comically satirising religious conversion? Perhaps something of all. Certainly Butler has a gift for seizing on an amusing idea or incident and seeing comic significance in it:

I read of a man who was cured of a dangerous illness by eating his doctor's prescription which he understood was the medicine itself. So William Sefton Moorhouse imagined he was being converted to Christianity by reading Burton's *Anatomy of Melancholy*, which he had got by mistake for Butler's *Analogy*, on the recommendation of a friend. But it puzzled him a good deal.

(Ibid. p. 311)

Here we have comedy based on sensible perceptions about psycho-somatic action and conversion; and such comedy is just about as common in Butler's novels as the more cranky sort.

It is by *Erewhon* and *The Way of all Flesh* that he stands or falls. Neither comes within hailing distance of Jamesian or Conradian standards of the well-wrought novel. *Erewhon* especially is like the notebooks, a patchwork of provocative brilliance, perversity and prejudices; a slender thread of story yokes together a number of pre-existing articles. *The Way of all Flesh* combines realistic (autobiographical) material with fantastic satire and 'notebook' bright ideas. Certain incoherences in the works arise because Butler believed or half-believed in some of the things he was ostensibly mocking—so that the mockery is sometimes indistinguishable from the didactic message. Again, attacks resulting from personal feeling and prejudice queerly intermingle with genuine intellectual comedy of inquiry. And there is the overinsistence—going far beyond a stimulating joke—on the positive *moral* virtue of good looks, good luck, and a private income.

Erewhon's title ('nowhere' backwards) is typical of the reversal technique that is the main method of his comedy. It may well be his best book; but if so, it is on account of the quality of separate parts, for the whole is a heap. Like the note-books, it sparkles with barbed asides:

> But the main argument on which they rely is that of economy; for they know they will sooner gain their end by appealing to men's pockets, in which they have generally something of their own, than to their heads, which contain for the most part little but borrowed or stolen property.
>
> (Chap. XII)

The Judge's speech to the tubercular culprit is a masterly, and morally shaking, pastiche. Humanity, sense, and brilliance are marvellously combined. But it is an unstable combination, for on the next page we see that Butler is inclined to *agree* with the Erewhonians (perhaps getting the repellent power of the court scene from this temporarily repressed, and surely perverse, inclination):

> I write with great diffidence, but it seems to me that there is no unfairness in punishing people for their misfortunes, or rewarding them for their sheer good luck; it is the normal condition of human life that this should be done, and no right-minded person will complain of being subjected to the common treatment.
>
> (Chap. XII)

Satire on the Churches (the Musical Banks) and Oxbridge (the Colleges of Unreason, specialising in the hypothetical language) is straightforward and rather dated. On the other hand, the Book of the Machines, and the following chapters on the Rights of Animals and the Rights of Vegetables are confused by the author's underlying belief in the things he is putting forward as Erewhonian absurdities. Two contradictory movements are going on at once, and the commonsensical style gives only an illusion of clarity. We come out with the paradoxical impression of *sensible* absurdities—for Butler, of course, does think that men are 'workshops,' 'toolboxes,' machines; so it does follow that machines could evolve and eventually supersede us. Moreover, he believes in elements of consciousness or purpose throughout matter, so the arguments for abstaining from animal flesh *and* vegetables—though put forward as absurdities—have some cogency, and have to be countered by two of Butler's other doctrines: that commonsense is preferable to logic, and that physical superiority is a form of moral superiority (from which it would follow that it is all right to eat the less dangerous animals and vegetables, but that we ought to do battle with the machines). The chapter on Mrs Grundy quite clearly approves of her, and approval of *laissez-faire* and money-worship crop up gratuitously and without even a pretence of mockery—complete with the suggestion that any man who has made a fortune should be regarded both as a work of art and a social benefactor, and therefore be exempted from taxation. In this comedy of ideas, then, some do not come off, but many do; and few could find it uninteresting or uninfuriating.

The Way of all Flesh is less inconsistent, though the first half is the more powerful. There, the ideas are purveyed through action and character—typical characters, but real types in a real society; and despite Butler's rage at having been bamboozled by spiritual fraud for so many years, it does show admirable self-knowledge. The barbed asides are more integral with the narrative and are prompted by it ('. . . tolerators, if not lovers, of all that was familiar, haters of all that was unfamiliar; they would have been equally horrified at hearing the Christian religion doubted, and at seeing it practised.' Chap. XV). Even the attitudes to money and parents are not too outrageous, given the awful Victorian context set up:

> Why should the generations overlap one another at all? Why cannot we be buried as eggs in neat little cells with ten or twenty thousand pounds each wrapped round us in Bank of England notes, and wake up, as the sphex wasp does, to find that its papa and mamma have not only left ample provision at its elbow, but have been eaten by sparrows some weeks before it began to live consciously on its own account.
>
> (Chap. XIV)

Similarly, his revisionist attitude to vice and virtue seems welcome because needed:

> 'Be virtuous,' says the copy-book, 'and you will be happy.' Surely if a reputed virtue fails often enough in this respect it is only an insidious form of vice, and if a reputed vice brings no very serious mischief on a man's later years, it is not so bad a vice as it is said to be.
>
> (Chap. XIX)

But surely it is utilitarian logic rather than commonsense that causes him almost immediately to narrow this to 'Pleasure—tangible material prosperity in this world—is the safest test of virtue.'

Much of the book seems a comic corrective to life-denying Victorian conventions, and thus predominantly an example of the third category (where *Erewhon* was predominantly of the first). Certainly, the idea that living 'in sin' represents a truer virtue than the legalism of marriage may be regarded as humanising, but the ideas of getting rid of family sentiment, regarding one's *own* welfare as the meaning of 'Christ', and regarding poverty, and ill-luck as being in principle what they were in practice, immoral, are progressively more dubiously so. Butler strives to patch over the impossibility of making a coherent scheme of such notions, tries also to give the impression of a consistent comic attitude, by his sharp, no-nonsense Shavian style. But it won't do. Nothing can disguise the fact that what he is against, in the first two-thirds of the book, is a good deal more convincing than what he is for, in the rest. This is because the one is based on the life and society of his times, which needed showing up; whereas the other is based on theory—often brilliant and stimulating, but finally too cranky to catch on.

Shaw too writes comedies of ideas that have not lasted as well as might have been expected, again mainly because clarity and cleverness of style cannot disguise their crankiness. Like Butler, too, he is much better at provocative, witty argument than at characterisation; all his characters are cold and unphysical—which helps with comic distance but not with humanisation. If you are hoping to convince an audience that a better world is attainable, this is a rather serious drawback. His plays are admirable as debates—forensic comedy *par excellence*—but they do lack body.

Mrs Patrick Campbell—Pat Cat to her many enemies—being naturally dissatisfied with a man who thought love-affairs best conducted by post, once accused Shaw of being all firecrackers and ashes: a perceptive comment. His major work comes between *Widowers' Houses* (1892) and *Back to Methuselah* (1921) and the one is all firecrackers, the other all ashes; the one is *against* the capitalist complexities of an inhumane society, the other is *for* Life, yet both are dehumanising.

Shaw was *not* daunted by the complexity of modern society, and, at least until *Heartbreak House*, was confident that the brave new world could be brought into being by socialism and a strong self-made man (such as Bernard Shaw) aided by a wise society woman (such as Lady Astor). Despite his philosopher-dustmen and avant-garde mechanics, he had little faith in the rationality of people in general; hence he admired both communism and fascism, for the same reason: they lent the people to organisation by men of power. Like Butler, he carries over into his rebellion against Victorian society and its conventions much more of its paternalistic authoritarianism than is evident at first sight. For all his socialism, he is utilitarian in his heartlessness: something tonally evident, and therefore tending to make the plays dehumanising, even when thematically they are concerned with abolishing suffering.

This characteristic is not simply a result of making plays as debates, of turning emotional responses into arguments; it is more deepseated than that (indeed, that is putting the cart before the horse). Their inner coldness, so effective in countering the sentimentality of his day, and now rather a handicap, seems to derive from the playwright's family upbringing. Both the coldness and the comedy it could produce are nicely compacted in this biographical fragment, on the cremation of Shaw's sister:

> The will of the deceased absolutely forbade any religious service. Yet Shaw found himself confronted, not with a solitary friend, but with a crowd that filled the chapel, all strangers to him, and all devoted to 'darling Lucy'. They expected a ceremony, and he told me how he met the difficulty. 'I could not let her be thrown on the fire without a word, like a scuttleful of coals. So I had to mount the pulpit and deliver a full dress elegy, concluding with the dirge from *Cymbeline*. Coal was very scarce then; and Lucy burnt with a steady white light like that of a wax candle'.
>
> (Hesketh Pearson, *Bernard Shaw*, London 1942, p. 301)

Note the effect of irreverence ('scuttleful . . .') masquerading as decent sensibility, and of irrelevance ('coal was very scarce'), while 'steady white light', with its mixture of esthetic and economic preoccupations unites both irreverence and irrelevance. But for a warmer comic mixture of these two elements, compare the burial scene in Joyce's *Ulysses*.

Admittedly, Shaw seems to envisage a time when the State has withered away, and, like Marx, to prefer it even to a time when it would be sensibly, rather than absurdly organised. But this was not because he thought *any* complex, industrial organisation dehumanising. On the contrary, it was because he thought none dehumanising enough. His plays lack body, ultimately, for religious reasons—that is to say, as an inheritance from his rejected Protestantism (no doubt in combination with the early coldness derived from an unloving mother). They lack body because he prefers mind; hence his Life Force paradoxically ends in a denial of all we know as living.

Shaw's dehumanising tendency becomes explicit in *Man and Superman*—the title, of course, being a significant indication—but is most clearly evident in *Back to Methuselah*. The conclusion of that work explains why the plays do not improve on further acquaintance. At first you are dazzled by the firecrackers, as you go on you become more aware of the ashes, begin to feel that somewhere there is criticism not merely of the follies and crimes of individuals or society but of life itself, and finally to suspect that this accounts for the disembodied quality of the style and the lack of sympathetic imagination in the personal relationships. It accounts too for the predominance of talk over action. Life is the positive, the standard by which the economy and conventions of Victorian and Edwardian man are measured (and usually found wanting). But what *sort* of life? Would it be any more satisfactory to live? *Back to Methuselah* gives the answer—and that is why this positive comedy is so drearily inferior to the negative, destructive ones. What is latent there, cropping up only occasionally is everywhere manifest here; witness the last scene:

> SHE ANCIENT The day will come when there will be no people, only thought.
> HE ANCIENT And that will be life eternal.

A vision confirmed and approved in the last speech of the play, by Lilith:

> They have taken the agony from birth [*these superpeople being born from eggs—and presumably by some form of artificial insemination*] and their life does not fail them even in the hour of their destruction. Their breasts are without milk, their bowels are gone.

And we may add, they don't eat, sleep, make love, dream or even talk to each other, the chief entertainment seeming to be sitting in gorse bushes like fakirs. Shaw's ideal society in fact seems to be peopled by a revolting combination of Swift's Struldbrugs and Houyhnhnms—compounds of physical monstrosity with moral smugness. *Man and Superman* is a better, and significantly earlier, play. It is also significant, however, that Don Juan and Tanner do not practise the freedom they preach. They *talk about*, where the characters of Restoration comedies *exemplify* their ideas.

The later plays can well be regarded as a special case of category-two comedies: withdrawal in disgust, though not disgust specifically with the brave new world of the industrial age. The earlier plays, however, come into the first category. Behind the clever demonstration of the tangled web of capitalist economics, which makes the most high-minded and well-intentioned a criminal by proxy, lies latent a blueprint for a better, communist web. *Widowers' Houses* seems the best example of this sort of play. The characters are not comic in themselves (so there is no great loss in their lack of roundedness) but only in relation to absurdities in society; indeed, within the limits allowed by the social structure they are fully competent and intelligent. Thus there is a perfectly good reason for the apparently absurd contrast in Sartorious of the desire to be gentlemanly and have a position for his daughter and his ruthless career as a slum landlord, and this is, almost cynically, made clear. He *needs* that position, because society itself is absurdly hypocritical—living indirectly on slum property but contemptuous of those who enable it to do so, unless they have 'position'. The play avoids any suspicion of dullness by a skilful deployment of all the arts of the Victorian well-made play that Shaw affected to despise: patches of farce, sensation, theatrically-effective entrances and exits and a careful buttressing of the main theme with many minor ones: the absurdity of 'gentlemanliness', prudery and so on. It is made quite clear, however, that the drama is fundamentally one of *social* ideas; Shaw is not interested in human nature *per se*. So every now and then the point is made so forcibly in Shaw's typically clear, cogent, colloquial prose, that one can hardly help feeling that only a change of society will do, not a Dickensian change of heart:

> SARTORIUS (*forcibly*) Yes: a mortgage on my property. When I, to use your own words, screw, and bully, and drive these people to pay what they have freely undertaken to pay me, I cannot touch one penny of the money they give me until I have first paid you your seven hundred a year out of it. What Lickcheese did for me, I do for you. He and I are alike intermediaries: you are the principal. It is because of the risks I run through the poverty of my tenants that you exact interest from me at the monstrous and exorbitant rate of seven per cent, forcing me to exact the uttermost farthing in my turn from the tenants. And yet, Dr Trench, you, who have never done a hand's turn of work in connection with the place, you have not hesitated to speak contemptuously of me because I have applied my industry and forethought to the management of *our* property, and am maintaining it by the same honourable means.
>
> (Act II)

One play, *Heartbreak House* (1919—but begun before the War), is usually attributed to the influence of Chekhov, and is generally regarded as Shaw's best. Here he is is more sensitive to human feelings than in any other play—indeed, the original source (leading to the Chekhovian method) seems to be a preoccupation with the 'inner light', which is brooded over in the postscript to *Androcles and the*

Lion. Shaw now seems to feel, like so many later writers of comedy, that human absurdities are not curable by any change of society, but only by an unlikely change of human nature. All the characters have what is lacking elsewhere, a shadow side; they are more than mouth-pieces; and the House is at once England seen as the *Titanic*, a techno-logical masterpiece drifting towards disaster, in an atmosphere of lavish frivolity, and the place where people's inner character comes to light—and is seen to be the most important reality. There is, too, a new awareness of the value of the emotional eccentric (as against the man who is eccentric merely because he is more rational than his fellows). So, though it is often farcical, it ends as depressing comedy, and though it is depressing, it is a third-category 'human' comedy, setting personal values above social ones, showing disillusion with social engineering. Not surprisingly, Shaw never liked to talk of *Heartbreak House*. Probably it expressed more than he intended, more indeed than he believed he had in him. Certainly, he seems to have been possessed, like Captain Shotover, by a demon which embodied many of his personal and Protestant repressions.

It is not as subtle, touching and humorous as Chekhov, but it is very unShavian. At the beginning of Act I I I, for instance, Hector maintains that what is wrong with the house is the inhabitants (not the structure): 'We are useless, dangerous and ought to be abolished'. Probably this links up with the strange doctrine of 'killing' (which in turn, perhaps, is a later manifestation of the suppressed psychological rage that gave the best speeches in *Major Barbara* to Undershaft—and left the puzzled audience to find the answer to Shaw's implicit approval of government by and for armament manufacturers).

Captain Shotover, the sage, lives by inventing weapons of war, and justifies himself in a strange dialogue with his son-in-law, Hector in Act I. Strange, because we find the sage putting forward the sort of doctrine associated with the choleric God of the Old Testament, and because Hector, the boastful hectoring hero, puts forward a Quakerish doctrine of the inner light. That each speaks for the shadow-side of the other seems clear from Shotover's last speech: 'We kill the better half of ourselves every day to propitiate them', which unites Hector's feeling about the need for the inner light with the idea of killing those who would prevent its development. The killing—in keeping with the mode of comedy—is in fact brought about by outside agency. The two robbers, the burglar and the capitalist, who run for shelter, are killed by bombs, while the impractical members of the household survive. All this gives a terrible thematic tangle, while leaving the impression of a humanising and potentially integrative play. The survival of the impractical, conflicts with the pessimism of Act III, for their uselessness is shown as having not only greater humanity, but also greater survival value than practicality. The idea of destroying such as Mangan and Dunn, contradicts not only Hector's doctrine of pity but also the theme of *Androcles*, for it simply reverses the persecution *of* Christians to a persecution *by* them. And finally the whole tone of the play is contradictory of all the former Shavian positives:* commonsense selfishness, social improvement as a key to moral improvement, and *cold* reason as a key to everything. The play does not resolve these contraries, and thus falls short of its potential achievement, but it does show itself *aware* of them, thus achieving some depth in ideas and characters, and some humility in the 'solution' —if pointing out, not a destination, but only a direction, can be called such:

> Capt. Shotover I tell you happiness is no good. You can be happy when you are only half alive. I am happier now I am half dead than I ever was in my prime. But there is no blessing on my happiness.
> Ellie (*her face lightening*) Life with a blessing! that is what I want. Now I know the real reason why I couldn't marry Mr Mangan: there would be no blessing on our marriage. There is a blessing on my broken heart. There is a blessing on your beauty, Hesione. There is a blessing on your father's spirit. Even on the lies of Marcus there is a blessing; but on Mr Mangan's money there is none.
> Mangan I don't understand a word of that.
> Ellie Neither do I. But I know it means something.
>
> (Act III)

Whatever it means, it suggests that the good life needs more than social engineering: beauty, sorrow, gaiety, fantasy. Whether the final lines are in keeping is an open question, but they certainly seem to record a very deep disillusion with the current world:

> Mrs Hushabye But what a glorious experience! [*the bombing!*] I hope they'll come again tomorrow night.

* A point made conscious and explicit several times over in the Preface to *Man and Superman*: e.g. in section IX: 'And so we arrive at the end of the Socialist's dream of "the socialization of the means of production and exchange", of the Positivist's dream of moralizing the capitalist, and of the ethical professor's, legislator's, educator's dream of putting commandments and codes and lessons and examination marks on a man . . . and pretending that his nature has been changed . . . We must eliminate the Yahoo or his vote will wreck the commonwealth.'

ELLIE (*radiant at the prospect*) Oh, I hope so.
    Randall at last succeeds in keeping the home fires burning on his flute.

But don't these lines reveal *still* a damaging inability to grasp what
people really feel?

B. II. WAUGH, HELLER

W. C. Fields is said to have remarked of somebody that no man who
hated children and dogs so much could be all bad. Waugh provokes
similarly paradoxical feelings; his work ought to be much more
unlikable than it is. Worse, it is the less cynical works that are least
likable. Few can like *Brideshead Revisited* whose ideas of 'morality'
and 'dignity' are a compound of Catholic snobbery and class snobbery;
but who can help loving the amoral callousness of *The Loved One?*
In fact, most of his works are amoral, and consequently tend towards
farce or divertisement; sometimes falling wholly into those categories,
more usually turning out to be farcical-comedies. Waugh is cooler in
tone than Nabokov or Shaw, more distanced from his characters than
West, and he opts out of the modern world more completely than
anyone else. The rejection of Butlerian, Shavian and Wellsian
'optimism' is total, and nothing is put in its place:

> I have succeeded, too, in dissociating myself very largely with the rest
> of the world. I am not impatient of its manifest follies and don't want
> to influence opinions, events, or expose humbug or anything of that
> kind. I don't want to be of service to anyone or anything. I simply
> want to do my work as an artist.
>
> ('Evelyn Waugh's Private Diaries'. *Observer Magazine*, 22 April 1973,
> 29 Aug. 1943)

The diaries also confirm the element of unsentimentality bordering
on cynicism. Witness 3 November 1943 (after sending his books out
of London during the bombing and bringing his son in):

> It would seem from this that I prefer my books to my son. I can argue
> that firemen rescue children and destroy books, but the truth is that a
> child is easily replaced while a book destroyed is utterly lost; also a
> child is eternal; but most that I have a sense of absolute possession over
> my library and not over my nursery.
>
> (Ibid. p. 19)

Refreshingly free of cant, and tending no doubt to produce the same
sense of liberation that Orwell found in Miller's *Tropics*: the sense
that here is someone who doesn't give a damn and, uninhibited by

ingrained social restraints, actually says what everyone has at some time guiltily felt. But it also reveals why we feel uneasy about the 'satire' of some of the books. After a time, one does hanker after *some* values.

Put Out More Flags (1942) is prefaced by a Dedicatory Letter whose contents suggest that this hankering is not entirely unreasonable. 'I find more food for thought in the follies of Basil Seal and Ambrose Silk, than in the sagacity of the higher command.' Well, any good history will cast doubt on that sagacity; but what do these follies consist in? Framing friends and innocent people with the secret police, for little more than a joke. No doubt it is an absurdity in society that the secret police should take such jokes seriously. One's unease comes from the fact that there is no trace of sympathy for the victims (for whom the results are by no means funny). Similarly, the Old Boy network is shown very clearly in operation, but with *no* sense of its possible wrongness or inefficiency.

The climate of his work, then, tends to be emotionally bracing but intellectually relaxing. To that extent it is releasing, though neither humanising nor integrative. One might expect it to be conserving, and certainly there occurs here and there an element of judgement by the standard of former glories, a suggestion that what was wrong with the upper class of his day was that it failed to be properly aristocratic. Thus in Chapter 8 of *Vile Bodies* (1930) the silly party of Bright Young Things, on the deck of a dirigible, is contrasted with 'a party of quite a different sort' full of real aristocrats, and 'behind and about them':

> a great concourse of pious and honourable people . . . their womenfolk well gowned in rich and durable stuffs, their men-folk ablaze with orders; people who had represented their country in foreign places and sent their sons to die for her in battle, people of decent and temperate life, uncultured, unaffected, unembarrassed, unassuming, unambitious people, of independent judgement and marked eccentricities, kind people who cared for animals and the deserving poor, brave and rather unreasonable people, that fine phalanx of the passing order, approaching, as one day at the Last Trump they hoped to meet their Maker, with decorous and frank cordiality to shake Lady Anchorage by the hand.

Hardly an adequate standard by which to measure the shortcomings of the modern world, especially if one takes due note of the implications of such items as 'uncultured,' 'rather unreasonable,' or 'animals and the deserving poor'—and to do Waugh justice, this is not central to his work. Centrally, he is a reactionary anarchist thinly disguised (by nostalgia) as a conservative. It seems an odd thing to say of the snobbish, bowler-hatted caricature of an English gentleman, who made a point in Italy of simply adding 'o' to the end of English words and shouting at the natives, that he was at heart a right-wing drop-out. But the witty bronze plaque at the entrance to his country house is a convincing symbol of the fact: 'No admittance on Business'. A consequence of this fact, the fact that his work is really hollow-centred, that he has no consistent comic vision but only a set of prejudices, is that he is better on topics where by chance judgement can concur with the prejudice concerned. Thus *Scoop* (1933) on contemporary newspaper lunacies, and *The Loved One* (1948) on the Californian death-cult, can be accepted wholeheartedly as brilliantly funny, if somewhat peripheral, comedies, where other apparently deeper books, like *A Handful of Dust* (1934) hover on the brink of some such monstrosity as farcical tragedy, and still others, such as the highly entertaining, cynical *Decline and Fall* (1928), with its elegantly circular structure, are outright divertisement. (West's *Cool Million*, as it were, without the implicit protest.))

It is no surprise to find, from *The Ordeal of Gilbert Pinfold* (1957), that Waugh never voted. His detestation of the modern world, though deriving from a reactionary temperament, was quite non-political and impractical:

> 'If you approve, head master, I will stay as I am here as long as any boy wants to read the classics. I think it would be very wicked indeed to do anything to fit a boy for the modern world.'
> 'It's a short-sighted view, Scott-King.'
> 'There, head master, with all respect, I differ from you profoundly. I think it the most long-sighted view it is possible to take.'
>
> *(Scott-King's Modern Europe (1946), conclusion)*

Behind the total rejection, however, seems to have been something not dissimilar to the attitudes of Huxley and others: a fear that the improvements of science and welfare-bureaucracy would lead to dehumanised sameness:

> The State had made him.
>
> No clean-living, God-fearing Victorian gentleman, he; no complete man of the renaissance; no gentil knight nor dutiful pagan nor, even, noble savage. All that succession of past worthies had gone its way, content to play a prelude to Miles. He was the Modern Man.
>
> His history, as it appeared in multuplet in the filing cabinets of numberless State departments was typical of a thousand others . . . . . .

In halls adorned with Picassos and Légers he yawned through hours of Constructive Play. He never lacked the requisite cubic feet of air. His diet was balanced and on the first Friday of every month he was psycho-analysed. Every detail of his adolescence was recorded and microfilmed and filed, until at the appropriate age he was transferred to the Air Force.

There were no aeroplanes at the station to which he was posted. It was an institution to train instructors to train instructors in Personal Recreation.

(Love Among the Ruins (1953), I)

This, however, is an attitude lying *behind* the novels more often than a theme in them. It is what enables him to seize on certain specific features of the modern world and see them as significant. He does not have to *say* they are significant but simply to focus on the vulgarian details betraying the fact. Thus, *Scoop* is farcically funny by focussing closely on one assignment. At the same time it reveals a general malaise in the modern press and, by implication, in its readers—and by further implication in the world which has spawned them both. Had Waugh felt it necessary to allow himself any explicit commentary he would almost certainly have blurred the general comic point (as well as, of course, diluting the fun) by revealing his approval of the Italian invasion of Abyssinia. A revelation certain to have cast doubt, for many readers, on the validity of his views on the values of the modern world.

The Loved One, too, nicely combines textural closeness and thematic distance. He is not on his home ground and therefore feels none of the unholy complicity with *these* vulgarities and asininities that he does with upper-class English ones, to the detriment of tonal consistency. There is no comment, yet by the end of the book, having been vastly amused by innumerable farcical events, dazzling verbal mimicry, brilliant pastiche of advertising and other literary horrors, we are left feeling that 'the American way of death' has been proved upon our pulses to be significant of the values of modern society at its most 'advanced' point. The novel acts therefore as an awful warning, in spite of its apparently cynical surface and abstention from moral or esthetic judgement. It is a black comedy uproarious enough for a blue farce.

In the second section of its fifth unnumbered chapter (p. 64 of the Penguin edition) *The Loved One* contains a paragraph that encapsulates the essential Waugh: the anarchy, the pure artistry, the negative-esthetic fascination, the perception of details as signs:

Dennis listened intently to the tones so often parodied yet never rendered more absurd or more hypnotic than the original. His interest was no longer purely technical nor purely satiric. Whispering Glades held him in thrall. In that zone of insecurity in the mind where none but the artist dare trespass, the tribes were mustering. Dennis, the frontiersman, could read the signs.

One of these 'readings'—which implicitly extends the idiot scientific improvements of Whispering Glades to the lunatic results of scientific improvements in the brave new world outside—compares and contrasts significantly with a key symbolic passage in Heller's one great comic novel *Catch-22* (1961):

> *This perfect replica of an old English Manor*, a notice said, *like all the buildings of Whispering Glades, is constructed throughout of Grade A steel and concrete with foundations extending into solid rock. It is certified proof against earthquake and*   *Their name liveth for evermore who record it in Whispering Glades.*
>
> At the blank patch a signwriter was even then at work and Dennis, pausing to study it, discerned the ghost of the words 'high explosive' freshly obliterated and the outlines of 'nuclear fission' about to be filled in as substitute.   (p. 35)

Where this goes from business to war by implication, Heller goes explicitly from war to business. In the one, it is taken for granted that laudable ideals have been perverted; in the other, they are explicitly obliterated:

> Milo Minderbinder's planes flew in from everywhere, the pursuit planes, bombers, and cargo ships streaming in to do what they were told. The planes were decorated with flamboyant squadron emblems illustrating such laudable ideals as Courage, Might, Justice, Truth, Liberty, Love, Honor, and Patriotism that were painted out at once by Milo's mechanics with a double coat of flat white paint and replaced in garish purple with the stenciled name M & M ENTERPRISES, FINE FRUITS AND PRODUCE. The "M & M" in "M & M" ENTERPRISES" stood for Milo & Minderbinder, and the & was inserted, Milo revealed candidly, to nullify any impression that the syndicate was a one-man operation.
>
> (Chap. 24)

Both novels end with the protagonist taking off, but in the case of Yossarian it is from the big complex ruthless world of war and international capitalism to the small welfare-state of Sweden, whereas in Dennis's case it is from the small world of Whispering Glades to the bigger world of which it is an emblem. There is a further difference.

Heller is less anarchistic and uncaring. Waugh rather revels in the brave new world he detests; so he can retire from it into himself and then make iconoclastic forays. *The Loved One* concludes:

> He was leaving it not only unravished but enriched. He was adding his bit to the wreckage; something that had long irked him, his young heart...
>
> He picked up the novel which Miss Poski had left on his desk and settled down to await his loved one's final combustion.

Beneath the cool surface beats a heart of stone. Heller, rather, seems to be preserving a humane sensibility beneath a buckler of comedy. True, Yossarian is not able to find civilised ideals being put into practice anywhere in 'the big picture' and after a conclusion like this naturally 'takes off' for a smaller picture:

> 'When I look up, I see people cashing in. I don't see heaven or saints or angels. I see people cashing in on every decent impulse and human tragedy.'

(Chap. 42)

But he himself has ideals, honest and humane, which show through: for instance, in his horror at Snowden's death, at the random massacres of the war, in his persistent attempt to find and rescue Nately's whore's little sister, in his desperation at instances of cruelty and callousness and corruption. And the reader is compelled by the coercion of various comic effects to wish to sustain these values and reject those of the dominant Korns, Cathcarts, Scheisskopfs and Peckems; so that the work borders on the third, humanistic kind. Sometimes indeed it is perhaps *too* explicit in its guidance. It lacks Waugh's economic artistry:

> ... a world that never yet had provided enough heat and food and justice for all but an ingenious and unscrupulous handful. What a lousy earth! He wondered how many people were destitute that same night even in his own prosperous country, how many homes were shanties, how many husbands were drunk and wives socked, and how many children were bullied, abused or abandoned. How many families hungered for food they could not afford to buy? How many hearts were broken? How many suicides would take place that same night, how many people would go insane? How many cockroaches and landlords would triumph? How many winners were losers, successes failures, rich men poor men? How many wise guys were stupid? How many happy endings were unhappy endings? How many honest men were liars, brave men cowards, loyal men traitors, how many

sainted men were corrupt, how many people in positions of trust had
sold their souls to blackguards for petty cash, how many had never had
souls? How many straight-and-narrow paths were crooked paths?
How many best families were worst families, and how many good
people were bad people?

(Chap. 39)

Despite the concluding series of paradoxes, it is perhaps rather out of
keeping in a comedy, and too overt for a work not purporting to be a
straightforward novel of ideas. Not that *Catch-22* is therefore inferior
to *The Loved One*. Rhetorical flourishes are in keeping with its
baroque style. Moreover, it is simply much bigger and therefore can
afford some superfluity; and it is not only bigger; it is greater.

It stresses the horrors of war and ruthless capitalism. Snowden's
death is gruesome, and when Milo has his own base bombed to make
money for the syndicate the emphasis falls not so much on the financial
ingenuity of the deal as on the maiming and death entailed. But the
main target—appropriately for a comedy—is the absurdities and
human muddles of them both; a theme insisted on time and again, as
in the ludicrous insistence on tight bombing patterns, the unnecessary
bombing of a friendly village, the briefing for peppy pre-mission
prayers (not mentioning morbid matters such as God or death), or the
squadron's paying seven cents for one-cent eggs in order to make an
illusory profit of one and a quarter cents for themselves as 'the Syndicate'—this profit (plus two and three quarter cents) going in fact to
Milo, whose capitalistic genius for wheeling and dealing enables him
to make it by selling seven-cent eggs for five cents! The following
quotation briefly exemplifies such muddles:

*Dear Mrs., Mr., Miss, or Mr. and Mrs. Daneeka: Words cannot express
the deep personal grief I experienced when your husband, son, father or
brother was killed, wounded or reported missing in action.*

(Chap. 31)

That Dr Daneeka is merely administratively 'missing' magnifies the
element of muddle and moral absurdity, and in no way minimises the
soullessness, so commonly associated with big bureaucracy.

Indeed, underlying all the other concerns, is the theme of the
complexity and bureaucracy of the modern world and its consequent
dehumanisation. Yossarian's sitting naked in a tree and going up for
his medal in the same state is a symbolic comic equivalent of King
Lear's similar urge to simplify. It indicates an ultimate belief in the
'poor, bare forked animal'—if he is not caught and corrupted in the

great, inhuman, mechanical web, of which Catch-22 is the central symbol:

> There was only one catch and that was Catch-22, which specified that a concern for one's own personal safety in the face of dangers that were real and immediate was the process of a rational mind. Orr was crazy and could be grounded. All he had to do was ask; and as soon as he did he would no longer be crazy and would have to fly more missions. Orr would be crazy to fly more missions and sane if he didn't, but if he was sane he had to fly them. If he flew them he was crazy and didn't have to; but if he didn't want to he was sane and had to. Yossarian was moved very deeply by the absolute simplicity of this clause of Catch-22 and let out a respectful whistle.
> 'That's some catch, that Catch-22,' he observed.
> 'It's the best there is,' Doc Daneeka agreed.

(Chap. 5)

> 'Catch-22,' Doc Daneeka answered patiently . . . 'says you've always got to do what your commanding officer tells you to.'
> 'But Twenty-seventh Air Force says I can go home with forty missions.'
> 'But they don't say you have to go home. And regulations do say you have to obey every order. That's the catch. Even if the colonel were disobeying a Twenty-seventh Air Force order by making you fly more missions, you'd still have to fly them, or you'd be guilty of disobeying an order of his. And then Twenty-seventh Air Force Headquarters would really jump on you.'

(Chap. 6)

This is the apotheosis of bureaucracy, as Milo's extraordinarily complicated international buyings and sellings under various names, and often to and from himself, are the apotheosis of capitalist complexity.

That the novel is so funny, however, comes structurally from the variety of comic incident—most of it directly related to the main themes, all of it indirectly related to them—and texturally from the extension of muddle and irrationality into the day-to-day details of life. Thus, structurally, there is the incident of Yossarian's taking someone else's bed in hospital and the consequence of his getting what he wants, as it were, but being obliged to let someone else have it who doesn't want it. Texturally there is the hilarious scene with the psychiatrist, trying to tell his own dreams, getting annoyed with his patient for having uninteresting dreams and sticking closely to his dossier (on A. Fortiori—a name in itself a neat textural detail). There is a good deal of tendency wit directed at this uncommonsensical 'science':

'Hasn't it ever occurred to you that in your promiscuous pursuit of women you are merely trying to assuage your subconscious fears of sexual impotence?'

'Yes, sir, it has.'

'Then why do you do it?'

'To assuage my fears of sexual impotence.'

(Chap. 27)

The same absurd logic that sustains such enterprises as Milo's deal with the American authorities to bomb a German-held bridge, and with the German authorities to defend the bridge with anti-aircraft fire against his own attack (on a cost plus six per cent basis in each case) informs Yossarian's anti-God argument with Scheisskopf's wife. Milo's deal represents a triumph for private enterprise 'since the armies of both countries were socialised institutions', but:

> Once the contracts were signed, there seemed no point in using the resources of the syndicate to bomb and defend the bridge, inasmuch as both governments had ample men and material right there to do so and were perfectly happy to contribute them, and in the end Milo realized a fantastic profit from both halves of his project for doing nothing more than signing his name twice.
>
> The arrangement was perfectly fair to both sides. Since Milo did have freedom of passage everywhere, his planes were able to steal over in a sneak attack without alerting the German anti-aircraft gunners; and since Milo knew about the attack, he was able to alert the German anti-aircraft gunners in sufficient time for them to begin firing accurately the moment the planes came into range. It was an ideal arrangement for everyone but the dead man in Yossarian's tent, who was killed over the target the day he arrived.

(Chap. 24)

Scheisskopf's wife is horrified at Yossarian's view of God as an incompetent bureaucrat and technician (pain as a warning system of bodily dangers! 'And who created the dangers?'):

> 'What the hell are you getting upset about? . . . I thought you didn't believe in God.'
>
> 'I don't,' she sobbed, bursting violently into tears. 'But the God I don't believe in is a good God, a just God, a merciful God. He's not the mean and stupid God you make him out to be.'

(Chap. 18)

This sort of logical absurdity, though comically heightened, is recognisable enough to act as a paradigm; and the second example of it (along with numerous other examples of specifically individual lapses of a similar kind) sufficiently suggests that the fault lies not only in the nature of society but also deep in human nature.

B. III. JOYCE, STOPPARD

For all its positives, its reformist laughter, *Catch*-22 is ultimately mithridatic comedy; its integrative tendencies seem designed to enable the individual to bear the modern world, till he can get out of it. Heller has energy but not buoyancy—a penalty to be paid, perhaps, for the advantages of a war-setting. The comedy of *Ulysses*, on the other hand, is ultimately celebratory. Joyce rejects his society but is not dejected by it. He has greater buoyancy both in spirit and form than any other comic writer of the age, and also a longer vision. Looking back down the ages, he sees that all periods have been, as Walpole said, tragedies for the man who feels, comedies for the man who thinks. Further, though not denying that people are affected by their society, he believes psychology to be prior to sociology; under superficial change people seem to remain *fundamentally* the same: falling, suffering guilt and division, being resurrected, uniting in harmony, and falling again. If societies do not seem to have become essentially better, at least human nature does not seem to have become essentially worse, in Joyce's view. At any rate, the human race has always got through its crises, if only just and ludicrously late in doing so. It is no accident that Thornton Wilder's play *The Skin of Our Teeth* (1942) made acknowledgements to *Finnegans Wake* for that theme is certainly there—and is an extension from the earlier book. When all the admissions, confessions, and qualifications have been made *Ulysses* finally says *Yes* to life; and its last chapter pointedly begins and ends with that word.

However, *Ulysses* is not only celebratory, but also innovatory comedy, technically, and also socially (insofar as it opposes the nationalism, Catholicism, militarism and prudery of the times). It is not only innovatory but also releasing (in its new tolerance); and it is not only releasing but also integrative, technically and psychologically (in showing all ages in one, in uniting eighteen stylistic viewpoints—and more—in the epic of one ordinary day to indicate the relativity and variety of life, and in reuniting body and mind):

> If a reader were asked to set down a list of the things that had impressed him about *Ulysses*, it might reasonably be somewhat as follows. First, the clarity with which the sights and sounds and smells of Dublin come to life, the rotundity of the character-drawing, and the

naturalness of the dialogue. Second, the elaborate way that the story and characters are parodied by being set against archetypal heroic patterns, notably the one provided by the *Odyssey*. Third, the revelation of character and incident through the searching use of the stream-of-consciousness technique. Fourth, the constant tendency to be encyclopedic and exhaustive both in technique and in subject matter, and to see both in highly intellectualized terms. It should not be too hard for us by now to see that these four points describe elements in the book which relate to the novel, romance, confession, and anatomy respectively. *Ulysses*, then, is a complete prose epic with all four forms employed in it, all of practically equal importance, and all essential to one another, so that the book is a unity and not an aggregate.

(Northrop Frye, *The Anatomy of Criticism*, Princeton 1957, pp. 313-4)

That is to say, it is the complete comedy: the only example in English of what Fielding tried for in *Joseph Andrews*, 'a comic epic in prose'. Joyce took comedy to be the highest form of art, provided that it was not propagandist, nor arousing desire and urging us to something beyond itself:

A comedy (a work of comic art) which does not urge us to seek anything beyond itself excites in us the feeling of joy. All art which excites in us the feeling of joy is so far comic, and according as this feeling of joy is excited by whatever is substantial or accidental in human fortunes the art is to be judged more or less excellent; and even tragic art (a tragedy) may be said to participate in the nature of comic art so far as the possession of a work of tragic art (a tragedy) excites in us the feeling of joy.

(*Notebooks* 13 Feb. 1903. Quoted by H. Gorman, *James Joyce*, London 1941, p. 97)

It is clear from this that he shared Aristotle's views: that comedy need not be hilarious, and that it should deal with permanent realities (the 'substantial'). Elsewhere he says that 'the great human comedy, in which each has share, gives limitless scope to the true artist, today as yesterday and as in years gone' (*The Critical Writings of James Joyce*, ed. Ellsworth Mason and Richard Ellman, London 1959, p. 45). Human life, then, was for Joyce permanently and inherently comic, however sad and bitter it might be in the short view; and *Ulysses* is above all a 'human' comedy—in three senses of the word. Firstly, it is human as opposed to *divine*: a comedy of Dantean scale, but affirming the essential glory of temporal life in *this* world. Secondly, it is human as opposed to *guiltless*: accepting the secret sins, selfishnesses, and sordidnesses that each thinks peculiarly his own, as 'only human'. And thirdly, it is human as opposed to *inhuman*—being to that extent not celebratory but satirical (of violence and hatred). The satire indeed is complementary to the celebration; the latter springs from warmheartedness and humane sympathies, and therefore must lead to opposition of what is their direct contrary. A technically complete, and a fully 'human' comedy, then, rooted in one milieu at one moment, but with universal import—though allowing that the big modern city does make it harder to be fully human.

In the *Portrait of the Artist* Joyce expressed the ambition to forge 'the uncreated conscience of my race,' a conscience uncreated owing to murderous nationalism, religious bigotry, and insular culture. Against these things Joyce sets a liberal socialism of the sort adumbrated by Wilde in his dazzling comic essay *The Soul of Man Under Socialism*, a socialism mocked by Shaw for such statements as the following: 'If the Socialism is Authoritarian; if there are Governments armed with economic power as they are now with political power; if, in a word, we are to have Industrial Tyrannies, then the last state of man will be worse than the first,' 'It is to be regretted that a portion of our community should be practically in slavery, but to propose to solve the problem by enslaving the entire community is childish,' and 'The form of government that is most suitable to the artist is no government at all.' A socialism, in fact, moving away from bureaucracy and towards humane flexibility—and therefore in the view of Wilde's and Joyce's pre-Stalinist contemporaries not socialism at all. Joyce himself, indeed, always mocks it when put forward in 'practical' terms by Bloom, its chief proponent in *Ulysses*. But as a desirable and possible state of mind it is a latent positive, especially in the three satirical chapters: 'Cyclops,' 'Circe,' and 'Ithaca'; and this tallies with Joyce's belief in the priority of psychology—and therefore gradualism—over sociology. Hodgart puts this point well:

> In the political discussion, Bloom does the rashest thing possible: he speaks up for liberalism, saying there is much to be said on both sides, thus irritating the Citizen still more.
>> But it's no use, says he. Force, hatred, history and all that. That's not life for men and women, insult and hatred. And everybody knows that it's the very opposite of that that is really life.
>> What? says Alf.
>> Love, says Bloom. I mean the opposite of hatred. I must go now. . .

Bloom is absurd and pathetic, as the digression on love that follows makes clear. But then liberalism, pacificism, broadmindedness *are* absurd, especially in tense historical situations. Joyce is implying that, but also stating clearly that liberalism and pacificism are the only possible political attitudes compatible with a humane view of life. They may be ridiculous, but they are the best we have got . . . Bloom [*gradually*] appears as an embodiment of Joyce's most treasured values.

(Hodgart, Satire, London 1969, p. 237)

Or there is Bloom's dream election-address in the Circe episode:

I stand for the reform of municipal morals and the plain ten command-ments. New worlds for old. Union of all, jew moslem and gentile. Three acres and a cow for all children of nature. Saloon motor hearses. Compulsory manual labour for all. All parks open to the public day and night. Electric dishscrubbers. Tuberculosis, lunacy, war and mendicancy must now cease. General amnesty, weekly carnival, with masked licence, bonuses for all, esperanto the universal brotherhood. No more patriotism of barspongers and dropsical impostors. Free money, free love and a free lay church in a free lay state.

(Ulysses, London 1969, p. 462)

Such instances, of the premature translation into social action of ideals designed rather to encourage one aspect of an inherently imperfect human nature and discourage another, could be multiplied; but to do so would be to belie the tenor of the book, which is more celebratory than satirical, more concerned to achieve the luminous stasis of 'joy' than the imperfect art of 'desire', more amused at life as it is than longing for life as it might be—and assuming 'the great human comedy in which each has share' to be, substantially if not accidentally, that of lives past and lives to come.

Early critics noted the sordidness in *Ulysses*, missing not only the wisdom and compassion, the sympathy for human nature that charac-terise it, but also as Joyce complained the fact that 'it's damn funny'. Later critics have often taken the structural symbolism of Homeric, Shakespearian, and Biblical reference to be working rather in the way it seems to in *The Waste Land*, and thus have turned the novel into a bitter satire on a debased modern world. For these critics the Oxen of the Sun chapter, in which all the main styles of English prose are parodied—linguistic growth thus matching foetal growth as the students debate birth and birth-control in the lying-in hospital—is merely a display of mind-boggling virtuosity. In a more considered view the chapter is central.

Joyce told Frank Budgen that he did not consider Odysseus a more heroic figure than Leopold Bloom, but rather the same sort of person, and in a letter to his brother Stanislaus (7 Feb. 1905) he stated his firm belief that 'the whole structure of heroism is, and always was, a damned lie.' And the book itself confirms these assertions. In *Ulysses* just as many modern styles are parodied as ancient styles; so the effect is not to debunk any one period, but to suggest—and mock—men's endless attempts to evade and falsify reality. Bloom walks past a long series of distorting mirrors, till the final effect is one of appreciation of the humdrum reality that has accumulated in the intervals between the mirrors. To put it another way: *Ulysses* condenses centuries of cloudy myth to one day of reality—and the fact that it is at least as much a naturalist, as a symbolist novel is important. For symbolism and mythopeia suggest that particulars are relevant to generalities, but as the area of generalisation widens the verifiable quality of symbolist work diminishes. Ultimately, its validity depends on the quality of the immediate reality given. The myths give significance to the particulars, but it is the particulars that give validity to the myths. In thinking of his work as essentially a system of 'epiphanies' Joyce confirmed this order of importance: starting from 'the now, the here, through which all future plunges to the past' (p. 186).

The main comic method of *Ulysses* is to blow up still further the swollen bladder of human pretentiousness and self-deception till it bursts in laughter, and we are left with the pea in the middle—but seen as something solid and worthwhile. Far from setting up titans of legend as standards by which to judge the present day, it tends to reduce *them* to human dimensions, to demythologise (though without thereby implying a devaluation: if Odysseus becomes Bloomlike, Bloom becomes Odyssean; they are 'the same sort of person' dressed in different styles).

The parody chapter shows in concentration man's perennial attempt to aggrandise himself by style, exaggerating first one aspect, then another of his human many-sidedness. Here, for instance, *David Copperfield* is used (very appropriately in the light of the situation of the hard birth of Mrs Purefoy's ninth—a situation shown realistically elsewhere) to exemplify the characteristic nineteenth-century tendency to flatulent sentimental self-inflation in family contexts:

> Meanwhile the skill and patience of the physician had brought about a happy *accouchement*. It had been a weary weary while both for patient and doctor. All that surgical skill could do was done and the brave woman had manfully helped. She had. She had fought the good fight and now she was very very happy. Those who have passed on, who have gone before, are happy too as they gaze down and smile upon the

touching scene. Reverently look at her as she reclines there with the motherlight in her eyes, that longing hunger for baby fingers (a pretty sight it is to see), in the first bloom of her new motherhood, breathing a silent prayer of thanksgiving to One above, the Universal husband. And as her loving eyes behold her babe she wishes only one blessing more, to have her dear Doady there with her to share her joy, to lay in his arms that mite of God's clay, the fruit of their lawful embraces. He is older now (you and I may whisper it) and a trifle stooped in the shoulders yet in the whirligig of years a grave dignity has come to the conscientious second accountant of the Ulster bank, College Green branch. O Doady, loved one of old, faithful lifemate now, it may never be again, that faroff time of the roses! With the old shake of her pretty head she recalls those days. God, how beautiful now across the mist of years! But their children are grouped in her imagination about the bedside, hers and his, Charley, Mary Alice, Frederick Albert (if he had lived), Mamy, Budgy (Victoria Frances), Tom, Violet Constance Louisa, darling little Bobsy (called after our famous hero of the South African war, lord Bobs of Waterford and Candahar) and now this last pledge of their union, a Purefoy if ever there was one, with the true Purefoy nose. Young hopeful will be christened Mortimer Edward after the influential third cousin of Mr Purefoy in the Treasury Remembrancer's Office, Dublin Castle. And so time wags on: but father Cronion has dealt lightly here. No, let no sigh break from that bosom, dear gentle Mina. And Doady, knock the ashes from your pipe, the seasoned briar you still fancy, when the curfew rings for you (may it be the distant day!) and dout the light whereby you read in the Sacred Book for the oil too has run low and so with a tranquil heart to bed, to rest. He knows and will call in His own good time. You too have fought the good fight and played loyally your man's part. Sir, to you my hand. Well done, thou good and faithful servant!

(pp. 417-8)

Much of the celebratory effect comes from form rather than content: partly negative form, the lack of blame or moral horror at furtive secrets, inner perversities—a result of the author's withdrawal, like the God of Creation, from his work; but mainly positive form, the immense gusto, élan, creative power and panache displayed in the complex structure and stupendous command of styles. However depressing the facts may be, this volume in which they are all bound together, is itself everywhere a counterbalancing example of human capacity. After its completion Joyce spoke of his 'emptiness':

I have not read a work of literature for several years. My head is full of pebbles and rubbish and broken matches and lots of glass . . . The task I set myself technically in writing a book from eighteen different

I

points of view and in as many styles all apparently unknown or un-
discovered by my fellow tradesmen, that and the nature of the legend
chosen would be enough to upset anyone's mental balance.

(Quoted by Chester G. Anderson, *James Joyce and his World*, London 1967,
p. 106)

Such a sustained projection of creative vitality into an incredibly
controlled and complex work means that the comic effect is cumulative. It comes from, for example, the contrast of Stephen's 'world'
and Bloom's at the same time and place, from the comparison of
different letters (Milly's and Martha's, both brilliant comic pastiche),
from the gathering implications of certain motifs as they occur in
different contexts, crossing and recrossing like the figures of the
'Dance of the Hours' which acts as a time-structure, from the same
incident seen from different viewpoints, from jokes planted in one
place and exploded chapters later, from serious, esthetic or bitter
parts contrasted with farcical, nightmare or humorous parts, and
finally from the sheer Rabelaisian exuberance of the whole. This
makes it difficult to illustrate briefly. One or two examples, structural
and textural, must suffice.

Thus, the opening chapters, the *Telemachiad*, featuring the guilt-
ridden, philosophising Stephen are not comic in themselves, though
they have many touches of wit and humour, abound in aphorisms,
and introduce the main themes of the 'human comedy': keylessness
in the big city, the clash of the brash and the sensitive, the difficulties
of family relationships, the problems of principles and practice, the
relative value of spiritual and physical kinship, and the matter of
alienation and persecution. The conclusion of the *Nestor* (School)
chapter may be taken as an example of both motif-comedy and textural
comedy:

Mr Deasy halted, breathing hard and swallowing his breath.

—I just wanted to say, he said. Ireland, they say, has the honour of
being the only country which never persecuted the jews. Do you know
that? No. And do you know why?

He frowned sternly on the bright air.

—Why sir? Stephen asked, beginning to smile.

—Because she never let them in, Mr Deasy said solemnly.

A coughball of laughter leaped from his throat dragging after it a
rattling chain of phlegm. He turned back quickly, coughing, laughing,
his lifted arms waving to the air.

—She never let them in, he cried again through his laughter as he
stamped on gaitered feet over the gravel of the path. That's why.

On his wise shoulders through the checkerwork of leaves the sun flung spangles, dancing coins.

(p. 42)

Perfectly realistic; Mr Deasy does and says the right things for his age. It is, though, funny in various ways: the somewhat ludicrous actions of a 'wise' man—made funnier by his symbolising Nestor—breathing hard, waving arms, stamping on gaitered feet; the inane cleverness ('honour . . . she never let them in'); then there is the coughball sentence gruesomely onomatopeic, perfectly descriptive, and lifting the spirits by its stylishness; and there is the tiny, unobtrusive touch that brings in the first hint of fun at Deasy's expense ('to say, he said . . . they say'). In addition, the beautiful image of sun-'spangles' completes the subdued picture of Deasy as clown, and the 'dancing coins' take us back to Stephen's salary, in sovereigns, to the discussion on money, and look forward to the many monetary matters to come. Structurally, too, this item links up with the persecution of Bloom later, in the Ithaca chapter. Wise Nestor is not only inane,but wrong. The Irish, it seems, will persecute a Jew if they can find one:

Gob, the citizen made a plunge back into the shop.
—By Jesus, says he, I'll brain that bloody jewman for using the holy name. By Jesus, I'll crucify him so I will. Give us that biscuitbox here.

(p. 340)

In larger structural terms, the *Telemachiad* as a whole sets off the much longer Bloomian odyssey, the part that is 'damn funny', giving depth to the comedy by contrast, linking up with the more sad and sombre of Bloom's reflections, and contributing to the larger vision of the human comedy: namely that maturity brings—may almost be defined as —a tolerance and acceptance uncharacteristic of youth. Moreover, Bloom's sensuousness, and therefore greater closeness to the bases of life, casts a retrospective comic air over Stephen's torment and abstract philosophising. At breakfast time Bloom is thinking of breakfast:

Mr. Leopold Bloom ate with relish the inner organs of beasts and fowls. He liked thick giblet soup, nutty gizzards, a stuffed roast heart, liver slices fried with crustcrumbs, fried hencod's roses. Most of all he liked grilled mutton kidneys which gave to his palate a fine tang of faintly scented urine.
Kidneys were in his mind as he moved about the kitchen softly . . .

(p. 57)

What was on Stephen's mind when we met him at the same hour was guilt, high principles, and the wrongs of religion. Here then is the sadder side of the human comedy, that man is the only animal to suffer for abstractions. Bloom, however, is not wholly free from such suffering, though much more down to earth than Stephen. Also, we recognise that in one respect at least Stephen represents a growth-point for something in humanity that will never amount to much in Bloom. So this contrast comedy cuts both ways, though mainly in Bloom's favour.

From breakfast to lunch (the *Lestrygonian* episode); and a plethora of mainly textural examples to choose from:

> His heart astir he pushed in the door of the Burton restaurant. Stink gripped his trembling breath: pungent meat juice, slop of greens. See the animals feed.
>
> Men, men, men.
>
> Perched on high stools by the bar, hats shoved back, at the tables calling for more bread no charge, swilling, wolfing gobfuls of sloppy food, their eyes bulging, wiping wetted moustaches. A pallid suetfaced young man polished his tumbler knife fork and spoon with his napkin. New set of microbes. A man with an infant's saucestained napkin tucked round him shovelled gurgling soup down his gullet. A man spitting back on his plate: halfmasticated gristle: no teeth to chewchew-chew it. Chump chop off the grill. Bolting to get it over. Sad booser's eyes. Bitten off more than he can chew. Am I like that? See ourselves as others see us. Hungry man is an angry man. Working tooth and jaw. Don't! O! a bone! That last pagan king of Ireland choked himself at Sletty southward of the Boyne. Wonder what he was eating. Something galoptious. Saint Patrick converted him to Christianity. Couldn't swallow it all however.
>
> (pp. 168-9)

The prose goes at a voracious rate, helped by the sparsity of punctuation as Bloom's consciousness becomes assimilated to the urgent scene. It is extraordinarily onomatopeic, both in its rhythms and its effects of consonance and assonance—witness respectively the first sentence of the last paragraph and the 'chewchewchew it. Chump chop off . . .' It has the economy of caricature ('hats shoved back' or 'an infant's saucestained napkin'); it is epigrammatic in a way appropriate to the observer ('New set of microbes'); it moves from the outer world to the inner ('Am I like that?'), from the present to the past ('that last pagan king of Ireland'), and it concludes with a pun that links this passage with Bloom's rather practical irreligiousness and contrasts it with Stephen's metaphysical mockery in such passages as the following:

He Who Himself begot, middler the Holy Ghost, and Himself sent Himself, Agenbuyer, between Himself and others, Who, put upon by His fiends, stripped and whipped, was nailed like bat to barn door, starved on crosstree, Who let Him bury, stood up, harrowed Hell, fared into heaven and there these nineteen hundred years sitteth on the right hand of His Own Self but yet shall come in the latter day to doom the quick and the dead when all the quick shall be dead already.

(pp. 197-8)

The playwright who wrote the folio of this world and wrote it badly (He gave us light first and the sun two days later), the lord of things as they are whom the most Roman of catholics call *dio boia*, hangman god, is doubtless all in all in all of us, ostler and butcher, and would be bawd and cuckold too but that in the economy of heaven, foretold by Hamlet, there are no more marriages, glorified man, an androgynous angel, being a wife unto himself.

(p. 213)

The impression of stylistic gusto and transmuting variety is strikingly confirmed in the seventeenth (*Ithaca*) chapter, which Joyce called his Ugly Duckling. It ought to be dull, since it represents Science and is done in the form of an impersonal catechism; its purpose being to show life as it would be if drained of all human emotion and sensation. Indeed, it has to be dull in order to fulfil the comic function of deflating the pretensions of science by contrast with the other, more human chapters, especially the one that follows, Molly Bloom's sleepy, sexy, meandering, material, illogical, basic, unordered and unpunctuated reflections. However, the *Ithaca* chapter is by no means so dull as might be expected. For one thing its accumulative thoroughness — for example on tapwater — both stuns with admiration and makes for a 'shaggy dog' amusement. For another thing, science is not guyed; its objectivity and chilly grandeur get due recognition, sometimes a remarkably evocative expression considering the dictional limits imposed; sometimes it is related, by an imaginative leap, to humanity — the extent of the gap rendering the leap an example of the 'joy' of the 'luminous stasis' of high imaginative perception:

What special affinities appeared to him to exist between the moon and woman?

Her antiquity in preceding and surviving successive tellurian generations: her nocturnal predominance: her satellic dependence: her luminary reflection: her constancy under all her phases, rising, and setting by her appointed times, waxing and waning: the forced invariability of her aspect: her indeterminate response to inaffirmative interrogation:

her potency over effluent and refluent waters: her power to enamour, to mortify, to invest with beauty, to render insane, to incite to and aid delinquency: the tranquil inscrutability of her visage: the terribility of her isolated dominant implacable resplendent propinquity: her omens of tempest and of calm: the stimulation of her light, her motion and her presence: the admonition of her craters, her arid seas, her silence: her splendour, when visible: her attraction when invisible.

(p. 623)

In general, then, the chapter puts 'human' life in perspective, making for comic acceptance by invoking the feeling that 'it will all be the same a hundred years hence', and at the same time places science in perspective by comparison with the more human chapters. But there is also an astonishing variety of more obviously comic items scattered about unobtrusively; in the following passage, for example, Bloom's (and Mr Deasy's) preoccupation with money is shown to be a more life-enhancing thing than Stephen's disregard for it, at least when romantic flummery is set aside. It is funny, partly because of the effect of hyperbole that turns out to be illusory (for these are quite possible events), partly because of the cold treatment (which however is reminiscent of scientific and bureaucratic ways of dealing with human suffering), partly by one's self-defensive reaction, but mainly by the celebratory creative élan shown in the thoroughness, the unexpected apt detail ('*deputy* cess collector') and the verbal invention within such strict self-imposed limits:

Reduce Bloom by cross multiplication of reverses of fortune, from which these supports protected him, and by elimination of all positive values to a negligible irrational unreal quantity.

Successively, in descending helotic order: Poverty: that of the outdoor hawker of imitation jewellery, the dun for the recovery of bad and doubtful debts, the poor rate and deputy cess collector. Mendicancy: that of the fraudulent bankrupt with negligible assets paying 1s. 4d. in the £, sandwichman, distributor of throwaways, nocturnal vagrant, insinuating sycophant, maimed sailor, blind stripling, eccentric public laughingstock seated on bench of public park under discarded perforated umbrella. Destitution: the inmate of Old Man's House (Royal Hospital), Kilmainham, the inmate of Simpson's Hospital for reduced but respectable men permanently disabled by gout or want of sight. Nadir of misery: the aged impotent disfranchised ratesupported moribund lunatic pauper.

With which attendant indignities?

The unsympathetic indifference of previously amiable females, the contempt of muscular males, the acceptance of fragments of bread, the simulated ignorance of casual acquaintances, the latration of illegitimate unlicensed vagabond dogs, the infantile discharge of decomposed vegetable missiles, worth little or nothing or less than nothing.

By what could such a situation be precluded?

By decease (change of state), by departure (change of place).

Which preferably?

The latter, by the line of least resistance.

(pp. 646-7)

We have already seen most of these misfortunes, expressionistically distorted, in the nightmare episode (*Circe*), a brilliant Freudian drama-tisation of the events of the day, fused with powerful fears and desires, and made hysterically comic in the grotesque way of surrealism. We have also met, in naturalistic setting, many such miserable people. So, were it not for the comic devices mentioned, and the ingenious puns, this would amount to a bitter indictment of social neglect and individual callousness; whereas in fact the treatment turns it into an unexpectedly funny piece of comic satire—behind it, of course, lying the humane positives on which *Ulysses* is built.

One could, however, go on quoting endlessly, and without repetition, for *Ulysses* is also 'the complete comedy' in that it uses every mood and every means known to comic literature (and probably a number previously unknown). It does, of course, necessarily lack pace, for the epiphanising method depends not on the accumulation of incident but the accumulation of significance, and fugal time-structure and sym-bolic reference sacrifice story-suspense for the rewards of implication, contrast, comparison and irony. It could not have more pace without being less complete.

In short, the symbolic structure universalises the local and temporal content, the stylistic range and vitality gives that content's drabness a celebratory comic vitality, and the depth and unflinching detail of characterisation reminds us that '*tout comprendre, c'est tout pardonner*'. The work's complexity reflects that of the modern city—especially in the labyrinthine cutting of the Wandering Rocks chapter—the difficulties of realising the more desirable human potentialities are fully acknowledged; humanity is revealed as pretentious, absurd and full of frailties at best, and at worst bigoted and brutal; living is seen to be inevitably shot through with sorrow and suffering; Bloom remains at the end unsuccessful in business, he does not find a spiritual son to replace his own, his Penelope has not been faithful, he has been snubbed and attacked—and yet, there seems no incongruity in the smiling satisfaction with which his day ends, in bed beside Molly's opulent curves. He has kept his head above water, controlled his feelings, given help where needed, forgiven wrongs; like humanity throughout its history he has come through by the skin of his teeth, remaining fully human. And it is just about by that margin that we agree with Molly's final affirmation, which goes back beyond 'civilisation' to the natural source of love and creative vitality:

> . . . and then I asked him with my eyes to ask again yes and then he asked me would I yes to say yes my mountain flower and first I put my arms around him yes and drew him down to me so he could feel my breasts all perfume yes and his heart was going like mad and yes I said yes I will Yes.

Joyce's final yea-saying is, of course, not founded on any dogmatic faith or optimistic metaphysic, but upon 'the incertitude of the void'. No guarantee is given to humanity from outside. In this he tends to preserve the greater distance that seems to be characteristic of British comic writers as compared with their American counterparts.

Tom Stoppard, writing today as a lesser man in a world of even greater menace both in its science and its bureaucracy, carries this tendency one step further by writing philosophic comedy on incertitude. In *Rosencrantz and Guildenstern are Dead* (1967) and even more in *Jumpers* (1972) both themes and subject-matter are philosophical. The questions they ask suggest a need to get back to base: What is it to be 'human'? What is identity, and its relation to impersonal structures or manipulation? Is there any place for idealism in a scientific, rationalistic world? Above all, how do we know if the answers are right? What, indeed, is knowledge: how do we know we really *know* what we think we know?

In the first play, these questions are not quite clearly sorted out. Like *Hamlet* itself it conveys a sense of the author's having bitten off a little more than he can chew; nor does the triple-perspective structure (of *Hamlet*, the Players, and the world of Rosencrantz and Guildenstern) help in such realisation. It does, however, help to emphasise the difficulty of knowing what is 'real' or what 'reality' is; and this is valuable, for Stoppard's comedy mainly purports to demonstrate the absurdity of dogmatic assurance. Like Joyce's, his work is balanced, but in a different way, and for a different reason.

Joyce made an immense effort to 'prove on the pulses'—by sharing the experience of deeply explored, finely rendered characters—that certain values *were* better than others, though man-made not God-given. Stoppard's 'distance' carried him further from humanity, not to cynicism or hardhearted amorality like Waugh, but to the philosophical problems underlying human ones. Stoppard has crystallised the modern writer's incertitude into the clear recognition that there is *a problem of knowledge*, perhaps insoluble. He is a genuine, thoughtful 'Don't-know', of a humane temperament. Naturally such comedies of incertitude carry no positive message, but rather the implicit negative one that cocksure manipulation of others, systematic or dogmatic, regardless of their feelings, seems unwarrantable. However, his philosophic neutrality does seem to incline just a little to one side, enough to suggest that scientific rationalism has no better claim to cocksureness than metaphysical idealism had.

The distance established between themes and characters, and between the author and both, means that Stoppard's comedy, like Waugh's in this one respect, can tolerate a great deal of farce and divertisement. Deep questions can be, and are, combined with a surface capable of rolling an audience in the aisles. *Rosencrantz and Guildenstern*, for example, brings in the question of pragmatism and metaphysics in the guise of Bloomian (and Everyman's) scientific thinking:

> GUILDENSTERN (*clears his throat*) In the morning the sun would be easterly. I think we can assume that.
>
> ROSENCRANTZ That it's morning?
>
> GUILDENSTERN If it is, and the sun is over *there* (*his right as he faces the audience*) for instance, *that* (*front*) would be northerly. On the other hand, if it is not morning and the sun is over *there* (*his left*) . . . *that* . . . (*lamely*) would *still* be northerly. (*picking up*). To put it another way, if we came from down there (*front*) and it is morning, the sun would be up there (*his left*) and if it is actually over *there* (*his right*) and it's still morning, we must have come from up *there* (*behind him*), and if *that* is southerly (*his left*) and the sun is really over *there* (*front*), then it's the afternoon. However, if none of these is the case—
>
> ROSENCRANTZ Why don't you go and have a look?
>
> GUILDENSTERN Pragmatism?!—is that all you have to offer? You seem to have no conception of where we stand! You won't find the answer written down for you in the bowl of a compass—I can tell you that. (*Pause.*) Besides, you can never tell this far north—it's probably dark out there.
>
> (Act II)

A paradigm of the official rebuke is imagined so:

> ROSENCRANTZ To sum up: your father whom you love, dies, you are his heir, you come back to find that hardly was the corpse cold

before his young brother popped on to his throne and into his
sheets, thereby offending both legal and natural practice. Now why
exactly are you behaving in this extraordinary manner?

(Act I)

And very naturally then the logic of uncertainty is theatrically conveyed in this flippant way:

ROSENCRANTZ He has moods.
PLAYER Of moroseness?
GUILDENSTERN Madness. And yet.
ROSENCRANTZ Quite.
GUILDENSTERN For instance.
ROSENCRANTZ He talks to himself, which might be madness.
GUILDENSTERN If he didn't talk sense, which he does.
ROSENCRANTZ Which suggests the opposite.
PLAYER Of what?
    (*Small pause.*)
GUILDENSTERN I think I have it. A man talking sense to himself is
    no madder than a man talking nonsense not to himself.
ROSENCRANTZ Or just as mad.
GUILDENSTERN Or just as mad.
ROSENCRANTZ And he does both.
GUILDENSTERN So there you are.
ROSENCRANTZ Stark raving sane.

(Act II)

What is common to these examples, and to all other cases of this
comic philosophy, is that any hint of a solution to the problem implied
is immediately undermined. Thus the coin-business raises the possibility that they are outside natural law, the creations of some god-
Shakespeare, but the logic leading to that conclusion patently collapses
and leaves the question open. So, too, the business of interpenetrating
stage-worlds leaves open the questions whether we are all actors ('the
opposite of people'), whether the manipulators ('Wheels have been set
in motion, and they have their own pace, to which we are . . . condemned') are themselves manipulated, or whether we are all puppets
in a deterministic machine, and whether we can know when we are
being authentic, real, as against performing for an audience. So too the
swiftness with which the two protagonists cease to know which is
which, leaves open the question whether or not personal identity
depends on one's habitat.

By setting *Jumpers* in a recognisable modern environment and
making the chief characters professional university philosophers of

different schools of thought, Stoppard has been able to clarify the questions, and even hint at an answer. It is in this play that the slight inclination of his balance becomes noticeable. Recognisable environment and characters, however, by no means make it a realistic play. In keeping with the philosophic preoccupation and the need for distance—so that we see the problems rather than feel with the characters—its mode is that of metaphorical and highly fictional comedy, the mood, satirical and humorous—satirical about Archie, dandy leader of the scientific rationalists (as we may stereotype the Jumpers), humorous about George Moore (the Third), dishevelled metaphysician fighting a losing battle against these acrobats. It is in this difference of mood that the inclination of Stoppard's comic balance is most evident. The chief method is that of travesty: texturally of philosophic debate, structurally of the detective-story, the two being mutually supporting, since both are concerned with trying to *find out* (neither, however, in this comedy of incertitude, being successful). What is to be found out, essentially, is whether the metaphysical standpoint is still tenable. And closely connected with this is the problem of knowledge...

Like the mystery of who murdered McFee, the metaphysical theme and the truth theme come to no clear conclusion—unless it is a clear conclusion that neither is an open-and-shut case. George's contorted attempt to prove the existence of God by adapting Zeno's mathematics—doomed to failure anyway as maths is a world of ideas (which, like wishes, are not horses) and existence is an empirical matter—reaches a triumphant, logical, but self-cancelling conclusion in the proposition that God exists but is nought. On the other hand, when he abandons logic, he does make a telling point or two, thus:

> DOTTY Archie says the Church is a monument to irrationality.
> GEORGE ... The National Gallery is a monument to irrationality!
> Every concert hall is a monument to irrationality!—and so is a
> nicely kept garden, or a lover's favour, or a home for stray dogs!
> You stupid woman, if rationality were the criterion for things
> being allowed to exist, the world would be one gigantic field of
> soya beans! ... The irrational, the emotional, the whimsical ...
> these are the stamp of humanity which makes reason a civilizing
> force. In a wholly rational society the moralist will be a variety of
> crank, haranguing the bus queue with the demented certitude of
> one blessed with privileged information—'Good and evil are
> metaphysical absolutes!'

(Act I)

But of course this is no answer to Archie's rational linguistic analysis of the problem of moral absolutes, as reported by Dotty in reply:

> ... Things do not *seem*, on the one hand, they *are*: and on the other hand, bad is not what they can *be*. They can be green, or square, or Japanese, loud, fatal, waterproof or vanilla-flavoured; and the same for actions, which can be *disapproved of*, or comical, unexpected, saddening or good television, variously, depending on who frowns, laughs, jumps, weeps or wouldn't have missed it for the world. Things and actions, you understand, can have any number of real and verifiable properties. But good and bad, better and worse, these are not real properties of things, they are just expressions of our feelings about them.

What in fact calls the Jumpers' viewpoint in question is the practical effects their logic leads to. Dotty, for instance, seems to have been driven dotty by *science* which has bleached out romance for her (signified by her horror at the astronauts on the moon who render her no longer capable of singing her spoony Juney moon songs) and by *reason* (George's philosophical remoteness having made her frigid, Archie's glib management having corrupted her into conniving at murder and supporting the sinister Rad.-Lib. Party). Her next speech, in fact, well conveys a sense of inescapable loss, and a deep need for something that nevertheless has to be abandoned since it cannot be justified by science or reason:

> ... If you like I won't see him. It'll be just you and me under that old-fashioned, silvery harvest moon, occasionally blue, jumped over by cows and coupleted by Junes, invariably shining on the one I love; . . . *Keat's* bloody moon!—for what has made the sage or poet write but the fair paradise of nature's light—and *Milton's* bloody moon! rising in clouded majesty, at length apparent queen, unveiled her peerless light and o'er the dark her silver mantle threw —And Shelley's sodding maiden, with white fire laden, whom mortals call thee—(*weeping*) *Oh yes, things were in place then!*

The very last words of the play are Dotty's 'Goodbye spoony Juney Moon' 'and', one inwardly seems to hear by that time, 'Hail, cost-efficiency!'

The play begins with a brilliant *coup de théâtre*: the Secretary, at the Rad.-Lib. victory party, swinging by her legs from a trapeze *'between darkness and darkness . . . into the spotlight and out'* doing a striptease. In retrospect, surely, a symbol of Truth, the naked truth, seen only in glimpses, flashes of illumination, and never quite whole (she crashes into the butler before the strip is completed). She never speaks during the whole course of the play (the truth is not self-explanatory). She is the mistress of McFee the arch-rationalist and the secretary of George Moore. Both press her into service, as it were, but in different ways, or, she 'takes down' for both, but in different senses. Both sides, that is to say, are theatrically seen to possess part of the truth, but neither knows the Whole Truth. There really is a problem of knowledge; and that is why nothing in the play is resolved: not the murder, not the status of Archie (glib self-seeker or necessary clever cynic?), not his relationship with Dotty (doctor or lover?) Indeed the whole movement of the work is appropriately Zeno-like, always approaching a conclusion, never reaching it. The two acts and the coda abound in uproarious slapstick (e.g. with the body), travesty (of police business and, in the Coda, of Justice), and of psychological and logical wit—and almost all of it, when examined turns out, like the striptease, to be relevant to the main themes. The action, too, is clever, funny and relevant. Indeed, since there is no answer in theory to the metaphysical problem—poised between arguments contradictorily entailing 'that though an arrow is always approaching its target, it never quite gets there, and Saint Sebastian died of fright', and that '. . . the first term of the series is not an infinite fraction but *zero*. It exists. God, so to speak, is nought'—the answer, or rather tendency, has to be given in practice, reality, where action naturally looms large.

The Party victory and the affair of the astronauts (in which the up-to-date rational Captain Oates clobbers his companion, climbs into the damaged spacecraft, and gets to safety), together with their consequences, represent *applied* philosophy and *applied* science. It is these which cause McFee to doubt his own standpoint (and, perhaps, bring about his murder as a traitor):

> CROUCH It was the astronauts fighting on the Moon that finally turned him, sir. Henry, he said to me, Henry, I am giving philosophical respectability to a new pragmatism in public life, of which there have been many disturbing examples both here and on the moon . . . he kept harking back to the first Captain Oates . . . Henry, he said, . . . if altruism is a possibility, my argument is up a gum-tree . . . Duncan, I said, Duncan, don't you worry your head about all that. That astronaut yobbo is good for twenty years hard. Yes, he said, yes *maybe*, but when he comes out, he's going to find he was only twenty years ahead of his time. I have seen the future, Henry, he said; and it's yellow.

(Act II)

Human emotions, it would seem, are not easily to be *permanently* caught in the web of rationalism and science. A point confirmed by one argument of George's that is subtle without being self-cancelling or muddled—though it does have to concede *most* of the case against goodness as an absolute. The speech, too long to quote in full, comes in a theatrically insistent place at the end of Act I:

> ... Professor McFee ... goes on to show ... that the word 'good' has also meant different things to different people at different times, an exercise which combines simplicity with futility in a measure he does not apparently suspect, for on the one hand it is not a statement which anyone would dispute, and on the other, nothing useful can be inferred from it. It is not in fact a statement about value at all; it is a statement about language and how it is used in a particular society ... Certainly a tribe which believes it confers honour on its elders by eating them is going to be viewed askance by another which prefers to buy them a little bungalow somewhere, and Professor McFee should not be surprised that the notion of honour should manifest itself so differently in peoples so far removed in clime and culture. What is surely more surprising is that notions such as honour should manifest themselves at all. For what *is* honour? What are pride, shame, fellow-feeling, generosity and love? If they are instincts, what are instincts? ... what can be said to be the impulse of a genuinely altruistic act? Hobbes might have answered self-esteem, but what is the attraction of thinking better of oneself? What is *better*? A savage who elects to honour his father by eating him, as opposed to disposing of his body in some—to him—ignominious way, for example by burying it in a teak box, is making an ethical choice in that he believes himself to be acting as a good savage ought to act. Whence comes this sense of some actions being better than others?—not more useful, or more convenient or more popular, but simply pointlessly *better*? What, in short, is so good about *good*? Professor McFee succeeds only in showing us that in different situations different actions will be deemed, rightly or wrongly, to be conducive to that good which is independent of time and place and which is knowable but not nameable. It is not nameable because it is not another way of referring to this or that quality which we have decided is virtuous ... The irreducible fact of goodness is not implicit in one kind of action any more than in its opposite, but in the existence of a relationship between the two. It is the sense of comparisons being in order.

A subtle and profound conclusion not undermined by the ivory-towerism that leads George to ignore Dotty's cries of Help, Rape,

Murder; whereas Archie's cool attention to it does undermine his human credibility as a man to follow:

> ARCHIE It's all right—just exhibitionism: what we psychiatrists call 'a cry for help'.
> BONES But it *was* a cry for help.
> ARCHIE Perhaps I'm not making myself clear. *All* exhibitionism is a cry for help, but a cry for help *as such* is only exhibitionism.

Such speeches, and such actions as his Pooh-Bah manipulation of a multiplicity of official positions to get away with murder (perhaps), do tend to discredit him as logic is not able to.

Nevertheless, the Coda forms a Conclusion in which nothing is concluded. George Moore's concern for absolute values, universal truths is once again shown to be a sort of fiddling while Rome burns, Clegthorpe's conversion may, but equally may not, show hope in humanity's capacity for transcending self-interest. Like Thomas à Becket, he changes character with the office, but also like Becket he is disposed of, as was the other renegade Radical Liberal, McFee. The final word—apart from Dotty's one-line song—is left with Archie; and a very callous, sane, and balanced statement it seems to be. But it gets a hint of taint from all we have seen of the Jumpers before, and its own conclusion, 'Wham, bam, thank you Sam' suggests a cynical theatricality. In fact it has to be taken in some degree ironically. The audience is balanced not, in the end, between two viewpoints, as in the beginning, but between belief and scepticism: belief in the facts (or most of them) and scepticism about the speaker:

> ARCHIE Do not despair—many are happy much of the time; more eat than starve, more are healthy than sick, more curable than dying; not so many dying as dead; and one of the thieves was saved. Hell's bells and all's well—half the world is at peace with itself, and so is the other half; vast areas are unpolluted; millions of children grow up without suffering deprivation, and millions, while deprived, grow up without suffering cruelties, and millions, while deprived and cruelly treated, none the less grow up. No laughter is sad and many tears are joyful. At the graveside the undertaker doffs his top hat and impregnates the prettiest mourner. Wham, bam, thank you Sam.

So does the play finally imply that 'the great human comedy in which each has share' may still have a happy ending, that under the dominion of the three thick-skinned giants of our day, totalitarianism, technology, and bureaucracy, we may still make life worth while, aided by the weapon of wit, the resilience of humour, the mockery of laughter, the critical distance of comedy? Well, accordant to a time even more menaced than his, the last word is clearly not a Joycean *Yes*, but something more appropriate to a comedy, and time, of such incertitude. Perhaps *Perhaps* . . .

Bibliography

Only those critical and creative works specifically used in the text are listed. (All titles are also indexed). Where a significant period has elapsed between the date of composition or performance and that of publication—as with many of Shakespeare's plays—the former is given, if known. Place of publication, London, unless stated otherwise. Publishers cited for all works after 1900.

Addison, J.
  (and Steele, R.) *The Spectator*, 1711-12
Anderson, C. S. *James Joyce and his World* (Thames and Hudson), 1967
Aristophanes *Comedies* (extant), c.426-388 BC
Arnold, M. *Literature and Dogma*, 1873
Ashley, M. *England in the Seventeenth Century* (Penguin Books), 1952
Auden, W. H. *Letter to Lord Byron* in *Letters from Iceland* (with L. MacNeice) (Faber), 1937
  Nones (Faber), 1952
  The Shield of Achilles (Faber), 1955
  Collected Shorter Poems 1927-57 (Faber), 1966
Austen, J. *Sense and Sensibility*, 1811
  Pride and Prejudice, 1813
  Mansfield Park, 1814
  Emma, 1816
  Northanger Abbey, 1818
  Persuasion, 1818
Bage, R. *Hermsprong*, 1796
Bamborough, J. B. *Ben Jonson* (Longmans), 1959
Beaumont, F.
  (and Fletcher, J.) *The Knight of the Burning Pestle* (performance), 1609
Beckett, S. *Waiting for Godot* (Grove Press), New York 1956
  No's Knife (Calder and Boyars), 1967
Bergson, H. L. *Le Rire* (Revue de Paris), Paris 1900
Blackmore, Sir R. 'Essay upon Wit', 1716
  In *Augustan Reprint Society, Series One*, Ann Arbor 1946
Boccaccio, G. *The Decameron*, 1348-58
  Printed Venice 1471
Bradbrook, F. 'Samuel Richardson', in *Pelican Guide to English Literature*, ed. Ford, Vol. 4, 1957

Jane Austen and her Predecessors (Cambridge U.P.), Cambridge 1966

Bradbrook, M. *The Growth and Structure of Elizabethan Comedy* (Chatto and Windus), 1955

Brower, R. H. *The Fields of Light* (Oxford U.P.), New York 1951

Bunyan, J. *The Pilgrim's Progress*, 1678

Burke, E. *Reflections on the Revolution in France*, 1790

Burns, R. *Poems Chiefly in the Scottish Dialect*, Edinburgh 1786

Butler, S. *Hudibras*, 1663 (Pt. I), 1664 (Pt. II), 1678 (Pt. III)

Butler, S. *Erewhon*, 1872
　　Erewhon Revisited (Grant Richards), 1901
　　The Way of all Flesh, 1884
　　　Printed (Grant Richards), 1903
　　Notebooks of Samuel Butler, ed. Jones (Fifield), 1912

Byron, G. G., Lord. *Beppo*, 1818
　　　　The Vision of Judgement, 1822
　　　　Don Juan, 1819-24

Canning, G. (ed.) *The Anti-Jacobin*, 1797-8

Capellanus, A. *The Art of Courtly Love*, late 12th century, trs. G. G. Parry (Columbia U.P.), New York 1941

Carnochan, W. B. Introduction to *The Man of Mode* (Arnold), 1967

Caudwell, C. *Romance and Realism*, ed. Hynes (Princeton U.P.), Princeton 1970

Chambers, E. K.
　and Sidgwick, F. *Early English Lyrics* (Sidgwick and Jackson), 1947

Chapman, G. *Eastward Ho* (with Jonson and Marston), 1605

Chaucer, G. *The Canterbury Tales*, 1387-1400
　　　　Printed 1478

Clark, A. M. *Studies in Literary Modes* (Oliver and Boyd), 1946

Cobban, A. *The Debate on the French Revolution* (Nicholas Kaye), 1950

Collier, J. *A Short View of the Immorality and Profaneness of the English Stage*, 1698

Congreve, W. *The Way of the World*, 1700

Cornford, F. M. *The Origins of Attic Comedy* (Arnold), 1914

Coulton, G. G. *Medieval Panorama* (Cambridge U.P.), Cambridge 1949

Craik, W. A. *Jane Austen, the Six Novels* (Methuen), 1968

Cruttwell, P. 'Two Scots Poets: Dunbar & Henryson' in *The Pelican Guide to English Literature*, ed. Ford, Vol 1. (Penguin Books), 1954

Cummings, E. E. *is 5* (Boni and Liveright), New York 1926

Dante, A. *Divina Commedia, c.*1313-1320. Printed Foligno 1472

Davenant, W. *The Wits*, 1636

Day, J. *Parliament of Bees* (performance), *c.*1607
  Humour out of Breath (performance), *c.*1608

Dekker, T. *The Shoemaker's Holiday*, 1600

Dickens, B.
  and Wilson, R. M. *Early English Texts* (Bowes and Bowes), Cambridge
    1954

Dickens, C. *Pickwick Papers*, 1836-7
    Martin Chuzzlewit, 1843
    Bleak House, 1852-3

Dobrée, B. *Restoration Comedy* (Clarendon Press), Oxford 1924

Downs, B. W. (ed.) Introduction to *Mrs. Shamela Andrews* (Cambridge
    U.P.), Cambridge 1930

Dryden, J. Preface to *An Evening's Walk*, 1671
    Absalom and Achitophel, 1681 (Pt. I), 1682 (Pt. II)
    MacFlecknoe, 1682
    The Medall, 1682

Dunbar, W. *The Tua Mariit Wemen and the Wedo, c.*1508. Printed Edin-
    burgh, incomplete, 1508

Edgley, R. 'The Object of Literary Criticism', *Essays in Criticism*, July 1964

Eliot, T. S. *Prufrock* (Faber), 1917
    The Cocktail Party (Faber), 1950
    The Confidential Clerk (Faber), 1954

Enright, D. J. 'Elizabethan and Jacobean Comedy' in *The Pelican Guide to
    English Literature*, ed. Ford, Vol. 2 (Penguin Books), 1955

Etherege, Sir G. *The Comical Revenge*, 1664
    The Man of Mode, 1776

Evans, M. *English Poetry in the Sixteenth Century* (Hutchinson), 1959

Eysenck, H. F. *Uses and Abuses of Psychology* (Penguin Books), 1953

Farquhar, G. *The Beaux' Stratagem*, 1707

Field, N. *A Woman is a Weathercock*, 1612
    Amends for Ladies, 1618

Fielding, H. *Shamela*, 1741
    Joseph Andrews, 1742
    Tom Jones, 1749
    Jonathan Wild the Great, 1743

Ford, B. (ed.) *Pelican Guide to English Literature* (*Vols.* 1-7) (Penguin
    Books), 1954-61

Freeman, A. M. *Thomas Love Peacock* (Martin Secker), 1911

Freud, S. *Jokes and their Relation to the Unconscious*, trs. James Strachey (Hogarth), 1960

Frye, N. *The Anatomy of Criticism* (Princeton U.P.), Princeton 1957
'The Argument of Comedy' in *Shakespeare's Comedies*, ed. Lerner (Penguin Books), 1967

Furbank, N. *Samuel Butler* (Cambridge U.P.), Cambridge 1948

Gibbon, E. *The Decline and Fall of the Roman Empire*, 1776-88

Gifford, W. (ed.) *The Works of Ben Jonson*, 1816

Goldsmith, O. *The Good-Natur'd Man*, 1768
She Stoops to Conquer, 1773

Gorman, H. *James Joyce* (John Lane), 1941

Greene, R. *The Famous History of Friar Bacon* (performance), 1584

Greene, T. 'The Self in Renaissance Literature', in *The Disciplines of Criticism*, ed. Demetz, Greene and Lowry (Yale U.P.) New Haven and London 1969

Guthrie, W. C. K. *The Greeks and their Gods* (Methuen), 1950

Harding, D. W. *Social Psychology and Individual Values* (Hutchinson), 1953

Hartnoll, P. *The Oxford Companion to the Theatre* (Oxford U.P.), 1951

Heller, J. *Catch-22* (Simon and Schuster), New York 1961

Henryson, R. *The Moral Fables of Aesop*, prob. late 15th century. Printed Edinburgh 1570

Hewitt, D. 'Entertaining Ideas: A Critique of Peacock's *Crotchet Castle*' in *Essays in Criticism*, April 1970

Heywood, J. *The Pardoner and the Friar*, 1533
John, Tib and Sir John (or Johan, Johan), 1533

Hobbes, T. *Leviathan*, 1651

Hodgart, M. *Satire* (Weidenfeld and Nicolson), 1969

Huxley, A. *Brave New World*, 1932

Jack, I. *Pope* (Longmans), 1954
English Literature 1815-1832 (Clarendon Press), Oxford 1963

Johnson, M. *Fielding's Art of Fiction* (Pennsylvania U.P.), Philadelphia 1965

Johnson, S. *Lives of the Poets*, 1779-81

Jones, H. F. (ed.) *The Notebooks of Samuel Butler* (Fifield), 1912

Jonson, B. (performance):
Eastward Ho (with Chapman and Marston), 1605
Volpone, 1605
Epicene, or the Silent Woman, 1609
The Alchemist, 1610

Bartholomew Fair, 1614
Timber, or Discoveries. Printed 1640

Joyce, J. *A Portrait of the Artist as a Young Man* (Huebsch), New York 1916
Ulysses (Shakespeare and Co.), Paris 1922
Bodley Head edn. 1936, 1937
Penguin edn. 1969
Finnegans Wake (Faber), 1939

Killigrew, T. *The Parson's Wedding* (performance), *c*.1637-42

Kinsley, J. *The Poems and Fables of John Dryden* (Clarendon Press), Oxford
1958
The Poems and Songs of Robert Burns (Clarendon Press), Oxford
1968

Kitto, H. D. F. 'Greece', in *The Oxford Companion to the Theatre* (Oxford
U.P.), 1957

Knights, L. C. *Drama and Society in the Age of Jonson* (Chatto and Windus),
1937
Explorations (Chatto and Windus), 1946

Langer, S. *Problems of Art* (Routledge), 1957

Larkin, P. *The Less Deceived* (Marvell Press), Hull 1955

La Rochefoucauld, F. duc de. *Maximes*, Paris 1665

Lawlor, J. 'Radical Satire and the Realistic Novel', in *Essays and Studies*,
ed. Low, Vol. 8 (Murray), 1955

Leavis, Q. D. 'Jane Austen', in *A Selection from Scrutiny*, ed. F. R. Leavis,
Vol. 2, Cambridge 1968

Lerner, L (ed.) *Shakespeare's Comedies* (Penguin Books), 1967
The Truthtellers (Chatto and Windus), 1967

'Letter to A. H. Esq., Concerning the Stage,' 1698. In *Augustan Reprint
Society, Series Three*, Ann Arbor, 1946

Locke, J. *Two Treatises of Government*, 1690

Loftis, J. *Comedy and Society from Congreve to Fielding* (Stanford U.P.),
Stanford 1959

Loftis, J. (ed.) *Restoration Drama* (Oxford U.P.), New York 1966

Lyly, J. *Endimion*, 1591

Mackenzie, W. M. *Poems of William Dunbar* (Porpoise Press), Edinburgh
1932

Marlowe, C. *The Jew of Malta* (performance), *c*.1589

Marston, J. *Eastward Ho* (with Jonson and Chapman), 1605
The Dutch Courtezan, 1605
What You Will, 1607

Marvell, A. 'To his Coy Mistress', *c.*1650. Printed in *Poems*, 1681

Mason, E.
  and Ellman R. *The Critical Writings of James Joyce* (Faber), 1959

Massinger, P. *A New Way to Pay Old Debts* (performance), *c.*1625
        The City Madam (performance), 1632

Meredith, G. *The Egoist*, 1879
        The Idea of Comedy and the Uses of the Comic Spirit, 1897

Middleton, T. *A Mad World My Masters* (performance), *c.*1606
        A Trick to Catch the Old One (performance), *c.*1606
        A Chaste Maid in Cheapside (performance), *c.*1612

Mills, H. *Peacock, his Circle and his Age* (Cambridge U.P.), Cambridge 1969

Muir, K. *The Comedy of Manners* (Hutchinson), 1970

Mumford, L. *The Condition of Man* (Secker and Warburg), 1944

Myers, A. R. *England in the Late Middle Ages* (Penguin Books), 1952

Nabokov, V. *Lolita* (Weidenfeld and Nicolson), 1959

Nashe, T. *Pierce Penniless*, 1592

Nicoll, A. *World Drama*, Vol. I (Harrap), 1949

Nottingham Evening Post. Nottingham 28 August 1971

Novak, M. E. 'Congreve's *Old Bachelor*: From Formula to Art,' *Essays in Criticism*, April 1970

Orwell, G. *Animal Farm* (Secker and Warburg), 1945
        Nineteen Eighty-Four (Secker and Warburg), 1949

Partridge, E. B. *The Broken Compass* (Chatto and Windus), 1958

Peacock, T. L. *Headlong Hall*, 1816
        Melincourt, 1817
        Nightmare Abbey, 1818
        The Four Ages of Poetry, 1820
        Maid Marion, 1822
        The Misfortunes of Elphin, 1829
        Crotchet Castle, 1831
        'French Comic Romances', in *The London Review*, 1836
        Gryll Grange, 1860

Pearson, H. *Bernard Shaw* (Collins), 1942

Peele, G. *The Old Wives' Tale*, 1595

Person, H. A. *Cambridge Middle English Lyrics* (Univ. of Washington Press), Washington 1953

Pickard-Cambridge, A. W. *Dithyramb, Tragedy and Comedy* (Clarendon Press), Oxford 1927

Pinto, V. de S. (and Rodway, A.) *The Common Muse* (Chatto and Windus), 1957

Plumb, J. H. *England in the Eighteenth Century* (Penguin Books), 1950

Pope, A. *Essay on Criticism*, 1711
    The Rape of the Lock, 1712
    The Dunciad (enlarged, revised version 1743), 1728
    Essay on Man, 1733
    Epistle to Dr. Arbuthnot, 1735
    The Characters of Women, 1735
    Imitations of Horace, 1733-7
    Epilogue to the Satires, 1738
Potts, L. J. *Comedy* (Hutchinson), 1948
Powell, A. *The Music of Time* (Heinemann), 1951- . . .
Quarterly Review. Anonymous review of Tennyson's *Poems*, 1833
Quennell, P. (ed.) *Byron, A Self-Portrait*, 2 vols. (Murray), 1950
Reed, H. *A Map of Verona* (Cape), 1946
Replogle, J. *Auden's Poetry* (Methuen), 1969
Reyher, P. *Essai sur les Idées dans l'œuvre de Shakespeare* (Didier), Paris 1947
Rice, E. *The Adding-Machine* (Doubleday), New York 1923
Robbins, R. H. *Secular Lyrics of the XIVth & XVth Centuries* (Oxford U.P.) 1952
Robinson, F. N. *Complete Works of Geoffrey Chaucer* (Oxford U.P.), 1957
Robson, W. W. *Modern English Literature* (Oxford U.P.), Oxford 1970
Rochester, Wilmot J., Earl of. *A Satire Against Mankind*, 1675
Rodway, A.
    (and V. de S. Pinto) *The Common Muse* (Chatto and Windus), 1957
Rodway, A. *The Truths of Fiction* (Chatto and Windus), 1970
Rossiter, A. P. *English Drama from Early Times to the Elizabethans* (Hutchinson), 1950
    Angel with Horns, ed. Storey (Longmans), 1961
Sedley, Sir C. *Poetical Works and Speeches*, c.1670-1700, printed 1702
Sewell, E. *The Field of Nonsense* (Chatto and Windus), 1952
Shakespeare, W. (performance):
    The Comedy of Errors, c.1592
    Love's Labour's Lost, c.1594
    Romeo and Juliet, c.1594
    A Midsummer Night's Dream, c.1595
    The Merchant of Venice, c.1597
    Henry IV Pt. I, Pt. II, c.1597-8
    Henry V, c.1599
    As You Like It, c.1600
    Twelfth Night, c.1601
    Troilus and Cressida, c.1602
    The Winter's Tale, c.1610

Shaw, G. B. *Widowers' Houses,* 1893
    Man and Superman (Constable), 1903
    Major Barbara (Constable), 1907
    Androcles and the Lion (Constable), 1916
    Heartbreak House (Constable), 1919
    Back to Methuselah (Constable), 1921

Shelley, P. B. *Peter Bell the Third,* 1819
    The Masque of Anarchy, 1819
    Oedipus Tyrannus, or Swellfoot the Tyrant, 1820

Sheridan, R. B. *The Rivals,* 1775
    The School for Scandal, 1783

Skelton, J. *Magnyfycence, c.*1516
    Printed 1533

Smith, H. *The Gay Couple in Restoration Comedy* (Harvard U.P.), Cambridge, Mass. 1946

Southam, B. C. (ed.) *Critical Essays on Jane Austen* (Routledge), 1968

Speirs, J. 'The Townley Shepherds' Plays', in *The Pelican Guide to English Literature,* ed. Ford, Vol. 1. (Penguin Books), 1954

Steele, Sir R.
    (and Addison, J.) *The Tatler,* 1709
        The Spectator, 1711-12

Sterne, L. *Tristram Shandy,* 1760-7
    A Sentimental Journey, 1768

Still, J. (?) *Gammer Gurton's Needle,* 1566
    Printed 1575

Stoppard, T. *Rosencrantz and Guildenstern are Dead* (Faber), 1967
    Jumpers (Faber), 1972

Swift, J. *The Tale of a Tub,* 1704
    The Conduct of the Allies, 1711
    Satirical Elegy, 1711
    The Drapier's Letters, 1724
    Gulliver's Travels, 1726
    A Modest Proposal, 1729
    Verses on his Own Death, 1731

Tawney, R. H. *Religion and the Rise of Capitalism* (Murray), 1926

Taylor, A. J. P. *English History* 1914-1945 (Penguin Books), 1970

Taylor, G. R. *Sex in History* (Thames and Hudson), 1953

Thackeray, W. M. *Vanity Fair,* 1848

Thomson, D. *England in the Nineteenth Century,* 1950

Tillotson, G. *Augustan Studies* (Athlone Press), 1961

Trevelyan, G. M. *English Social History* (Longmans), 1942

Trotter, W. *Instincts of the Herd in War and Peace* (Fisher and Unwin), 1916

Twain, M. *Huckleberry Finn* (Chatto and Windus), 1884

Udall, N. *Ralph Roister Doister, c.*1553
   Printed 1567

Underwood, D. *Etherege and the Seventeenth-Century Comedy of Manners* (Yale U.P.), Yale 1957

Waugh, E. 'Evelyn Waugh's Private Diaries', *Observer Magazine*, 22 April 1973
   Decline and Fall (Chapman and Hall), 1928
   Vile Bodies (Chapman and Hall), 1930
   A Handful of Dust (Chapman and Hall), 1934
   Scoop (Chapman and Hall), 1938
   Put Out More Flags (Chapman and Hall), 1942
   Brideshead Revisited (Chapman and Hall), 1945
   Scott-King's Modern Europe (Chapman and Hall), 1946
   The Loved One (Chapman and Hall), 1948
   Love Among the Ruins (Chapman and Hall), 1953

Waddell, H. (ed.) *Mediaeval Latin Lyrics* (Penguin Books), 1952

Wells, H. G. *Kipps* (Macmillan), 1905
   The History of Mr. Polly (Nelson), 1910

West, N. *Miss Lonelyhearts* (Liveright), New York 1933
   A Cool Million (Covici, Freide), New York 1934

Wilde, O. *The Soul of Man Under Socialism*, 1891
   Intentions, 1891
   The Importance of Being Earnest, 1899

Wilder, T. *The Skin of Our Teeth* (Harper), New York 1942

Wilson, A. 'The Neighbourhood of Tombuctoo: Conflicts in Jane Austen's Novels', in *Critical Essays on Jane Austen*, ed. Southam (Routledge), 1968

Wright, A. *Henry Fielding: Mask and Feast* (Chatto and Windus), 1965

Wycherley, W. *The Country Wife*, 1675
   The Plain Dealer, 1677

Index